# Memoirs of an Obscure Professor and Other Essays

# Memoirs of an Obscure Professor and Other Essays

## Paul F. Boller, Jr.

Texas Christian University Press / Fort Worth

Books by Paul F. Boller, Jr.

*This Is Our Nation*, with Jean Tilford (1961)
*George Washington and Religion* (1963)
*Quotemanship* (1967)
*American Thought in Transition, 1865-1900* (1967)
*American Transcendentalism, 1830-1860* (1974)
*Freedom and Fate in American Thought* (1978)
*Presidential Anecdotes* (1981)
*Presidential Campaigns* (1984)
*A More Perfect Union*, with Ronald Story (1984)
*Hollywood Anecdotes*, with Ronald L. Davis (1987)
*Presidential Wives* (1988)
*They Never Said It*, with John George (1989)
*Congressional Anecdotes* (1991)

Copyright © 1992, Paul F. Boller, Jr.

       Library of Congress Cataloging-in-Publication Data
Boller, Paul F.
   Memoirs of an obscure professor and other essays / by
      Paul F. Boller, Jr.
    p.    cm.
   ISBN 0-87565-097-X (cl). — ISBN 0-87565-098-8 (pbk.)
   1. Boller, Paul F.  2. Historians—United States—Biography.
  3. United States—Historiography.  I. Title.
  E175.5.B65A3   1992
  973'.07202—dc20                    91-30356
                                            CIP

Cover illustration by Charles Shaw
Designed by Whitehead and Whitehead

# Contents

# Acknowlegments

I WOULD like to thank former students David Broiles, David Carlson, Paul and Karen Faler, Marilyn Hill, George and Elaine Hopkins, Lee Milazzo, Peggy Nash, Diane Orr, Douglas Sloan, Marshall Terry, and Patricia Wallace for helping me get my facts straight in my reminiscences about Southern Methodist University in the years I taught there. A nod, too, to former SMU colleagues, Gene Benton and Larry Perrine, for helping me with my memories.

I'm enormously grateful as well to the following people for writing me, sometimes at great length, about the life and work of the Japanese Language Officers (JLOs) at Boulder, Colorado, and in the Pacific Ocean area during what Studs Terkel called "the Good War": Harry Allen, Carl Bartz, Wendell Furnas, Carl Nelson, Roger Pineau, Griff Way, and Ed Whan.

TCU Press director Judy Alter and editor Tracy Row were a pleasure to work with and I appreciate their helpful suggestions for improving the manuscript.

TCU professor of history Donald L. Worcester deserves special mention. Not only was he the first to encourage me to write this manuscript for the TCU Press; he also read the first draft and helped me make crucial decisions about what to include and what to leave out. Don is an emeritus professor, but he is as busy as he ever was, teaching and writing, though never too busy to help students, friends, and colleagues in their own research and writing. Don honors the academic profession.

# Preface

**B**ACK in 1953, when the *Chicago Tribune* took umbrage
at something I had written and contemptuously dismissed me
as "an obscure professor," I was amused, but my friends and
associates at Southern Methodist University, where I was
teaching, were gleeful.

"How's the Obscure Professor today?" they asked when
they met me on the campus. Or: "Well, Your Obscurity,
how are things going? Are you still hiding your light under a
bushel?" "Look," I told them, "what's so bad about obscurity? It's a helluva lot better than celebrity! You don't have to
truckle to public opinion if you're obscure, or do any grand-
standing. Also: you can change your mind about things without provoking hoots and hollers. And, best of all, you don't
have to sound off on everything under the sun."

In the years since then I have published books that won
favorable attention, and I have even gone on book-promotion
tours. But I haven't really changed my mind about the advantages of obscurity, and I still recall the *Tribune's* choice of
words with amusement and even affection. Soon after retir-
ing from teaching at Texas Christian University, thirty years
after the *Tribune's* blast, it occurred to me that it might be
fun, even instructive, to describe what it was like being an
obscure professor at one of America's less renowned cam-

puses during the McCarthy years. There have been many books and articles about the tussles with extreme rightists that took place at the nation's top ten universities during the McCarthy period, but next to nothing written about the experiences of people working at less celebrated campuses during those years. It was high time, I thought, to present a minority report on the subject, and the first essay here attempts to do so.

While working on the McCarthy essay for this book, I came across the excellent *American Heritage* series, commencing in 1989, with the title "My Brush with History," and I couldn't help recalling that I had had a few minor "brushes" of my own during World War II. Some of the *Heritage* pieces were by celebrities, but most of them were the recollections of people like me who were not famous but who had had chance encounters with some of the Big Events of the twentieth century or had happened to meet a few of the Great and Powerful People in this world at some point in their lives. The topic fascinated me. So after completing my memoir of the McCarthy years, I started in on another essay that ended by dealing not only with my own personal little "brushes" with history, but also with a larger topic that has yet to be studied in detail: the work of specialists in *Nihongo* (the Japanese language) whom the U.S. Navy trained to translate captured documents and interrogate Japanese prisoners during the Second World War.

Most of the other essays here are reprints, dealing with special topics that have meant a great deal to me, and which I think are still of interest. In keeping with the semi-autobiographical nature of the first two essays, however, I have written brief introductions to each of them, explaining how I came to write them and what the responses were when they first appeared in print. The Coolidge essay is new. It's not that I admire Calvin Coolidge the way, say, Ronald Reagan did; it's just that someone, some day, somehow, I decided, had to do something with all those amusing Coolidge stories. I have also added some "Academic Anecdotes" about my experiences as a student and teacher, and some "Afterthoughts" that probably reveal as much about me as they do about this curious universe in which we live, move, and have our being.

The original title for the book was *Memoirs of an Obscure Professor and Other Popular Essays,* meaning essays directed to the general reader rather than to the specialist, but I soon decided against it. In my mind I could hear my friends and associates at it again. "Well, how is the Popular Essayist today?" "How does it feel to be so popular?" "Good morning. Your Popularity, how is the dog and pony show these days?" I ended by keeping "obscure" in the title, skipping "popular," and settling for the non-committal "And Other Essays."

Paul F. Boller, Jr.
*Department of History*
*Texas Christian University*

# 1

# Memoirs of an Obscure Professor:
## McCarthy Days in Texas

**H**ow does one begin a memoir?

Augustine started off by invoking his God. So did Rousseau, but he made it clear that the deity he adored had to take him on his own terms: good, bad, indifferent. Rousseau's way of putting it amused Henry Adams, but Adams skipped the invocation and simply announced his birth date and then stated the theme of his book: he was a child of the seventeenth and eighteenth centuries required to play the game of the twentieth. Benjamin Franklin was pedagogical (and a bit proud); he wanted to show his son, he said, how he rose from "Poverty and Obscurity" to "a State of Affluence and some degree of Reputation in the world." Lincoln Steffens was cutesy; he was born in San Francisco, he wrote, "a remarkable child," according to his mother, "a remarkable woman." Benevenuto Cellini was solemn. "All men of whatsoever quality they be, who have done anything of excellence, or which may properly resemble excellence," he declared, "ought, if they are persons of truth and honesty, to describe their life with their own hand; but they ought not to attempt so fine an enterprise until they have passed the age of forty."

Well, I'm past forty — way past it, in fact — and perhaps it is time to say something, that is, if I have something to say, and I think I do. But the gifted men whose memoirs I have just cited are men of fame; they are what the present era calls celebrities. How does a mere obscurity — "an obscure professor" — commence his remembrances of things past, especially when he plans to confine them to a short period in his life: his encounter with McCarthyism in Texas in the 1950s and 1960s? Perhaps the best strategy is to start by explaining the appellation.

The *Chicago Tribune,* ultra-conservative Robert R. McCormick's pride and joy, did the christening, and did so when I was just beginning my academic career. Not long after I took my doctorate at Yale and began teaching history at Southern Methodist University, the *Tribune* huffily dismissed me as "an obscure professor" in an editorial attack on an article I wrote in 1953 defending Franklin Roosevelt's 1933 inauguration of diplomatic relations with the Soviet Union. I was already being referred to as a "junior personality" by John O. Beaty, English professor at SMU, because I had criticized his anti-Semitic views in a letter to the student newspaper. Soon I was to be attacked as an outright Communist by McCarthyites in Texas and even blamed for SMU's football losses one season, though, as one of my conservative senior colleagues jocularly admitted to a student who had heard I was a Communist, but thought I was nice, "Yeah, he's a nice Communist!" But Texas McCarthyites didn't think I was nice; and when a high school textbook of mine came up for adoption in 1961, they raised such a rumpus that they succeeded in killing the book in the Lone Star state on the ground that it was "soft on communism."

It was all very ironic. I was, in fact, an old-fashioned Norman Thomas anti-Stalinist, who knew his Orwell and Koestler and was aware of the crimes of Stalin long before Nikita Khrushchev exposed them to his colleagues in his famous speech in 1956. It amused me at first, and then disturbed me, that people who knew nothing whatsoever about Communism talked so glibly about it. But, as Lady Bird Johnson was fond of saying, "If you're talkin', you aren't learnin'."

My years at SMU coincided with the heyday of McCar-

thyism in the United States. But what was called McCarthyism lasted longer in the Dallas area and in Texas generally
than it did in other parts of the country. In Dallas, McCarthyism actually antedated the sudden leap of the Republican
senator from Wisconsin from obscurity to fame in February
1950; and it didn't really subside until after the assassination
of President John F. Kennedy in November 1963. Long before Joseph R. McCarthy began talking about "twenty years
of treason," the *Dallas Morning News* was treating President
Truman "like a pickpocket," as he once put it, and there were
plenty of opportunities to get in trouble with Dallas reactionaries without even half trying. Years before I began
teaching at SMU, Henry Nash Smith, a young instructor in
the English department, was summarily fired by Professor
Beaty, then chairman of the department, for writing the preface to a story by William Faulkner which Beaty regarded as
lewd and profane. SMU quickly found a berth for Smith in
another department, and he went on to take his doctorate at
Harvard and achieve celebrity in the field of American literature at the University of Minnesota and the University of
California in Berkeley. One of his books, *Virgin Land* (1950),
a study of attitudes toward the West since colonial times,
became something of a classic in scholarly circles.

Professor Beaty himself was by no means lacking in scholarly achievement. A courtly Virginian who had been teaching
at SMU even before taking his doctorate at Columbia University in 1921, he published a monograph and several textbooks in English literature while he was at SMU and he also
wrote novels and published a bit of poetry in the *New Yorker*.
His specialty was Old English, but he taught the survey of
English literature and period courses in the field as well. But
Beaty thought that modern literature was largely decadent.
In *Image of Life* (1940), a book about evils in modern life and
literature, he charged that "purveyors of foul literature" in
the United States were undermining the Christian religion
and Anglo-Saxon ideals, and he urged the publishing industry to exercise self-censorship (much as Hollywood was doing at the time) in order to restore "decency and morality" to

American books and magazines. During World War II, while serving in the army and rising to the rank of colonel, Beaty shifted his attention from literature to politics, and after the war he began devoting his energies to safeguarding the Anglo-Saxon "heritage and ancestral rights," as he put it, against "twentieth century newcomers of alien race" in American politics as well as in literature. But what might be called Beatyism didn't become a serious problem for SMU until the fifties and it coincided with McCarthyism. McCarthyism held that Communists were taking over the country. Beatyism agreed, but added that most of the Communists were Jews.

During my salad days at SMU I first squared off with Professor Beaty (or, Colonel Beaty, as he liked to be called) in a debate over President Truman's dismissal of General Douglas MacArthur for criticizing the administration's conduct of the Korean War. In a column for the student newspaper, the *Daily Campus,* in April 1951, I emphasized the principle of civil supremacy over the military and held that Truman had no alternative but to dismiss a military officer who repeatedly violated instructions from his civilian superiors. I also pointed out that MacArthur's desire to extend the Korean War into Manchuria threatened to involve the United States in a gigantic war on the Chinese mainland and might even touch off a Third World War. To my astonishment, Beaty addressed himself to none of these issues in the column he wrote taking the other side. Instead, he called Truman a "puppet of sinister forces," said critics of MacArthur were "playing the Communist game," and insisted that the dismissal "shows people the full measure of the treason in our executive branch in Washington." After our exchange, Beaty began expressing doubts to students about my loyalties.

By the time of the presidential campaign of 1952, tensions were acute in Dallas, and being a supporter of Adlai Stevenson (whom McCarthy accused of following "suicidal Kremlin-directed policies") placed one beyond the pale with ultrarightists like Professor Beaty. Stevensonians were a distinct minority on the SMU campus, among both faculty and students. Still, there were enough of us on the faculty to form a little group called Volunteers for Stevenson and plan an evening of speeches on his behalf. We arranged for our rally to be held off campus and made it clear in all our publicity that we spoke only for ourselves as citizens and not in any way for SMU. Our precautions were to no avail. The news that people at SMU were planning a pro-Stevenson rally raised such a storm among metropolitan reactionaries that the SMU administration (which depended on local fund drives for its annual budget) somewhat embarrassedly asked us to call it off. In the end, though, there was little to call off. As opposition to the rally mounted, one after another of our little group defected and soon there was only a handful left. Our disappointment at not being able to stage a pro-Stevenson event was exceeded only by our chagrin over the failure of so many of our colleagues to stand firm in a crisis.

Professor Beaty was not, so far as I know, involved in the anti-Stevenson agitation. From his point of view Dwight D. Eisenhower was almost as bad as Adlai Stevenson and his special *bete noir* was Harry Truman. He liked to post pictures of Truman on the English department bulletin board outside his office in Dallas Hall with nasty comments written below. By 1952, he was also busy pushing a book entitled *The Iron Curtain over America,* which he had published in Dallas in December 1951. Beaty's book was unusual in the subliterature of hate. Unlike the frenetically demagogic outpourings of Gerald L. K. Smith (whose vicious magazine, *The Cross and the Flag,* I received as a gift subscription for many years from anonymous donors eager to set me on the right path), Beaty's book gave the appearance of sober, serious, and carefully researched scholarship. It was, however, an amazing collection of truths, half-truths, and outright distortions held together by a conspiratorial view of all major happenings in the world during the twentieth century. According to Beaty, the Khazar Jews (a people of mixed stock with Mongol and Turkish affinities who conquered southern Russia in the seventh century and adopted Judaism in the ninth century) were responsible for all of America's — and the world's — ills beginning with World War I. An aggressive minority within Russia, the Judaized Khazars, said Beaty, were bent on destroying Germany, bulwark of western Christianity, and establishing communism throughout the world. They infiltrated the Democratic Party under Woodrow Wilson, pushed the country into war against Germany in 1917, engineered the Bolshevik Revolution, persuaded FDR to recognize the Soviet Union in 1933, forced the United States into another war with Germany in 1941, and, in their latest undertaking, took the country into the Korean War in order to kill off non-Jewish boys. This *"powerful Eastern European element dominant in inner circles of the Democratic party,"* Beaty insisted, *"regarded with complete equanimity . . . the killing of as many as possible of the world-ruling and Khazar-hated race of 'Aryans.'"* Beaty's pseudo-erudition and his tone of sweet reasonableness (he claimed to be anti-Khazar but not anti-Jewish) made him unique in the history of bigotry. According to *Zion's Herald,* a Methodist magazine, Beaty's book was the "most extensive piece of racist propaganda in the history of the anti-Semitic movement in America." It was also the most appalling: by implication throughout, and in some places openly, the book was friendly to Hitler and the Nazis.

Beaty's book made little stir at first. Most of us at SMU had heard that Beaty had published a "hate" book at his own expense, but few of us had seen it or knew anything of its precise contents. By 1953, however, the book was attracting national attention. Millionaire J. Russell Maguire (who had bought up the *American Mercury* and turned H. L. Mencken's delightful old journal into a mouthpiece for prejudice and reaction) put up money to distribute the book and it was hailed with enthusiasm by hate groups throughout the country. Gerald L. K. Smith called it "the greatest . . . of its kind ever to appear in print" and Gerald Winrod's *Defender Magazine* and Robert H. Williams' *Williams Intelligence Summary* (both anti-Semitic hate magazines) were energetically promoting it. In the fall of 1953, Margaret L. Hartley, associate editor at the SMU Press, released the first careful study of the untruths contained in Beaty's book in the *Southwest Review* (published at SMU) and was called on the carpet by some of the SMU trustees for her effort. Late in 1953, Lon Tinkle, SMU French professor, created a special category for Beaty's book in his Sunday book column for the *Dallas Morning News:* books that should never have been published. Shortly afterwards, I decided to join Margaret Hartley and Lon Tinkle in repudiating the book. Having plowed through *Iron Curtain* with mounting distaste, I wrote a letter to the *Daily Campus* on November 25, calling the book "a dreary performance, full of distortions, omissions, and half-truths," which "shows not the slightest understanding of either modern history or the dynamics of Soviet communism." I also pointed out that Beaty's disclaimer of anti-Semitism was "surprisingly similar to that of the Stalinists [who were persecuting Jews in Czechoslovakia and in the Soviet Union itself during the early fifties], a fact which, along with many others, seems to have escaped him entirely." It was an arrogant letter, but how else was one to deal with an ignorant book professing to dwell on a high level of intellection? In any case, Beaty's response was to refer to Tinkle as a "novice" in the rank of full professor and to me as a "junior personality." Privately, however, he referred to me as a Communist, though not, so far as I ever heard, as a Khazar Jew.

Early in 1954, Beaty published an eight-page pamphlet entitled "How To Capture a University" in which he announced that "a certain powerful non-Christian element in our population" was trying to take over SMU. B'nai B'rith, a "Jewish Gestapo," he said, was trying to get control of SMU's theology school; the SMU bookstore (which stocked a pamphlet by Karl Marx for a history class) was "an outlet for official Soviet propaganda"; and the *Southwest Review* (because of Margaret Hartley's article) had a "non-Christian and leftist slant." Both in his pamphlet and in interviews with the *Daily Campus,* Beaty stressed the fact that only a few "junior personalities" on the faculty had criticized his book and that there had been no official repudiation of his views by the university administration. At this point SMU President Umphrey Lee announced that he had referred Beaty's pamphlet to the board of trustees for "such action as they may see fit to take," seven Dallas clergymen issued a statement expressing "outraged Christian consciences" over Beaty's views, and a group of SMU law professors, led by Roy Ray, sent a letter to the campus paper repudiating the opinions set forth in *Iron Curtain*.

What about the faculty as a whole? *Time* magazine, I learned, was planning to do a story about Professor Beaty; and I couldn't help feeling that it was important for the SMU faculty to distance itself publicly from his views before the story appeared. Late in February 1954 I went into a huddle with Allen Maxwell and Margaret Hartley, my friends at the SMU Press and the *Southwest Review,* and they suggested I discuss the possibility of general faculty action with my history department chairman Herbert P. Gambrell. It was important, we agreed, for a senior faculty member to take the initiative in such a matter. I called Professor Gambrell at once and at his invitation dropped by his house around five o'clock that afternoon. His wife Virginia joined us, invited me to dinner, providing, she said impishly, I had no objection to ham, and I ended by staying with the Gambrells until after midnight. Both the Gambrells were gifted raconteurs. Not only did they have at their disposal a prodigious collection of amusing tales, funny remarks, choice malapropisms to report, and outrageous puns for just about every occasion, they also had a talent for talking about their encounters with other people in this world in such a way as to transmute the most commonplace situations into little dramas filled with charm, good humor, and a bit of absurdity.

The Gambrells plied me with drinks that evening as well as with food and anecdotes, and as the evening progressed I began wondering whether my suggestion for faculty action in the Beaty matter was being taken seriously. Between stories, however, Dr. Gambrell (he was amiable but dignified and I never learned to call him anything but that in all the years I knew him) made phone calls to friends on the faculty and in the administration, and one of them, I couldn't help overhearing, was to Roy Ray, sponsor of the SMU law school professors' letter to the *Daily Campus,* and another to Hemphill Hosford, the provost, one of the most civilized members of a university administration whom I have ever encountered. "Paul Boller is here," Dr. Gambrell announced each time, "and thinks we ought to do something about Dr. Beaty at our faculty meeting tomorrow." But he always resumed his story-telling when he put down the receiver, and he never said anything about the responses he was getting to his exchanges with his associates. When I finally left the Gambrells, late that night, a bit dazed, I wasn't sure I had accomplished anything, but I knew I had had a great time.

The following morning I was still doubtful about what was to come, and after I had met my classes and eaten lunch and was ready to attend the general faculty meeting set for 4 P.M., I was still wondering. But as I made my way over to Hyer Hall, where the faculty was assembling, Dr. Gambrell took me aside for a moment and told me that Roy Ray had a resolution to introduce that would interest me. It did interest me; it was, in fact, one of the most interesting resolutions introduced into a faculty meeting at which I was present during all my years in the groves of academe.

Professor Ray's resolution repudiating Beaty's philosophy was brief, but strongly worded, and Ray handled faculty discussion of it masterfully. It didn't come until the end of the meeting and it transformed a typical dreary faculty meeting into one charged with excitement. Professor Beaty (perhaps sensing what was to come) absented himself from the meeting, but some of his supporters were there, and they voiced objections to the wording of Ray's resolution. So did several other members of the faculty known for their garrulousness at meetings. "Most of us haven't read Dr. Beaty's book," they said, "and we don't know enough about his views to repudiate them." To this Professor Ray finally exclaimed: "What do you mean, you don't know what his views are? There isn't a person in this room who doesn't know what his views are! I want this resolution to be voted on as it stands; otherwise, I will withdraw it." Provost Hosford then put the resolution repudiating Beaty's views as "without any foundation in fact" to a standing vote and it passed by a vote of 114 to 2.

A few days after the SMU faculty's action (which *Time* reported in an article about Dr. Beaty, with his picture, entitled "The Friendly Professor"), the SMU trustees issued a mild statement chastising Beaty. Some of the trustees appointed to look into the matter had, in fact, been at least as critical of the *Southwest Review* as they were of Beaty, and Margaret Hartley had been obliged to appear before the trustees' committee to explain that her article did not contain her own opinions about Beaty but was a lengthy review of Ralph Lord Roy's *Apostles of Discord* (1953), in which she summarized Roy's criticisms of Beaty's book. Beaty claimed, not unnaturally, that he had not really been reprimanded by the trustees and issued another pamphlet charging that the label "anti-Semitic" was simply a smear aimed at good anti-Communists.

Still, the faculty resolution and the trustees' statement, weak as it was, helped put an end to Beaty's crusade against the Khazars. But he remained busy all the same. He next turned his attention to the English department and began mailing out pamphlets to the parents of SMU students complaining that SMU's English professors required their classes to read dirty books and plays by people like William Faulkner and Clifford Odets. At this point, Willis Tate, a sociology professor who had succeeded Umphrey Lee as president of the university, called Dr. Beaty into his office and made it clear to him that he was to send out no more pamphlets without first clearing them with the administration. Beaty remained quiet after that; and Beatyism ceased being a problem at SMU. But a few years later, after his retirement, Dr. Beaty got even with Tate; in January 1960, the *American Mercury* ran an article written by Harold Lord Varney, but obviously inspired by Beaty, entitled "Southern Methodist University Pampers Leftism" which gave high praise to *The Iron Curtain over America* and accused President Tate of coddling leftism.

In *Iron Curtain* Professor Beaty made a special point of

attacking Franklin Roosevelt for extending diplomatic recognition to the Soviet Union in November 1933. By recognizing the Soviet government, he said, FDR gave a new lease on life to a tottering regime and furthered the cause of Communist expansion. Beaty was not alone in seeing something sinister in Roosevelt's action. The nefariousness of Soviet recognition was stock in trade for all the McCarthyites in the early fifties and the "twenty years of treason" they talked about with such vehemence commenced, they said, with Soviet recognition. Writers like William F. Buckley and newspapers like the *Chicago Tribune* and the *Dallas Morning News* charged that recognition planted the seeds of Communist subversion in the United States and they all blamed FDR for it. As the *Dallas Morning News* put it angrily on November 17, 1953: "Russia was recognized solely because Franklin D. Roosevelt as President insisted upon it."

It was difficult for me to believe that the question of Soviet recognition was that simple — or that sinister. Late in 1953, therefore, I began spending part of each day in the stacks of SMU's Fondren Library turning the pages of countless magazines and newspapers back in 1933 to see if I could learn with some precision just how Soviet recognition came about and what the American people thought about it at the time. The results were surprising, even to me; the majority of newspapers and the bulk of the American business community, I found, favored recognition at the time. They saw the possibility of profitable trade with Russia, for one thing; for another, they thought Russian recognition might serve to check Japanese aggression in China. The *Dallas Morning News,* I discovered to my delight, had been especially eager for recognition. "Some object to recognition," said the *News* late in 1933, "on the ground that Russia's system of government is communistic and in general antireligious. Internationally, however, each State in theory has the right to determine its own form of government and sphere of activity. . . . The general opinion in this country is that Russia and the United States should resume normal and diplomatic relations, since they have many common interests, especially in the Far East, and can readily develop trade relations, mutually profitable. . . ."

To the *Dallas Morning News,* Russia was "Just Another Customer." A *News* cartoon portrayed a Russian woman waiting before the counter in a grocery store to make her purchases while Uncle Sam, the clerk, tells two protesting women (the American Federation of Labor and the Daughters of the American Revolution): "Listen! I ain't goin' to marry the gal!" But my favorite finding was the report of the love feast held in Manhattan's Waldorf-Astoria Hotel on November 24, 1933, to celebrate recognition. It was an elegant party attended by Soviet officials (including Maxim Litvinov, chief Russian negotiator) and by prominent businessmen representing just about every major corporation in the United States. The high point of the evening came when the 2500 guests stood and faced a stage behind which hung a huge American flag beside the Red flag with Soviet hammer and sickle while the organ played "My Country 'tis of Thee" and then switched into the "Internationale." I wrote up my findings in an article entitled "The 'Great Conspiracy' of 1933: A Study in Short Memories," which appeared in the *Southwest Review* in the spring of 1954.

The *SWR* article attracted considerable attention. Not only were its findings summarized in newspapers around the country, the *New York Post* requested and received permission to reprint the article in its weekend magazine section on August 22 and accompanied it with an editorial commenting favorably on its conclusions. The *Chicago Tribune* picked up the story, reprinted the *Post* editorial on September 6, and added an editorial of its own, sternly reminding the *SWR* writer, "an obscure professor" in Texas, that the *Tribune* itself had adamantly opposed recognition to the bitter end. Unlike the *Tribune,* the *Dallas Morning News* could scarcely claim it had opposed recognition in 1933; in an editorial commenting on the *SWR* article on March 16, however, the *News* insisted that the Roosevelt administration had concealed information about Russia from the American people and that if the *News* had been privy to such information it would have opposed recognition. When Larry Perrine, my good friend in the English department, wrote the *News* to say he thought the editorial was a weak one, Colonel Beaty denounced him at an English department meeting and tried to block his promotion to associate professor.

For all its McCarthyism, the *Dallas Morning News*, it must be said, did have one anti-McCarthyite section in the paper in the 1950s: the Sunday book page edited by SMU Press director Allen Maxwell and carrying French professor Lon Tinkle's lively book column. I did several reviews for the Sunday *News*, taking the anti-McCarthyite point of view where appropriate; and on April 4, 1954, I even had a confrontation with Harry C. Withers, executive editor of the *News*. In our exchange on the book page he praised and I criticized *McCarthy and His Enemies,* a defense of the Wisconsin senator by William F. Buckley and L. Brent Bozell. To my delight, I received a nice card from the elder Maury Maverick (who had been a lively Democratic congressman from Texas in the 1930s) about one of my anti-McCarthyite reviews; but the usual response to my pieces, if any, was an anonymous card linking me to the Communist conspiracy. From time to time I also received anonymous notes from students at SMU (or from their mothers) calling me a Commie. Once I mentioned D. H. Lawrence casually in one of my classes and the next day to my amusement received two unsigned letters accusing me of following "the good ole party line." For the fun of it, one day I put a Lenin quotation (which argued for restricting free speech) on the blackboard, without identifying the source, and asked students in one of my classes to talk about it. To my immense gratification, the majority of the youngsters felt uneasy about the statement and voiced misgivings about its general tone. The only student who defended the statement with ardor was a young woman who always made a special point of her ultraconservatism. When the discussion ended and I revealed the source of the quotation, she flushed with surprise and embarrassment. I felt truly sorry for her; but I hoped she had learned something from the incident.

Despite the McCarthyite atmosphere in Dallas and the conservative nature of SMU's faculty and student body, I think I can honestly say I never felt restrained in expressing my opinions while teaching at SMU. When I debated Lynn Landrum, conservative columnist for the *Dallas Morning News,* about McCarthyism in the fall of 1953, the majority of students in the audience were on my side; one Korean veteran, in fact, told Landrum he thought he had been fighting for free speech, not for McCarthyism, when he was in Korea. But this took place in the Perkins School of Theology, which was always far more liberal than the other schools at SMU. Most of the students in the College of Arts and Sciences were, I think, conservative; and those who were liberally inclined were not very far out in left field. Still, most of the students, even the conservatives, believed in good manners and fair play, and when I happened to mention some anonymous student letters I had just received to one of my classes, all the students there were genuinely shocked.

In SMU's next big crisis, after the Beaty affair, during the 1950s — the Gates crisis — the student body in my opinion behaved admirably throughout. It was students, indeed, who precipitated the crisis, though that was not the way the *American Mercury's* Harold Lord Varney saw it. In his attack on President Tate, Varney gave the impression that Tate himself was responsible for what he called the "booking" of John Gates, "a notorious Communist," as a university lecturer in the spring of 1958.

Varney, as usual, garbled things. SMU did not "book" Gates as a university lecturer, and when Gates appeared on the campus he was not "a notorious Communist," but a disillusioned defector from the American Communist Party. He had been a faithful Stalinist, it is true, for many years; and in 1949 he was indicted, along with ten other Communist leaders, for Communist activities, and sent to the Atlanta penitentiary (in flagrant violation of the Bill of Rights, in my opinion) for four years and eight months. Upon his release, he became editor of the *Daily Worker,* but not for long; in 1956, after Soviet Premier Nikita Khrushchev delivered his

impassioned speech to Soviet Communist Party officials denouncing Stalin for his criminal activities, Gates, like so
many other American Communists, lost faith in the Soviet
system and quit the Communist Party soon after, though
continuing to think of himself as a "democratic socialist."

When reports of Gates' disaffection with communism began appearing in the newspapers, some of the students at
SMU thought it might be fun to invite him to the campus to
give a talk on why he had left the party. In January 1958, the
SMU Student Center Forum Committee (on which some of
my students served, but with whom I had never discussed
Gates) sent a telegram to Gates in New York inviting him to
speak at a dinner seminar in the Grand Ballroom of the Student Center in April. News that Gates had accepted the invitation hit Dallas like a bombshell. There was a violent outcry, on and off campus, followed by efforts to induce the
administration at SMU to cancel the invitation. "Who but a
communist, or a communist supporter, would want a communist spouting his views for the benefit of college students?" exclaimed one protester. Angry letters poured into
President Tate's office from SMU parents and alumni around
the country, the American Legion and the Daughters of the
American Revolution condemned the invitation, Federal
Judge Whitfield Davidson deplored the idea of an atheistic
Communist appearing on the SMU campus, and civic
groups in Dallas (especially the Public Affairs Luncheon
Club) passed resolutions protesting plans for a talk by Gates
at SMU.

Despite the fury, President Tate stood firm. "One thing
worse than having John Gates speak at SMU would be to
veto his appearance," he told the Student Council. "Confin-
ing freedom in any area cripples freedom in all areas. Free
expression is the cornerstone of democracy." Tate insisted
that ideas must be aired so their worth could be evaluated.
"College students are adults," he said. "I believe that the
purpose of a university is to confront them with the real
issues of life. I don't believe that facts, ideas or people should
be withheld from them — as long as they are expressed in

good taste." At Rice University the administration flatly turned down student requests for permission to invite Gates to the campus after his SMU appearance. The University of Texas also barred an appearance by the former Communist.

SMU's student newspaper was hostile to the Gates talk from the outset. The editors compared members of the Student Center Forum Committee, who had asked Gates to speak, to a group of Boy Scouts helping an old lady off the curb into the path of an eight-axle fruit truck. Inviting Gates to speak at SMU, they complained, was like inviting Satan to speak on sin. And when some of the students said they would like to hear Satan on sin, the editors retorted: "They know where they can go!" But most of SMU's students disagreed with the *Daily Campus*. They may have been conservative, but they also resented outside interference with the college's internal affairs and rejected the assumption that they were not bright or mature enough to hear a former Communist speak and decide for themselves what they thought about him. Undoubtedly, too, they looked forward to a little fun and excitement on the campus. The *Daily Campus* received more letters from students favoring the Gates talk than from those opposing it, and the editors finally gave way grudgingly and announced that "we recognize the right of free speech and consider it proper that SMU students should attend the meeting for whatever it might be worth."

Despite the *Daily Campus'* change of heart, hostile pressure from off campus continued undiminished and in the end President Tate arranged a compromise; he replaced the dinner seminar with an afternoon meeting in McFarlin Auditorium, the school's largest gathering place, and arranged for Gates to appear on a panel with Herbert Philbrick, former FBI agent who had infiltrated the Communist Party years before (and whose testimony at the trial of party leaders in 1949 had helped send Gates to prison). Gates at first exploded when he learned that Philbrick was going to be on the panel, but at length he regained his composure and agreed to face his old enemy at SMU. There were other members of the panel besides Philbrick: J. Claude Evans, SMU chaplain; Douglas

Jackson, professor in the Perkins School of Theology; and Lloyd Wells, professor in the Department of Government. The first floor of McFarlin was reserved for students and faculty and the two balconies were opened to the general public. The proceedings were to be piped into the Student Center ballroom, in case of a McFarlin overflow. As it turned out, approximately 3000 people filled McFarlin on April 23, 1958, the day of the event, and an additional 1500 listened to the discussion in the Student Center.

April 23 was a hot day: ninety degrees by three o'clock in the afternoon, the time of the Gates appearance. I prepared my one-o'clock class (about eighty students) for the Gates panel by finishing a three-part lecture I had commenced the previous week on Marxism-Leninism-Stalinism and the history of the American Communist Party, from the 1920s onward. When the class period ended at 2:30, we all walked over to McFarlin Auditorium (then without air-conditioning), and though we got there early, we found the place already jampacked with students, faculty members, and townspeople, and were forced to stand in the aisle. When Gates rose to speak after the student chairman's introduction, people in the galleries started hissing and booing noisily, but this only touched off a round of applause among the students below. When the auditorium quieted, Gates began his talk by thanking the Public Affairs Luncheon Club (the Dallas group that had been agitating against his appearance for weeks) for making the meeting such a success. This set off another chorus of boos in the balconies and another round of applause on the main floor. Several more exchanges between town and gown followed, as Gates proceeded with his remarks, and at length the moderator pleaded for restraint and saw to it that things went off in an orderly fashion after that. Gates spoke for about forty minutes on why he had left the Communist Party and then fielded questions from Philbrick and the professors, and after that responded to written questions sent up to the platform from students occupying the main floor. Gates made no secret of the fact that although he had lost faith in the Soviet system he was still opposed to capitalism and hoped for the triumph of democratic socialism in the United States some day. The *Dallas Morning News* reported that he "still thinks like a Communist" and quoted Philbrick as saying that he revealed the "communistic mind at work."

The Gates afternoon was a stunning triumph for academic freedom at SMU; and for me it almost made up for the cancellation of the Stevenson rally in 1952. April 23 was a triumph for seriousness at SMU, too, for hundreds of students, ordinarily quiescent, were roused for weeks to a high pitch of excitement by a discussion of ideas and issues of high importance for the nation. "It was a thrilling meeting," wrote Gates afterward, "and I learned as much from these students as they from me." But partly because Gates came across as brighter and wittier than Philbrick, Dallas McCarthyites began referring to SMU as "Southern Marxist University" and charging that the place was full of leftists. Of course, if Gates had gone from communism to McCarthyism when he left the Communist Party, as so many former Communists did, he would have been welcomed with open arms in Dallas. But he didn't; and he was regarded as untrustworthy at best and a crypto-Communist at worst. The *Dallas Morning News* complained that Gates had talked too long at the meeting and that no one had tried to stop him. "SMU's advertised debate of 'free' ideas," grumbled the editors, "turned out to be 40 minutes for Communism, 15 for Americanism."

I was only peripherally involved in the Gates affair, for I am not, as a matter of fact, much of an activist. Still, though I don't regard myself as an Organization Man, I did help establish three new groups while I was at SMU: the American Studies Association of Texas (1956), the Dallas Citizens for Peaceful Integration (1957), and the Dallas Civil Liberties Union (1960). The ASA of Texas was a scholarly group and posed no problems; nor did the DCLU, for some reason, provoke any opposition when it was first founded. With DCPI, the integrationist group, however, it was quite otherwise. The association of SMU professors — which included my history department colleague Richard H. Powers and my friend Robert F. Smith in the government department — with an organization favoring compliance with the Supreme Court's 1954 ruling on public school integration produced severe criticism from Dallas conservatives and considerable pressure from public school administrators in Dallas to discipline or fire us. Looking back on those days, though, I find it hard to see why. DCPI (or "Dipsy," as one of our members, jumbling initials, facetiously called it) wasn't particularly effective. We assembled only a handful of members, met about once a week Thursday evenings at homes and churches for lectures, discussions, and occasional parties, and in 1958 sent a letter to the Dallas school board encouraging compliance with Supreme Court decisions outlawing racial segregation in the public schools. DCPI's letter, when quoted in the press and on radio and TV, produced furious protests to President Tate from the superintendent of schools and other prominent Dallasites, and it also touched off a series of irate phone calls to Powers, Smith, and me. Still, it seems clear that when integration finally came to Dallas a few years later our little group had little, if anything, to do with it. Prestige and profit, not pressure from "Dipsy," turned the trick. The city fathers finally decided they wanted Dallas to become a convention city in which the big national organizations — business, educational, political — would hold their annual meetings (filling the city's coffers) and there was no place for violent resistance to integration in such a scheme of things.

Despite Dipsy's ineffectiveness, I enjoyed my association with the organization, mainly because for the first time in my life I began meeting blacks socially on a fairly regular basis. Georgia Battle, the plucky local NAACP official who worked with us, was a favorite of mine; it was she, Bob Smith, and I who drafted DCPI's constitution in the Dallas NAACP office one searingly hot summer afternoon, with a beer or two to spur us on. While working with Dipsy, I also joined the younger members of the SMU faculty, prompted by the English department's Larry Perrine, in meeting with President Tate from time to time to encourage integration at

SMU. The first black undergraduate entered SMU in 1961; Dallas began integrating its schools in 1964.

Before becoming involved with DCPI, both Dick Powers and I joined the Southern Conference Educational Fund (SCEF), an integrationist organization whose field secretaries, Carl and Anne Braden, had visited Dallas in 1957 and encouraged us to organize a local integrationist group. DCPI had no connection with SCEF; Mrs. Battle insisted from the outset that we form a completely autonomous group, with no ties to SCEF or any other national organization. But the SCEF connection eventually proved troublesome for Powers and me, for its enemies charged that it was Communist-controlled. The attorney general's list of subversive organizations did not include SCEF, to be sure, but Mississippi Senator James Eastland's Committee on Internal Subversion had unfairly branded the organization a Communist-front group. And the House Un-American Activities Committee (HUAC) also cited Carl Braden, SCEF leader in Louisville, Kentucky, for contempt, and sent him to jail for a year for refusing to answer questions about his political beliefs. Braden announced elsewhere that he was not a Communist, but he refused to say so to HUAC because he thought the Bill of Rights prohibited government agencies from inquiring into a citizen's personal beliefs. I thought then and still think he was right, and I refused to sever my association with SCEF simply because know-nothing groups like the John Birch Society, the Circuit Riders, and Texans for America called it subversive and used my membership in it as an excuse for calling Powers and me Communists. I did, though, tongue in cheek, write the Department of Justice inquiring about SCEF and received a letter from the assistant attorney general, Internal Security Division, informing me of what I already knew: that SCEF was not listed as subversive. I wrote the letter reluctantly, but angry SMU alumni were bombarding President Tate with letters about my SCEF membership and it seemed at the time the only decent thing to do.

McCarthyism reached the peak of its influence in Texas in the early 1960s (despite McCarthy's death in 1957) and in the

Dallas area even Beatyism made something of a comeback. In January 1960, an organization called Texans for America, headed by J. Evetts Haley, a Canyon, Texas, cattleman and author of books on ranching, reprinted the *American Mercury's* article on leftism at SMU (which had praised Beaty's anti-Semitic book) and mailed 8000 copies of it to SMU alumni and parents. The following month former FBI agent Dan Smoot, an extreme rightist commentator in the Dallas area, got into the act. In his monthly newsletter, the "Dan Smoot Report," and on his Sunday afternoon TV show, he praised the *Mercury* article, and, since President Tate had publicly denied the *Mercury's* charges, he presented evidence gathered from SMU students to prove that the *Mercury* (and Professor Beaty) were correct in their charges. Smoot's student informants singled out six of us on the faculty at SMU as leftists; but Smoot gave me special attention because a couple of my students had turned class notes over to him and he was able to quote from them at length.

Some of what the students told Smoot about my views was false; most of it was accurate enough, though misinterpreted. It was not true, as one student alleged, that I had called the Chinese Communists "agrarian reformers" and that I had followed the Soviet line on China. I always made it clear to my classes in Far East history that Mao Tse-tung and other Chinese Communist leaders regarded themselves as orthodox Marxist-Leninists who departed from Stalinism only in building their movement on the peasants rather than on the proletariat. But the students were quite correct in telling Smoot that I denied that the United States "lost China" and insisted, instead, that Chiang Kai-shek and the Nationalists had gone down to defeat through their own inefficiency, corruption, military ineptitude, and inability to win the allegiance of the Chinese masses. This of course ran counter to the McCarthyite charge (which no one who knew anything about China took seriously) that we had "lost China" because of subversion in Washington. When it came to my large class, "History of Ideas in America," students reported my lectures accurately enough; I was friendly, as they told

Smoot, to FDR and the New Deal. They ignored the fact, though, that I was careful in lectures to point out weaknesses in the New Deal and to present both conservative and radical criticisms of Roosevelt's policies. Smoot found one student's summary of my opinions particularly alarming: "FDR's sympathies for the poor people was no abstract thing with FDR. His humanitarianism grew out of his love of people."

Smoot's biggest "scoop" — in his newsletter and on TV — was that in lectures on American Communism I told SMU classes that Communist influence through the years had been vastly exaggerated. He was also puzzled and disturbed by the distinction I made (borrowed from Hannah Arendt) between "former Communists" (who shed the Bolshevik mentality when they left CP, USA, and took up the liberal democratic faith) and "ex-Communists" (who retained the Bolshevik frame of mind when they moved from Left to Right). Shortly after the Smoot Report began making the rounds, the *Daily Campus* sent a reporter to interview me about Smoot's "revelations," but I refused to "roll around in the gutter" with Smoot, as I put it, somewhat superciliously, and refrained from making any comments on his charges. I also refused to appear before the textbook committee of the Texas House of Representatives in Austin to "defend myself against the charge of Communism," because, as I told the committee chairman, I had nothing to defend.

Pressed by students, however, I finally agreed to give a talk on American Communism in the Student Center. On March 15, I lectured to a large audience on "The Rise and Fall of the Communist Party in the United States" and answered questions afterward. In my talk, I made it clear that the twists and turns of the Stalinist line from the 1920s until 1953, when Stalin died, were absolutely indefensible from an American point of view, though the Bill of Rights, I pointed out, did not forbid the airing of views I regarded as erroneous. But I also noted that only a small minority of Americans had ever joined CP, USA, and that the party had enjoyed a certain amount of popularity in this country only when the Stalinist line happened to coincide with what most Americans believed at the time (the anti-Nazi line, 1935–39, and the wartime line, 1941–45). I pointed out, moreover, that during World War II, such impeccable conservatives as Eddie Rickenbacker, Congressman John Rankin of Mississippi, and Douglas MacArthur (to say nothing of the *Dallas Morning News*) had been extravagant in their praise of Stalinist Russia, our wartime ally. But in 1960, I concluded, CP, USA, was at the lowest ebb of its influence; for all practical purposes, I said, the party was dead and "deserves to be." I later wrote up my lecture for the *Southwest Review* and it was published that fall with the title, "CP, USA: An American Irrelevance." I got in the habit of sending copies of the essay to angry letter-writers and that always abruptly ended the correspondence.

On a panel discussion with three other professors during "Religious Emphasis Week" at SMU in February 1961, I reiterated my belief that CP, USA, was "practically defunct and really irrelevant to the important problems facing this country." When someone in the audience quoted J. Edgar Hoover to the contrary, I made so bold as to differ with the FBI chief, whose opinions I found something less than infallible. There were shocked gasps in the audience (which included townspeople as well as students, some of them with tape recorders) and my *lèse majesté* went into the record to haunt me for the next few years. Probably nothing I did at SMU — not even associating with SCEF — damaged me more with the Paranoid Right in Texas than my insistence that American Communism was a negligible force in American life. To minimize American Communism was, in those days, like taking the Wicked Witch out of *The Wizard of Oz,* or Captain Hook out of *Peter Pan,* or the wolf out of the Little Red Riding Hood story. What is a fairy tale, after all, without witches, wizards, and goblins? Dallas reactionaries needed the Communist Party far more than I did. Without CP, USA, to blame, how could they explain America's vast problems after World War II despite the triumphant victory in that war? And how else could they account for the drive for social and racial justice after the war when Americans should, they thought, have resumed their old pre-war ways of living?

Sometimes I thought I was being cold-hearted in trying to deprive reactionaries of their beloved Communist Party.

On February 15, the *Dallas Morning News* (which had launched an investigation and triumphantly produced eight Communists in Dallas and 200 in Texas as a whole) lectured me sternly on the subject and quoted FBI Chief J. Edgar Hoover at length for my edification; a few days later Hoover wrote the *News* a letter commending the editors for their wisdom. In a talk to the Dallas Federation of Women's Clubs a little later, Colonel John W. Mayo, head of the Dallas City Council Civil Defense Committee, denounced me severely and warned Dallasites that there was "something wrong at SMU." The *Park Cities-North Dallas News* joined Mayo in excoriating my "unusual views," and, like the *Dallas Morning News*, quoted Hoover chapter and verse to confound me. Later on, it began calling me SMU's "rotten apple."

But my critics all ignored one ironic point I had made on the Religious Emphasis Week panel: that there were many FBI plants in the tiny American Communist Party and that they always voted the ultra-left line at meetings. They also overlooked the statement that Attorney General Robert F. Kennedy made, not long after the panel met, to the effect that CP, USA, was a "political organization of no danger in the United States," and that, although objectionable, it "had no following and has been disregarded by the American people for many, many years." And they all kept quiet about an essay of mine on "The *Dallas Morning News* and Communist Russia" appearing in the March issue of the *Southwest Social Science Quarterly* which showed, by copious quotations from editorials, that the *News* had been extremely friendly in the past toward FDR, the New Deal, Russian recognition, and (during World War II) the Soviet Union. (I still treasure the letter I received from former President Truman praising the article and suggesting that I take on "one or two other newspapers in the same class with the *Dallas Morning News*, whose ideas of fairness and truth are nonexistent.") In any case, my minimization of the Communist threat within the United States made me a prime target of the ultra-right in Texas. By

September 1961, President Tate felt obliged to issue a public statement defending me as a teacher, scholar, and citizen. He was receiving hysterical calls in the middle of the night (though he never told me about them until I left SMU for another position) ordering him: "Fire Boller!" I was sorry when I heard about these calls, and I was impressed by the fact that he did not mention them to me at the time. As far as I was concerned, he had certainly earned the Alexander Meiklejohn Award which the American Association of University Professors conferred on him in 1965 "for significant action in the support of academic freedom."

The timing of the controversy over communism in America could not have been worse for me. In 1961, a high school textbook, *This Is Our Nation*, which I had written with Jean Tilford, a Cincinnati public school teacher, came up for adoption in Texas. When hearings were held before the state textbook advisory committee (made up of teachers and principals) in September, cattleman J. Evetts Haley, head of Texans for America, went to Austin to testify that *This Is Our Nation* was "dangerous as a textbook and deleterious to the character of the children reading it." He went on to say that I was "soft on communism or short on logic and learning, or perhaps both." Harris Holmes, the hard-working Texas representative of Webster Publishing Company in St. Louis, which had published the book, made a valiant defense of my integrity before the committee. Lon Tinkle, Rabbi Levi Olan, SMU faculty friends, Allen Maxwell and Margaret Hartley at the SMU Press, and many of my students gave me their warm support. And the American Studies Association of Texas passed a resolution, written by Martin Shockley, doughty English professor at North Texas State University (who for years fought hypocrisy, humbug, and hysteria in the academic world), expressing complete confidence in me and "no confidence whatsoever" in Haley. Haley, of course, was unmoved by all this. In an article on American reactionaries about this time, *Life* referred to Haley as a "crackpot," but in Texas he was thought of as a "good ol' boy."

*Teaching at SMU (author's collection).*

Haley's organization had a textbook committee of its own, headed by Don Riddle, a veterinarian from Paris, Texas. Riddle made a cursory reading of all the American history texts submitted for adoption and issued criticisms of most of them. But he gave *This Is Our Nation* special attention, since I taught in Texas, and it was necessary for Wally Stees, the hard-working editor whom Webster had assigned to the book, to call an emergency meeting with Jean Tilford and me to prepare detailed replies to his long list of criticisms. Riddle's critique was shabbily written: awkward, repetitive, and filled with errors in spelling, punctuation, and grammar. The critique was also filled with inaccuracies: it accused us of omitting vital facts about American history which we had actually included in the book. But it was harder to respond to other charges. What was one to say to the allegation that we spent too much space on the Indians and on the subject of slavery? Or that it was "sadistic" to mention the Salem witch-hunt? Or that we failed to point out that the United Nations was a world government infringing on American sovereignty?

Riddle was particularly upset by a quotation from Anzia Yezierska (an immigrant from Russia who published several books in the 1920s about her life in America) appearing in the book. He kept coming back to the Yezierska quote in his critique and complaining that we could have selected "a more truly American" figure to cite. We did in fact quote Washington, Jefferson, and Franklin. But when it came to the twentieth century, we also quoted John Dewey, Lincoln Steffens, Ida Tarbell, and Upton Sinclair; and all of these people, from Riddle's point of view, were suspect. Dewey, he said, had been cited twenty-one times by HUAC. He also saw something sinister in a cartoon the book contained illustrating America's purchase of Alaska from Russia in 1867. The cartoon pictured Secretary of State William Seward (who had had trouble getting the U.S. Senate to ratify the Alaska treaty) laboriously pushing a wheelbarrow, called "treaty," on which was perched a huge rock labeled "Russian America" (the name of Alaska before our purchase). "The authors," Riddle warned, "purpose [sic] to instill in the students [sic] mind a Russian America." The book was of course accused of being too friendly to Roosevelt and the New Deal and faulted for not saying that FDR had tricked the United States into recognizing the Soviet Union. What bothered Riddle above all else was that in a chapter on American culture in the twentieth century we mentioned scores of people — Ralph Bunche, Aaron Copland, Charlie Chaplin, Albert Einstein, William Faulkner, Ernest Hemingway, Sinclair Lewis, Eugene O'Neill, Willa Cather, Carl Sandburg, "and many more!" — whose loyalty to the United States was in question. "Our students," lamented Riddle in the grand conclusion to his report, "are supposed to learn more of the true heritage of their country by reading the works of men who are [sic] government investigating committee had sighted [sic] as being affiliated with subversive organizations; than by studying the lives and history of the men who formed our government." The tone of the reply we framed to Riddle was moderate and unruffled; we took up his points one by one and yielded ground on none of them.

The battle of the textbooks went on for weeks. When the textbook committee, made up of fifteen high school teachers and administrators throughout the state, met to make its recommendations to the State Board of Education in October 1961, it selected five textbooks, including *This Is Our Nation,* for the state's multiple-adoption list. The committee also asked for minor changes in all of the books, including ours. We agreed to the revisions; they involved changes in wording in three places for clarification and replacing one picture because its reproduction was poor. One of the writers for the *Texas Observer,* liberal biweekly, called me from Austin to ask about the changes. To my astonishment, he simply refused to believe that we had not altered our book to please the Haleyites; and in his coverage of the textbook controversy in the *Observer,* he gave the impression that we had "sold out." I found it hard at this point to decide who had a lower opinion of me: Haley or the *Observer* writer.

In November 1961, the State Board of Education approved

the textbook committee's recommendations (despite Haley's efforts to have my book stricken from the list), and the multiple-adoption list was sent to local school districts throughout the state. Up to this point, Texas educators had withstood admirably the enormous pressure brought on them by the Haleyites and deserved high praise, I thought, for their refusal to be intimidated. But when the multiple-adoption list went to the local districts, the Haleyites renewed their efforts to kill off my book (including attacks on me at the textbook committee hearings of the state legislature in 1962) and in the end they succeeded. It didn't make sense to people at the local level to risk trouble with the Haleyites when there were four other books, just as good as mine and perhaps better, from which to choose. Two or three districts did lean toward *This Is Our Nation* for a time; but when Haley's TFA sent out a four-page circular denouncing the book and threatening "indignation meetings" if it was selected, the local committees gave way and picked other textbooks. In the end, though the book did well in other states, the only place where it was chosen in Texas, so far as I know, was Uvalde, the home of FDR's first vice-president: John Nance Garner.

In Dallas, when the school board met in February 1962 to hear the recommendations of the local textbook committee, some townspeople who were friends of mine and some of my students went to the meeting and told me afterwards what happened there. The high school auditorium where the meeting was held was crowded with grim-faced citizens, they said, holding copies of *This Is Our Nation,* filled with marginal notations in red, ready to spring into action if the book was recommended. When the meeting came to order, the Dallas superintendent of schools (who had been trying to get SMU to fire me) reassured the crowd at once: "I want you to know right away that we have not picked the Boller book!" There was an outburst of applause, and then he went on to give the name of the chosen textbook. It was University of Wisconsin historian Merle Curti's *Rise of the American Nation* (written with L. P. Todd). Well, I thought, when I heard the news, perhaps Haley hadn't won after all; Curti and I see eye to eye on most issues and I hold him in highest esteem. But I felt sorry for Webster Publishing Company, which had invested a lot in *This Is Our Nation* and counted on doing well in Texas with an SMU author.

The textbook controversy was accompanied by numerous hate calls to my home. Even after the fight was over, the anonymous calls continued and even increased in rancor. Sometimes people would call up and scream: "Gotcha Commie!" and then hang up. On other occasions, they would pretend to be friendly, ask what I taught, and then burst out: "I have a son coming to SMU next year, but he won't be taking any of your awful courses!" A favorite ploy was to breathe heavily for a few moments when I lifted the receiver and then hang up. Some evenings I received calls regularly every fifteen minutes, with the caller slamming down the phone as soon as I lifted the receiver. By the spring of 1963, the number of anonymous calls and hate-filled letters I was receiving became so numerous that, for the first time in all my years at SMU, I began to feel a bit jittery. Then, out of the blue, Texas historian Joe B. Frantz, my good friend in Austin, called to invite me to be visiting professor at the University of Texas the following year. I accepted with alacrity; the prospect of obscurity on another campus was enormously appealing. I taught at UT in 1963 and 1964, took a semester off to work on a book, and returned to SMU in the spring of 1965. By that time, I had the feeling that, after the terrible shock of the Kennedy assassination in November 1963, there was a far more tolerant atmosphere in the metropolitan area than there had been two years earlier. Still, I wasn't absolutely sure of this.

Toward the end of my last semester at SMU (I left Dallas in the summer of 1966 to take a position at the University of Massachusetts in Boston), I was asked by a student group to take the negative side of a panel discussion on the Vietnam War. I was reluctant to do so; I was trying to finish the first draft of a book and I hated to interrupt work on it to make the kind of careful preparation I regarded as essential for talking about the Vietnam War in public. But when students told me they couldn't get anyone else on the faculty with the knowledge or inclination to take the negative side, I agreed to appear on the panel, took a couple of weeks off from my writing to do my homework, and was more than ever convinced by my research that involvement in the Vietnam civil war was a tragic error for our country.

The Vietnam debate, held in the SMU law school auditorium, went off nicely. The exchange of views with my colleagues on the panel was courteous and friendly, though at times sharp, and, somewhat to my surprise, the majority of students in the audience seemed friendly to the position I took, even enthusiastic about it. But at three o'clock that night I was awakened by the insistent ringing of the telephone. "Here we go again!" I sighed; I let the phone ring until it gave up, and went to sleep again after a while, somewhat discouraged by the thought of renewed strife with Texas reactionaries. A few days later, though, I learned that my apprehensions had been unfounded; some friends in Austin had decided in the midst of a beer party to call and wish me farewell and good luck before I left Texas.

When I left for the East Coast a few weeks later, I did so with mixed feelings. I had had enemies in Texas, of course, during the long McCarthy years there, and it was a relief not to have to "roll around in the gutter" with them any more. But I had also had good friends, among enlightened conservatives (like Dr. Gambrell) as well as among common-sense liberals (like Margaret Hartley) in the Lone Star state, and I knew I would miss them. They were a plucky bunch. They had to be.

★ ★ ★ ★

At the University of Massachusetts in Boston (UMB), where I taught from 1966 to 1976 (and then became Lyndon Baines Johnson Professor of United States History at Texas Christian University in Fort Worth), the tables were turned. It was the extreme leftists who were in the ascendancy in the Boston area in the late 1960s and early 1970s and they proved to be as dogmatic, intolerant, repressive, and mean-spirited as the extreme rightists I had encountered in Texas.

At UMB I managed to stay out of trouble, for I shared the opposition of the Left to the Vietnam War (though I was dismayed by the way radicals shouted down Vice-President Hubert Humphrey when he tried to speak in Boston during the 1968 presidential contest). But I was so outraged by the campaign of slander and vilification waged by some campus radicals against Dick Robbins, chairman of UMB's sociology department, because he didn't rehire a young leftist who was on a one-year contract, that I finally drafted a letter deploring the vile treatment Robbins was receiving: the sit-ins, day after day, in his office, the posters around the campus calling him a racist, fascist, and imperialist, and the venomous attacks on him in *Mass Media,* the student paper controlled by ultra-leftists.

After finishing the letter, I made the rounds seeking as many signatures as I could from my associates on the faculty. It took some time, for UMB is a commuting school, but I finally secured about twenty signatures and was ready to send the letter to the school paper. By this time, however, the young leftists had stopped hounding Robbins and were pouring all their energies into a new agitational enterprise, and it occurred to me that it might be wise to consult Robbins before publicizing the letter.

"Dick," I said, "here is a letter offering you our moral support. It may be of some help to you to know that so many of your colleagues are on your side." After Robbins had read the letter and expressed gratification, I told him that I planned to take it to *Mass Media* for publication and wondered whether that was all right with him. Not surprisingly, he questioned the wisdom of releasing the letter at that point. He had ceased to be a target, he reminded me, and making the letter public at this juncture might well revive the sit-in campaign, which, he said, had badly disrupted the work of the department. His preference, he said, was for holding the letter in reserve and making it public only if he thought the need for it arose later on.

I'll be honest: I was secretly relieved by Robbins' decision. I was well aware of the fact (and no doubt Robbins was too) that once the letter appeared in print I was likely to join him as a target of leftist hate, abuse, and contumely. Having tussled with the extreme Right in Dallas, I was not eager to get embroiled with the extreme Left in Boston. Luckily for both Robbins and me, the leftists never renewed the anti-Robbins campaign, and I never had to make the letter public.

# 2

# Some Brushes with History:
## Handling the Japanese
### Language During World War II

WILLIAM JAMES once said that life was a series of interruptions, and I have always found this to be so. One afternoon, shortly after the Japanese attack on Pearl Harbor, I was chatting with Bob Wade, a fellow graduate student, in Yale's Sterling Memorial Library, when suddenly he broke off and cried: "Sorry, I've got to leave. I have to see Commander Hindmarsh." "Hindmarsh? Who's he?" I asked puzzledly. "Here, read this," said Bob, handing me a flyer as he left. It was an announcement that Lieutenant Commander A. E. Hindmarsh, USNR, was appearing on the Yale campus to recruit students for the Navy's Japanese Language School in Boulder, Colorado. I was at once intrigued. I liked languages; I had studied Latin and French in high school and German in college, and I even knew a few simple Japanese phrases I had learned from Nisei (Japanese-American) friends in New York City. The upshot: I saw Hindmarsh, too, and ended up at Boulder with Bob and a couple hundred other college students trying to master the intricacies of *Nihongo* (Japanese).

The Navy's program, which used the dormitories, dining halls, and classrooms of the University of Colorado, was a rigorous one: it compressed a three-year course the Navy had sponsored in peacetime into one year. We met four hours a day in classes of five or six (two hours of reading, an hour of conversation, and an hour of dictation) and had a four-hour examination every Saturday morning, as well as periodic oral exams in the middle of the week. We were supposed to speak *Nihongo* at meals, but usually didn't. We needed to get away from our studies whenever we could ("We owe it to ourselves," as my tall, genial Texas friend Carl Bartz liked to put it), for we were moving ahead at breakneck speed, memorizing a dozen or so new *kanji* (Japanese characters) each day and rushing from one chapter to the next in *Naganuma,* our multi-volumed Japanese text. Falling behind in assignments was fatal. My first roommate, a likable fellow just out of Yale, tried the old college trick of leaving everything until Friday night, when he would suddenly begin cramming for Saturday's exam, right after supper. It didn't work; he lasted only a few months.

Some evenings we saw Japanese movies. The school had acquired a handful of old pre-war B-movies in *Nihongo*, including one featuring a big fellow who was an obvious take-off on America's silent-film comedian, Fatty Arbuckle, and who sang *"Aozora"* ("My Blue Heaven") whenever he couldn't think of anything else to do. The movies were just plain awful, and we saw the same ones so often that we couldn't help hissing and booing, to our instructors' chagrin, as soon as the titles appeared on the screen. Saturday nights, though, when we were free to do as we pleased, we saw some good movies in Boulder's movie palaces — classics (though we didn't know it at the time) like *The Maltese Falcon* and *Casablanca.* We saw some of Hollywood's war movies, too, and were amused by the way Chinese performers handled the role of Japanese villains. The Chinese language has an *l* but no *r; Nihongo* has an *r* but no *l.*

In addition to classwork there was *undō* (exercise) for an hour every afternoon during the week and twice-a-week drills supervised by petty officers who could scarcely conceal their humiliation at having to deal with a bunch of college kids, some of them decidedly bookish, who entered the Navy as yeomen, second class, but weren't scheduled to wear uniforms until they were commissioned as ensigns upon completing the language course. One of my friends, Wendell Furnas, regarded the *undō* period as a waste of time; he soon got into the habit of edging unobtrusively off the playing field during the workouts and then sneaking to the library to study his *kanji*. The petty officers never seemed to notice what he did, or if they did, they didn't care. Furnas was no bookworm; he had spent time in a Japanese prison camp in China after Pearl Harbor and was anxious to get on with the war. He did, though, take part in the display of mass calisthenics which we students put on, clad in skivvy shirts and gym shorts, before a large crowd in the stadium celebrating Colorado University Days. Unfortunately, the chief petty officer who was giving us commands over the public-address system got rattled half-way through the exercises, began counting wrong, and threw us all out of sync. The result was chaos on the field and cachinnation in the stands.

Our *sensei* did better by us. They were a mixed lot. Some of them were academics, like Florence Walne, University of California specialist in Oriental languages, who was director of the school. Others were missionaries who had mastered *Nihongo* while trying to save souls in Japan during the 1920s and 1930s. There were also a fair number of *Nisei* who had been released from internment camps in Arkansas, New Mexico, and elsewhere to teach at Boulder. The *Nisei* were surprisingly lacking in bitterness about the way they had been uprooted from their homes on the West Coast after the attack on Pearl Harbor. One of them told us with some amusement that she took a copy of Tolstoy's *War and Peace* with her to the relocation center, expecting a long internment, only to have an army officer confiscate the book because he thought there was something suspicious about it. Only one of our *sensei* (a Japanese national who somehow had received clearance to teach) brought politics into the classroom. To our surprise — and wry amusement — he took time off from *Nihongo* one day to explain that Japanese imperialism was no different from Europe's or even America's; and though no one in my class, so far as I know, ever tattled on him (or "named names," to use Victor Navasky's term for informing), his sloppy teaching eventually became known to the authorities and he was dropped from the teaching staff.

Upon graduating late in 1943, a few Boulderites went into the Marine Corps, but most of us entered the Naval Reserve as ensigns and then headed for Pearl Harbor, where we joined the Translation Section of the Joint Intelligence Center, Pacific Ocean Area (JICPOA), headed by Lieutenant Commander John W. Steele, a retired Navy officer who had been called back to duty after Pearl Harbor because he had learned *Nihongo* before the war. Steele, a short, gritty, and slightly deaf man in his late thirties, was one of the hardest working human beings I have ever known. There were three eight-hour shifts at JICPOA, but, unlike the rest of us, he always worked two shifts, busily translating captured documents himself as well as supervising the work of two hundred or more language officers under his command. He never took a leave, not even for a weekend. Then came V-J Day, and, the story goes, he stayed in his quarters, got drunk, fell down some stairs, and spent the next few days in the hospital.

If Steele was diligent he was also straightforward and down-to-earth. He was, in fact, the saltiest officer I ever encountered during my three and a half years in the Navy. His instructions were invariably such a mixture of slang, Navy lingo, and profanity that sometimes I had to think them over a bit before I could figure out precisely what he wanted me to do. At a general meeting of the translation section shortly after he became head, one of the ensigns asked if we were expected to salute him every time we met him on the base. "Salute me the first time you see me in the morning, if you want to," croaked Steele, "but for Christ's sake don't go on saluting me the rest of the day!" One day the chief personnel officer, a fussy fellow with the rank of lieutenant, sent a solemn memo around for posting in all sections: "It has been observed that junior officers are addressing Lieutenant-Commanders as Commanders. This is incorrect. Only full Commanders are to be addressed as Commanders. Lieutenant-Commanders are to be addressed as Mister." Lieutenant

*Some Boulder students, newly commissioned. Left to right: Scribner McCoy, Paul F. Boller, Jr., Carl Bartz, Herbert Dean, Addison Parker, Lance LaBianca (author's collection).*

Commander Steele posted the memo with a notation of his own at the bottom: "Correct as hell. Button up your pants, Madam."

What did Z Section (Translation), JICPOA, contribute to the naval war effort? Its job was to process the tons of documents captured from the Japanese during the fighting in the Pacific and translate into English anything that contained information which might be of importance for American military and naval operations against the enemy. To facilitate the work, Z Section was divided into *han* (subsections), eventually fifteen, specializing in documents dealing with various subjects: aviation, land forces, radar and sonar, ordnance, ships, shipbuilding, geography, and the like. For a time I worked in the *han* devoted to naval vessels; then I became one of the sorters, that is, I went through the documents pouring into JICPOA from the islands captured from the Japanese, and assigned them to the appropriate *han*. We sorters were sometimes called "Sparrows," because, as Captain Winfred J. Holmes (deputy officer in charge of JICPOA, which included cryptanalysts as well as translators) put it, they "scratch through a mound of horse manure and select the few grains of potentially important information."

Much of the material we sorted was of little or no interest to JICPOA and was sent to the Washington Document Center (called the "Over the River Burial Association") for handling. At one point JICPOA sorters began labelling low-priority documents "crap" before transmitting them to Washington, but this produced such vehement protests that eventually my friend Carl Nelson, a zealous sorter, went through all the documents designated for Washington and carefully prefixed an "S" to the labels. This mollified but did not overjoy the Washington Document Center people, which included WAVES who had begun receiving language training at Boulder about the time I left.

Some of the documents coming into JICPOA from the Marshalls and other islands captured from the Japanese were extremely valuable. There was a rush job, I recall, shortly after I got to JICPOA, when eighty-five top secret Japanese hydrographic charts containing invaluable information about the location of mine fields around all of Japan's main ports came into our hands, and it was important to translate and transmit the information to American submarines on patrol as quickly as possible. But few of the captured documents were that crucial; most of them were of longer-range interest to JICPOA. By the time the war ended, JICPOA had issued thirty-nine volumes of translations and interrogations (there was a prisoner-of-war camp at Pearl Harbor) and about ninety special translations. In his memoirs, Captain Holmes singled out five JICPOA translations he regarded as having been of immense strategic importance: 1944 Japanese Army Mobilization Plan; Hypothetic Defense of Kyushu; Kagoshima Defense Battle Plan; Digest of Japanese Naval Air Bases; and Manual of Anti-Aircraft Defense.

Captain Holmes took a more indulgent view of Japanese Language Officers (JLOs) than our petty officers did back in Boulder. "It is not surprising that, with their academic backgrounds, many language officers found it difficult to adjust to a military routine," he wrote after the war. "No relationship has ever been established between punctilio and military effectiveness, as attested by Washington's Ragged Continentals, Sherman's Bummers, and Stonewall Jackson's Foot Cavalry, or, for that matter, some of [our own] outstanding regular Navy cryptanalysts." Holmes' senior colleagues occasionally complained about the unmilitary behavior of the men in Z Section (popularly known as the "Zoo Section" as well as the "Salt Mines"), but he advised them to relax. "We have always won our wars with a bunch of civilians in uniform anxious to get back to their own affairs," he told them, "and we will win this one the same way."

From time to time members of the Z Section were assigned temporary duty with combat units, and, before the war was over, they had taken part in the invasions of the Marshalls, Marianas, Leyte, Iwo Jima (which, we linguists knew, the Japanese called Iōtō), and Okinawa. No language officer lost his life or was even seriously wounded during these operations, though, of course, anything could have happened. He usually landed with the third wave during invasions and his task was to interrogate prisoners captured during the assault and translate any documents of immediate value falling into American hands. Back in our Boulder days one of the students had drawn a cartoon for *Sono Hi no Uwasa (Today's Gossip)*, the language-school paper, picturing a beleaguered Boulderite clutching a big book as bombs burst around him and crying: *"Chotto matte kudasai! Jibiki wo mimasu!"* ("Just a minute! I'm looking it up in the dictionary!") It was never like that, to be sure, but language officers did take pocket dictionaries with them for emergencies; mostly, though, they relied on the *Nihongo* they had learned at Boulder and Pearl Harbor, and it served them well. During the fighting on Iwo Jima, a story came floating back to JICPOA that one Boulderite, who had landed with the Fifth Marine Division, went into a cave looking for documents and came hurtling out moments later in stupefaction. "Jee-zus Christ!" he was quoted as yelling. "Those Japs tried to kill me!" It was a good tale but apocryphal. "Respect for language officers and appreciation of their value increased with each succeeding operation," according to Captain Holmes. "It was a privilege to serve with the Navy language officers. They contributed their fair share to the victory in the Pacific."

Several of my best friends (Ed Whan, a mischievous Michigander, for one, and Griff Way, a sedate Seattleite, for another) took part in combat operations during 1944, and I naturally became eager to be assigned to one myself. Finally my great day came: Lieutenant Commander Steele picked me for the Iwo Jima invasion and I began assembling equipment, taking shots, studying combat manuals, and attending briefings to prepare myself for the experience. I also began compiling a dictionary of Japanese military and technical terms I thought might come in handy in the field and it was later published in an expanded form by JICPOA. Then, abruptly, came a dark day: Steele called me over to his desk and informed me that he was taking me off the Iwo Jima assignment and sending me to Guam where Admiral Chester Nimitz was establishing his advance headquarters as Commander in Chief, Pacific Fleet (CinCPac). I was to act as senior translator in the language section of the Advance Intelligence Center there. Swallowing my disappointment, I packed my things, took leave of my buddies, and was soon en route to Guam, via Johnson Island and the Marshalls, in the very first plane trip I ever took.

Guam proved depressing at first. CinCPac's language section was small (about thirteen of us). The material Lieutenant Commander Steele sent from Pearl for translation was of minimal interest, and the officer to whom I reported for special assignments from time to time, Captain Edwin Layton, Admiral Nimitz's chief intelligence officer, was brutal in his treatment of subordinates. I never walked over to Layton's office across the square without steeling myself beforehand for the vehement dressing-down that was sure to come. Only in retrospect can I bring myself to acknowledge that Layton's high competence made up for his extreme unpleasantness. "He has whiskey ulcers," someone explained to me, "and he's mad about something all the time!" About the only thing I liked at first about my assignment on a tropical island, with its spells of what we called Sadie Thompson weather (rain! rain! rain!), was the prevailing informality: khaki shorts and short-sleeved shirts without ties and practically no saluting to speak of. Early one morning, however, when I headed for the mess hall, I suddenly encountered Admiral Nimitz himself, together with Admiral Raymond Spruance and several high-ranking officers on their staffs. Startled, I froze in my tracks, did one of the snappiest salutes of my entire Navy career, and waited until some of the U.S. Navy's biggest shots gravely returned my lowly ensign's salutation, and passed on.

Gradually things improved. To escape the tedium of translating Japanese military manuals and geography books, hour after hour, seven days a week, I began slipping out of the office and making my way to the prisoner-of-war stockade, two or three miles away, to chat with the prisoners there. I had almost no opportunity to engage in *kaiwa* (conversation) in Pearl Harbor, and I was anxious to improve my facility in spoken Japanese. Who knows? I might get in on an operation some day after all, and I wanted to be as well prepared as I could be for the eventuality. One of the first prisoners, a colonel I think, to whom I talked in the stockade, was nasty. *"Su-pi-ku I-nu-gu- ri-su!"* ("Speak English!"), he sneered when I addressed him in *Nihongo*. I then shot a stream of English at him and he gave way at once, though not at all gracefully. I never saw him in later visits to the stockade without thinking of the cruel and arrogant officers encountered by Americans captured during the war.

But the other prisoners I approached were friendly and polite; and talking Japanese with them turned out to be great fun. I enjoyed trying out new words and phrases on them; I also liked to spring outrageous puns (*Nihongo* is full of homonyms) of my own contriving, some of which were not half bad. At the same time I began striking up an acquaintance with several of the prisoners (including an army major named Yanagi who was a physicist in civilian life and heartily disliked military life), who, like me, were eager for novelties to interrupt the daily routine. My immediate boss, Lieutenant Frank Huggins, a rugged, heavy-set, and hedonistic B.J. (born in Japan) who spoke *Nihongo* fluently, took an indulgent view of my absences from the office. He was bored, too, drank heavily (in our free time we all frequented the quonset hut housing the officers club, where drinks were a dime apiece), and sometimes came wearily into the office in the morning, sat down, leaned back, put his hairy legs up on the desk, and slept off hangovers.

One day, out of the blue, came one of those "turning points" that fascinated Mark Twain so much that he wrote an essay in 1910 discussing the turning points in his life. A Navy lieutenant named Robert Morris, a specialist in psychological warfare, who had a desk at one side of the language section, came over to my desk and began quizzing me about the prisoners I had gotten to know in the stockade. "Do you think," he asked me, "it would be possible to persuade any of them to help out on a project I am trying to devise, if they thought it would help shorten the war?" I was almost certain some of them would; the prisoners I knew best, I told Morris, all realized that Japan was headed for defeat and they longed for a speedy end to the war. Morris then explained what he had in mind. With the capture of the Marianas and the establishment of air bases on Guam, Saipan, and Tinian, he noted, our B-29 Superfortresses were beginning to make daily attacks on the Japanese home islands. Why not prepare leaflets for some of them to drop, warning inhabitants ahead of time when Japanese cities were going to be hit during the next few days? With the conquest of Iwo Jima, Morris went on, our B-29s had such control of the skies over Japan that advance announcements of their raids would in no way put them in jeopardy and would probably have the psychological effect of dramatizing American superiority and the futility of Japan's continued resistance.

Morris' plan appealed enormously to me. We headed for the POW stockade at once, and I rounded up the POW's I had befriended, about five in all, and explained the project to them. As I had expected, they all volunteered to help out; they were enthusiastic about the idea of doing something to help shorten the conflict. A few days later, Morris handed me the English text which he and one of his associates had prepared for use on the leaflets:

Read this carefully as it may save your life or the life of a relative or friend. In the next few days, the military installations in four or more of the cities named on the reverse side of this leaflet will be destroyed by American bombs.

These cities contain military installations and workshops or factories which produce military goods. We are determined to destroy all the tools of the military clique which they are using to prolong this useless war. But unfortunately bombs have no eyes. So, in accordance with America's well-known humanitarian principles, the American Air Force, which does not wish to injure innocent people, now gives you warning to evacuate the cities named and save your lives.

America is not fighting the Japanese people but is fighting the military group which has enslaved the Japanese people.

The peace which America will bring will free the people from the oppression of the military and means the emergence of a new and better Japan.

You can restore peace by demanding new and good leaders who will end the war.

We cannot promise that only these cities will be among those attacked, but at least four will be. So, heed this warning and evacuate these cities.

On the reverse side of the leaflets was to be a picture of a B-29 unloading bombs, with the names of ten or twelve Japanese cities, enclosed in circles, and appearing under the bombs.

When I took the message Morris had prepared to the stockade, my POWs went energetically to work on it in a room assigned us. *"Issho kemmei ni hatarakimasu!"* ("We will work very hard!"), one of them assured me. All of my collaborators were college-educated and had a reading knowledge of English (though they did not speak it well at all) and in a couple of hours the five of them had prepared a Japanese translation of the Morris text which I knew was far better than any literal translation I might have made myself. Upon its completion, one of the POWs named Kitagishi, an excellent calligrapher, copied it all over in large and graceful *kanji* for photographing, and I turned his handiwork over to Morris. Morris then flew to Saipan with it, where the Office of War Information (OWI) prepared and printed the leaflets, wrapped them in rolls, packed them in 500-pound bomb cases, and delivered them to the Air Force. Jim Garcia, intelligence officer for the 21st Bomb Command (headed by General Curtis LeMay) had arranged for the 73rd Bomb Wing, stationed on Saipan, to assign three B-29s to drop the leaflets on regular weather runs to Japan. During the next few weeks the 73rd Bomb Wing dropped millions of the leaflets, principally on Honshu, Japan's main island, warning thirty-one cities of raids to come (fourteen of which were subsequently fire-bombed). We also devoted a special leaflet to the Potsdam Declaration, issued on July 26, calling for "unconditional surrender," a policy originally adopted by the United States in 1943.

It got to be a routine: toward the end of every week I would call up my contact in the Air Force, a graduate of the Boulder school named Ardath Burke, and ask: "Well, what are the cities for next week?" Ardie would then reel off the names of the cities (almost like listing movies, I thought, for the outdoor theater's coming week) and I would head for the stockade and see to it that the leaflets were modified accordingly. How far off can the war's end be, I wondered, when we were in a position to give advance warning each week of the cities we intended to bomb? To my surprise and delight, the directors of the Advance Intelligence Center were so pleased with the whole operation that they turned a brand-new quonset hut over to the language section in which to do the leaflet work. The building contained a large central room, with a long table and chairs at which we could work, surrounded by four small separate rooms for individual interrogations. We didn't use the little rooms much; every so often, though, Japanese soldiers who had been holding out in the caves and jungles of Guam gave themselves up (sick and tired, we joked, of the Republic and Monogram movies they watched from afar at night) and we brought them in for questioning. The only really interesting interrogation, though, took place in the language section office itself, not the quonset. When a *kamikaze* pilot survived a suicide dive and was taken to the stockade, Huggins brought him to the office, plunked him down on a chair in front of his desk, and for an hour or so shot noisy questions at him. But the pilot refused to talk. "Say, Frank," murmured a fascinated bystander (men from other sections had crowded into our office to see the show), "why don't you tell him if he doesn't talk you won't let him commit suicide!"

One week Ardie had no cities for me. "There seems to be a special deal of some kind planned for next week," he told

日本國民に告ぐ

自分や親兄弟友達の
ことはもとより思ひをよせくん讀かの

命を助けるために
米軍が数日でけた
部品をこの空製の都市は
人ちは全か部の爆撃は
らで避難すること
れないすつあ
す樹に書かれ
るんくこかがて戦んば
するんで都市の爆撃と書裏に
下に書かめいて注意してあるる都市からさ避難しらて裏

*Front and back of a leaflet warning of raids to come (author's collection).*

me. "I really don't know what's going on." I didn't think much about it at the time. I joined Huggins for a flight to Saipan that afternoon and a trip out into the boondocks there with him and an army intelligence officer to try to persuade a Japanese army lieutenant, holding out in a cave, to surrender peacefully. Shortly after we got back to the army base, having failed in our mission, I heard the news over the radio: the United States had dropped an atomic bomb, with the explosive force of 20,000 tons of TNT, on Hiroshima. A wave of depression instantly engulfed me; as if war weren't already terrible enough, I couldn't help thinking, here, now, we have this frightful new weapon for future conflicts.

But there was no time to brood about what the Japanese call "the sadness of things." Lieutenant Morris got in touch with me soon after the news of Hiroshima came through, gave me a statement he had prepared, quoting President Truman's warning to Japan about the new weapon and calling for unconditional surrender, and I flew back to Guam to work with my POWs on a new leaflet. I was struck by the fact that my collaborators put the word, atomic bomb, at once into Japanese (*genshi bakudan*) and went ahead with the translating as if there wasn't anything special about the Truman statement. When they had finished, I couldn't help saying, "It's really awful, isn't it, this *genshi bakudan?*" "You mean, it's real?" they cried in evident surprise. Their surprise surprised me; they had translated a statement which they had taken for granted was mere propaganda just as diligently as they had statements they knew were true. More than that: they didn't seem especially upset, so far as I could tell, when they learned the *genshi bakudan* was for real.

Events now moved rapidly. Two days after Hiroshima, Russia declared war on Japan and a day later came the atom-bombing of Nagasaki. Right after Nagasaki, Morris called to tell me that Philip Morison, the Cornell University physicist with the Manhattan Project who had assembled the A-bombs for loading on the planes which took off from Tinian, wanted to meet Major Yanagi, the physicist who was working with me, and was planning to fly over to Guam for a visit. A few

*On Guam, spring 1945 (author's collection).*

hours later Professor Morison arrived at the Advance Intelligence Center and I took him to the quonset hut where we did our leaflets and introduced him to my POWs. As soon as we sat down around the long table to talk, Morison handed Major Yanagi some reprints of scientific articles he had brought with him. Yanagi eyed them lovingly. "Scientists," he murmured, in halting English, "scientists hate war. Scientists love peace." Morison and I exchanged glances. I didn't doubt that he was thinking what I was thinking: "and yet scientists produced the terrible atomic bomb!" It didn't surprise me to read later on about Morison's earnest anti-war activities after the war.

On August 10, the day after Nagasaki, the Japanese government expressed readiness to accept the terms of the Potsdam Declaration, "with the understanding that said declaration does not comprise any demand which prejudices the prerogatives of His Majesty as a sovereign ruler." The United States then quite sensibly, in my opinion, backed off from the unconditional surrender demand to which FDR had committed us in 1943 and expressed willingness to negotiate with the Japanese without insisting on the abdication of the Emperor. On August 14 Japan accepted Allied terms and President Truman announced an armistice that night. I was standing watch in front of the Advance Intelligence Center building the night Japan surrendered and I knew that the big news was likely to break any moment during my watch. Our building was dark and empty, but across the street, in Admiral Nimitz's headquarters and in the news correspondents' building nearby, all the lights were on and from the sounds drifting over to where I stood I got the impression that the place was filled with people as tense and hopeful and expectant as I was. Suddenly I heard a tremendous explosion of shouts and cheers in both buildings. "This must be it!" I cried. I was tempted to desert my post, or ask the Marine guard who was with me to desert his post and run across the street to learn the news. Fortunately I did nothing so rash; and within minutes Frank Huggins came rushing up in a jeep to tell me that Japan had just surrendered and he almost "busted out crying" when he heard the news. "But I told my brother to go to hell!" he added angrily. "I just phoned him and he said he wouldn't have minded if the war had gone on, because he liked Navy life. The little bastard!"

The next day was hectic in our office; we had a rush translation job to perform. When Japanese envoys met American officials in Manila to arrange for the formal surrender, they turned over documents revealing the disposition of all of Japan's armed forces, military and naval, in eastern Asia and the Pacific Ocean areas, and the document dealing with the Imperial Fleet, hastily prepared in ink, came to Guam for translation. When it arrived, Captain Layton ordered me over to pick it up posthaste and I got to his office in a New York minute. First he raised hell with me about something or other and then got to the business at hand. "Get this thing translated as fast as you can and have Frank telephone me the information while you're working on it," he ordered. He then handed me the document and added: "When you're finished, make two copies of it. Send one copy to Washington and bring me the other copy. Send the original to JICPOA in Pearl." "Aye, aye, sir," I said, excited by the new assignment, and I was on my way.

Back in the language section we all went to work with zest on the document Layton gave me. As we read it aloud, correcting and prompting each other, to keep things moving as rapidly as we could, Lieutenant Huggins, who was on the phone, dictated our translation to one of Captain Layton's secretaries, putting it in dispatch form as he did so for transmittal to all the appropriate authorities as soon as possible. Translating the document was, in fact, quite easy, particularly since some of us already knew a great deal about the composition of the Japanese navy and about the losses it had sustained. First, I remember, came a list of the battleships (*senkan*): *Fuso,* sunk in Surigao Strait, October 25, 1944; *Haruna*, half-sunk in shallows off Kure, July 27, 1944; *Hiei*, sunk off Guadalcanal, November 13, 1942; and so on and on until it was clear that there was only one *senkan* left. Next came aircraft carriers: four lost at Midway in June 1942, and all but one of the others sunk in later engagements with the American fleet. And so it went: heavy cruisers, light cruisers, destroyers, until we got to the end and marveled at the terrible beating the Imperial Navy had taken during the war.

Afterwards, even Captain Layton seemed momentarily in good spirits (at least he didn't abuse me) when I delivered a copy of the document to him, after having arranged to send the original to Pearl and a copy to Washington, as he had instructed. "Okay," he said. "Did you send the original to Pearl? And copies to OWI in Washington? And to Army Intelligence? And to the British?" My heart sank; he had asked for two copies and I had made three, just to play it safe, but now he was adding new places to his list. The war was about over, but I was still under his command, and I knew better than to call attention to the discrepancy between his original instructions and his present ones. When I left his office, hoping never to see him again, I wondered what to do. Then it came to me in a flash: send the extra copy I had made to Army Intelligence and shoot off instructions to the JICPOA people to make a copy of the original I had sent them and transmit it to the British.

My plan seems to have worked; at least I never heard anything more about it. And I saw Captain Layton only one more time. On that occasion, though, I outranked him, i.e., I was a civilian. I was in Washington soon after I got out of the service, walking some papers through the Naval bureaucracy there to get some money still owed me, when suddenly the door of an office I was passing opened and out popped Layton. I had always told my Navy buddies that if I encountered Layton after the war I would bump into him as I passed. But I did no such thing; instead, I did a double-take and almost stopped short. Layton peered intently at me as I passed, but I resolutely declined to recognize his existence. It was my finest hour with him.

V-J Day was on August 15, and a few days later the Ninth Anti-aircraft Artillery Battalion (U.S. Marine), ordered to take over the island of Rota (one of the Marianas about forty miles north of Guam) where there remained 3000 soldiers

and 5000 civilians, sent a request to our office for an inter-
preter to go along. I volunteered at once; it didn't promise to
be much of an operation, but it was better than nothing, and
clearly my last chance to get an assignment of that kind. The
9th's commanding officer, Lieutenant Colonel Kenneth A.
King, USMC, seemed unfriendly at first; like Boulder's
petty officers he seemed to take an exceedingly dim view of
servicemen whose specialty was *Nihongo*. I found it impossible to persuade his outfit to issue the gear I needed for the
operation — dungarees, helmet, cot, K-rations — and spent
so much energy chasing around Guam that afternoon round-
ing up the equipment elsewhere that I was still perspiring
profusely, even after two showers, when I reported in to him.
"Boller," he exclaimed, eying my damp khaki shirt doubtfully, "when I need you, I want you to be there!" "Aye, aye,
sir," I blurted out, astonishing myself (and him, too) with
the vehemence of my response. But Lieutenant Colonel King
seemed to like it; he was pleasanter to me after that, and later
on he sent a letter of commendation about me to the Navy
department in Washington. That night we shoved off for
Rota — several LCTs and a couple of destroyers — and soon
after he called me up to the deck to tell me he planned to stage
a formal surrender ceremony after the landing. He then
handed me a set of questions to ask the Japanese officer in
command on Rota during the ceremony and I went to work
at once putting the questions into *Nihongo*.

The Rota surrender ceremony, which took place near the
dock soon after we landed, went swimmingly. With the Japanese commanding officer, a major named Imagawa, and his
staff lined up in full dress uniform on one side, facing Lieutenant Colonel King and his staff, I began the proceedings, as
directed, by announcing in a loud (and amusedly authorita-
tive) voice: *"Beikoku no namae de, kono shima wo senryō shi-
masu!"* ("In the name of the United States of America we take
possession of this island!"). Then Imagawa and his men
turned their *samurai* swords over to Lieutenant Colonel King
and his staff, and I began asking Imagawa if he had complied
with all the orders transmitted to him: "Have you issued an

order ending all resistance on Rota?" "Have you attempted to bring in all stragglers?" "Have you assembled all your troops in the spot designated for processing and evacuation from the island?" Imagawa's answers were of course all emphatically in the affirmative; and when I finished with the exchange Lieutenant Colonel King seemed pleased. "Tell him, Boller," he said amiably, "that they are now on good behavior."

The expression, good behavior, is a military term; there was, I knew, a Japanese equivalent, but for the life of me I couldn't quite think what it was on the spur of the moment, and I was forced to make a quick literal translation of my CO's words. I knew the word for behavior (*gyōgi*) and the word for good (*yoi*), and I at once framed a sentence with those words in it to convey what Lieutenant Colonel King wanted me to tell Imagawa. Literal translations are perilous when it comes to *Nihongo*, and the clumsy way I expressed myself surprised and offended the Japanese. "Look," Major Imagawa said plaintively (I do not, of course, remember his exact words after all these years), "We've done everything your commanding officer instructed us to do. We've surrendered. We've turned our swords over to you. We've assembled all our men at the place you designated and they're waiting to be evacuated. Why, why, after all of this, why do you make such an insulting remark to us?" I was obliged to say something at this point, and since the excessive solemnity of the proceedings (we had been going on, in the hot sun, for close to two hours) was beginning to oppress me, I decided to have a little fun. "Look," I said, "it's all very simple. I'm only a *chūi* (lieutenant junior grade). My CO is a Marine colonel. He ordered me to say that to you!" At this, Major Imagawa started laughing and the men on his staff all joined in. "What're they laughing at?" Lieutenant Colonel King asked me suspiciously. "Nervousness, I think, sir," I said innocently.

Following the surrender, I helped some Marine officers process close to 3000 Japanese soldiers assembled at a nearby village, ascertaining their ranks and grades, and separating them into three groups — officers, NCOs, and privates —

for transportation to Guam. For hours we worked at the task — with the blistering sun giving way periodically to mighty tropical downpours — and for the first time I got to use some of the military commands I had learned at Boulder: *"Ki wo tsuke!"* ("Attention!"); *"Isoge!"* ("On the double!"); *"Yasume!"* ("At ease!"). The following day I accompanied Lieutenant Colonel King and Major Imagawa on a tour of the island and put all the compliments they showered upon each other, as military professionals, into the appropriate languages. The third day I joined a Marine patrol looking for stragglers in the caves, jungles, and villages of Rota. We found only one: an enlisted man who was obviously a bit deranged and had long since been discharged from the army. But he still wore a cap that looked like a soldier's headgear and the patrol leader insisted on taking him along on our ten-hour trek and putting him in my keeping. I had a series of strange exchanges in *Nihongo* with him as we made our way around the island. Boulder hadn't prepared me for that kind of *kaiwa* (conversation).

But the ditsy guy we picked up that day wasn't the only civilian on Rota who wore what looked like a military cap. All the men — even the boys — in the villages wore little baseball caps similar to those worn by Japanese enlisted men. One of our very first encounters that day, in fact, was with a farmer named Nakayama who was wearing that kind of head covering. And after I questioned him a bit and then assured the Marine lieutenant in charge of the patrol that the man had no connection whatsoever with the Japanese army, that he hated it, in fact, and was glad the war was over, the lieutenant told me sternly: "Well, he's wearing a military cap, isn't he?" Nakayama and I talked that one over a bit and I then explained to the lieutenant that according to Nakayama the cap he was wearing was not a military cap, though it looked like one, and that most of the men in the villages wore similar ones. "Well, tell him to get rid of it!" said the lieutenant stolidly. "It looks like a military cap, and, damn it, if he goes on wearing it, one of our boys is liable to make a mistake, and then it'll be too bad for him!"

When I relayed the lieutenant's warning to Nakayama, he became quite agitated, whipped off the cap, tore it apart, threw it on the ground, and savagely ground it into the mud. Then he calmed down, looked thoughtful, and asked wonderingly: "But what will I do now when it rains?" I was on my own at that point; the lieutenant had lost interest in Nakayama and was preparing to move on. "Oh, we'll see to it that you get proper headgear eventually," I told him; and we left him standing rather doubtfully by the roadside, eyeing the remains of his cap a bit wistfully.

After the encounter with Nakayama, my patrol leader seemed obsessed with caps, and during the next two days we succeeded in de-capping the entire male population of Rota. At a small village we came upon shortly after our meeting with Nakayama, the lieutenant warmed to his work. He had me track down the village boss, whom I called *hanchō* (group leader), and seemed disbelieving when I assured him, after talking to the *hanchō*, that there were no soldiers hiding out there. Then, at his request, I had the *hanchō* assemble all the men in the village, all the way from a doddering *ojiisan* (senior citizen) down to a couple of twelve-year-olds, for inspection. The *hanchō* organized the men into four rows, called them to attention, and was just ordering them to dress right, when the lieutenant intervened. "Tell them to knock off all that military stuff!" he cried. "If they aren't soldiers, what're they acting like that for? And tell what's-his-name there to knock off his damn saluting!" I quickly explained things to the *hanchō;* here, after all, was an opportunity to educate some Japanese civilians in democracy. After I had expounded a minute or two on the principle of civil supremacy over the military, I asked him: *"Wakarimasu ka?"* ("Do you understand?") *"Wakarimasu!"* ("I understand!"), he responded briskly, and, turning to the villagers, commanded: *"Yasume!"* ("At ease!")

While I was contemplating another lecture on non-military behavior, the lieutenant began scrutinizing the little baseball caps most of the men were wearing. "Tell him to collect all those caps and burn them!" he exclaimed. When I transmitted the order to the *hanchō*, he became quite upset, and I was forced to use the arguments on him that had worked with Nakayama: 1) "You wouldn't want an American Marine to mistake you for a Japanese soldier, would you?" 2) "We'll try to fix you up with new civilian caps later on." This turned the trick; the *hanchō* ordered the two twelve-year-olds to go through the lines collecting the caps and then built a fire and tossed them all into it. I was glad when we left at this point. To this day, though, I still feel a bit remorseful about the way we went from one village to another the next two days decapping all the males on Rota without providing any replacements.

Rota was a fascinating experience, but Japan — my last Navy assignment — was the best of all. During the occupation of Japan I spent four weeks in Sasebo, a naval base in southern Kyushu, and then went up to Tokyo, where I spent the next three months, along with scores of other Boulderites, working for the United States Strategic Bombing Survey (USSBS, which we called Us-Bus). My duties were fairly interesting. In Sasebo I was attached to the Naval Technical Mission to Japan and accompanied naval technicians to factories, arsenals, and warehouses in the area and supervised the Japanese workmen who packed and crated military weapons of interest to the Navy to send to the States for inspection and testing. In Tokyo I joined the other Boulderites in translating documents throwing light on the effects of strategic bombing on the Japanese war effort and interviewing officials in the police department, municipal government, and in the War Ministry (now called the "Demobilization Department").

One USBSS interrogation took me to Hachioji, a city about thirty miles from Tokyo, which had been so thoroughly destroyed by our B-29s that there was only one building with four walls left standing. During the course of conversations with the mayor and some of the city officials I learned for the first time something about the leaflets we had prepared on Guam. The Japanese, I learned, had given the B-29 a nickname. They combined the word for two (*ni*) with the word for nine (*ku*) and added a diminutive suffix (*chan*), giving a wry twist to the translation: *Nikuchan* ("the 29 kid"). One week, the mayor told me, the *Nikuchan* dropped a bunch of leaflets on Hachioji warning of a possible raid to come and he had given people permission to evacuate the city if they wanted to. Most of them did, he said, and escaped the raid that came a few days later, leveling the city. Of those who remained, he added, 360 were killed.

Devastation and defeat did not, so far as I could determine from numerous conversations I had while in Japan, produce resentment and bitterness. The Emperor had decreed surrender; *kamaimasen* (So be it!). The most common attitude I encountered was one of resignation, acceptance, eagerness to rebuild, and, with American help, to develop a more democratic society. The words I heard most frequently whenever conversations touched upon the damage Japan had suffered during the war were: *"Shikata ga nai!"* ("It can't be helped!") This was true even when I expressed sorrow after one of the men I interrogated happened to mention, almost casually, that he had lost his entire family at Hiroshima. *"Shikata ga nai,"* he said, matter-of-factly, when he saw my reaction. He then started laughing. In Sasebo I asked a Japanese rear admiral with whom I worked for a few days if there were any bookstores or theaters in the city, and he said emphatically: "None whatsoever." Then he exclaimed: "You bombed them all!" He started laughing at this point and all the men on his staff broke into laughter. When I began smiling, he pointed his finger at me and chortled: "Look at him laughing!"

But the rear admiral took a liking to me. He got in the habit of bringing me little presents — tangerines, persimmons, picture postcards — every day, while I supplied him with American *shi-ga-ret-to* (cigarettes) in return. One day, when I went to his office, he was reading the morning newspaper at his desk, and for the fun of it I started reading the lead story aloud. Everyone in the office stopped to listen. As I proceeded, the admiral glanced down the page and fixed his eye on a difficult Japanese compound, toward the bottom, as if wondering whether I could handle it. Luckily I was able to; I had come across it for the first time a day or so before. When I read it aloud, everyone began applauding. The admiral then delivered a little lecture to the younger men there: "You men have studied years of English in school and still can't read or speak it very well. Here is an American who studied Japanese only a year and look how well he does!" The following day the admiral and I had another little exchange that tickled him. During the course of our conversation he used an English word, but gave it the Japanese pronunciation, and, since I was expecting *Nihongo*, I failed to recognize it and had to ask what it meant. He at once grabbed a pencil and some paper and gleefully wrote down an English word that I recognized immediately. "Listen," I cried, in mock-consternation, "I've been talking so much *Nihongo* that I've forgotten all my English! Please get me an English dictionary right away!" He and his associates went into peals of laughter.

Tokyo was of course far more exciting than Sasebo. Though much of the city lay in ruins from B-29 raids, the Imperial Palace and the area around it were untouched and there were enough buildings left intact or only partially destroyed in other parts of the city to support a lively commercial and social life from the beginning of the occupation. From the outset, too, there was an amazing outburst of fraternization (and sororization) between the GIs and the Japanese; the hatred that Americans had felt for the "Japs," even more than for the Germans, during the war dissolved almost overnight among the occupation forces in Tokyo and elsewhere. General MacArthur, high and mighty in his offices on the twelfth floor of the Dai Ichi Building in the heart of Tokyo, took a benign view of the startling new camaraderie and calmly issued one order after another (many of them with a New Dealish flavor) providing for the democratization of the occupied country. And at one o'clock every day he descended from his twelfth-floor sanctuary, strode rapidly and erectly to his limousine, which was to whisk him off to the American embassy for lunch, seemingly indifferent to the hundreds of GIs and Japanese who had been gathering on the

*Japanese Naval officer (above), with whom the author worked in Sasebo. At left, in Tokyo during the Occupation (both photos from the author's collection).*

**61**

streets for an hour and more to catch a glimpse of him and take his picture.

In my free time I explored Tokyo as much as I could, hitching rides in jeeps, boarding jampacked subway cars and electric trains, traveling on foot in outlying areas, and speaking *Nihongo* everywhere I went. Knowing *Nihongo* was like possessing a magic key; it turned my every venture in the city into an adventure, with exchanges of *meishi* (calling cards) and gifts, long conversations, and frequently invitations to tea. Whenever I stopped to read signs and posters along the streets, crowds gathered and I knew I had to read the *kanji* aloud to prove myself and then bask in the kudos that followed: *"O-jozu desu ne!"* ("How skillful!") A request for directions invariably produced crowds plus carefully drawn little maps on slips of paper, with all the railroad tracks painstakingly penciled in for good measure.

In my quest for *kaiwa* I went everywhere, sometimes with friends, sometimes alone: to the Imperial Theater, where I saw the first play presented there after the war ended; to a movie theater that showed the first American movie in Japan after the war: a Republic Pictures programmer called *Yukon no Sakebi (The Call of the Yukon)*, with *kanji* floating down the right side of the screen as the performers talked; to Hibiya Hall, for a program of Japanese music and dances, concluding with swing music by a GI band that brought the house down; to a motion picture studio on the outskirts of the city, where the "Clark Gable of Japan" was filming a scene with the "Bette Davis of Japan" in the first post-war movie, and where the producer told me: "We used to make war movies; now we make peace movies!"; and to the baths, where I soaked contentedly in hot water during cold winter nights and chatted with my companions. I also met the aging Tsubouchi, the great Japanese actor, whose father, a playwright, critic, and novelist, had translated Shakespeare's plays into Japanese, and spent an afternoon discussing American, British, and Japanese drama with him over tea. And I walked into a *Me-to-di-su-to kyōkai* (Methodist church) on the Ginza one day, got to talking with the minister and his wife, and ended by playing the organ (an old reed organ you pumped with your feet) for a service in *Nihongo* the following Sunday.

My fondest recollections, however, are of encounters with the families of some of the POWs I had gotten to know on Guam. Thinking I might get to Tokyo sooner or later, I had taken the addresses of the Tokyoites when I made a farewell visit to the Guam stockade before leaving for Japan. Major Yanagi's was the first family I got to visit, but locating his house took some doing, for there were no street names and house numbers in Tokyo. But I managed to land in the general vicinity of the Yanagi residence, and then, as always, sought the help of the local policeman, who, after serving tea, took me promptly to the wrong district. When he discovered his error, he apologized profusely and we retraced our steps and soon reached the right district; but it took another policeman (and more tea) to get me to the Yanagis'. When the second policeman knocked at the door and announced that there was someone from the *Shinchugun* (Army of Occupation) outside, there was a flurry of activity in the house, and after a moment or two the door slid open and a woman in her early forties peered out anxiously. "My name is Paul Boller," I told her, handing her one of the *meishi* I had acquired soon after arriving in Tokyo. "I know some *Nihongo*. I came by to tell you that I saw your husband, Major Yanagi, recently. He is in good health. He will be home in a few weeks." Mrs. Yanagi stood there, a bit dazed, for a moment, and I repeated my words. She then began repeating what I had said in great excitement: "You have seen my husband recently! He is in good health! He will be home in a few weeks!"

The Yanagis had three daughters, all in their teens, and after Mrs. Yanagi invited me in, they shyly made their appearance, one by one, as we were having tea. With each appearance, Mrs. Yanagi made the same introduction: "This is *Bo-ra chūi* (Lieutenant Boller). He has seen Major Yanagi recently. He is in good health. He will be returning home in a few weeks." News of my visit seems somehow to have gotten around the vicinity soon after my arrival. The next thing I knew friends and neighbors began dropping in, taking my hand and introducing themselves, and repeating the only news I had given Mrs. Yanagi: "I understand that you have seen Major Yanagi recently and that he is in good health and will be returning home in a few weeks!" No one, not even Mrs. Yanagi, asked for more information; and I carefully refrained from explaining that I had met the major in a POW camp after he was captured on Okinawa. Before I left, I gave Mrs. Yanagi some C-rations and promised to return for dinner. When I went back with my friend Griff Way for another visit a few days later, we were impressed by the skillful way she had blended the C-rations with the Japanese food she prepared for us. Before leaving Tokyo I found time to call on the families of two more of the prisoners I had gotten to know on Guam and both times the visits turned into neighborhood events.

One night I found myself in front of the *Tokyo Hosokyoku* (Tokyo Broadcasting Station) and decided to go in to listen to some of the radio programs to improve my skill in understanding spoken Japanese. I caught the nine o'clock news, did pretty well with it, and was about to leave when the young man monitoring the program expressed amazement that I knew some *Nihongo* (Japanese), struck up a conversation, and then, when the announcer came out, insisted on introducing me to him. The announcer and I exchanged *meishi,* chatted a bit, and when he left, the monitor told me: "You know, Mr. Yamagiwa is one of our best announcers. He's a graduate of *Teidai* [the Imperial University] and knows English too!" A night or two later I dropped by the broadcasting station for more *Nihongo,* listened to another news program, saw Yamagiwa again, and accepted his invitation to join him in the newscasters' sitting room for green tea and cigarettes. Yamagiwa, it turned out, had taken several years of English at *Teidai,* but he found it so difficult to converse in *Eigo* (English) that he preferred talking to me in *Nihongo.*

About the time I was getting to know Yamagiwa, a young woman named Hirose Takako, whom I had met in Sasebo when she was working in the mayor's office there, accompanied the mayor to Tokyo for a mayors' conference lasting about a week, and she got in touch with me soon after reaching town. Takako was a plain and simple country girl, about eighteen, who had grown up in southern Kyushu (regarded as the sticks in Tokyo), but she was bright and lively and unusual in at least one respect: though not a college graduate she had studied at an American mission school and learned to speak surprisingly good English. Showing her around Tokyo was a delight. Her excitement at seeing the big city, even in its dilapidated condition, for the first time, reminded me of my own excitement when, as a small-town boy from Watertown, New York, I made my first trip to New York City.

One night I decided to take Takako to the broadcasting station for a visit. I timed our arrival at Studio 2 for around nine, and, sure enough, there, through the window, we could see Yamagiwa busily feeding vertical columns of *kanji*, so to speak, into the microphone. When he finished with the news and sighted me through the window, his face lit up, and he came hurrying out. "You are very wise to listen to these broadcasts," he told me. "We use the very best Japanese for them and there's no better way for you to learn a language than by hearing the best." At this point I broke in to introduce Takako, whom he noticed now for the first time, and they exchanged the usual formalities in Japanese. Yamagiwa then turned back to me and said hesitantly: "I was planning on introducing you to some of the other announcers, but. . . ." I assured him that both Takako and I liked the idea, so we took the elevator to the newscasters' room on the fifth floor where Yamagiwa introduced me to three of his colleagues (all *Teidai* graduates, I learned, like Yamagiwa) and I presented Takako to them in my best Japanese. As we sat down for tea, one of the newscasters looked over at me and made the usual remark: *"Nippongo wa o-jozu desu ne!"* ("Your Japanese is very good!") "Have you ever been to Japan before?" "This is my first time," I replied, after making the usual denials of proficiency. "It's really surprising," he said, "that you should have learned to speak it so well in America." Everyone in the room joined in on the praise, including

**65**

Takako. "Listen, Takako," I exclaimed, turning to her and lapsing into English, "just because you're speaking Japanese, you don't need to be so darned polite! You know very well that my pronunciation is lousy!" "It's not so bad," she insisted, speaking English, too, at this point. "I think you're improving all the time."

Yamagiwa and his colleagues seemed a bit put off by this aside in English, but when it was over, Yamagiwa resumed the Japanese conversation by saying: "Those B-29s of yours were pretty good, weren't they?" Everyone laughed at the *fausse naiveté* of this remark, but since he had used English for B-29, I told him I had heard that during the war the Japanese called them *"Nikuchan,"* which could be translated as "the 29 kid." "Oh, it's more than that," Takako interjected, going into English again. "You know, *niku* — twenty-nine — is close to the word, *nikui,* which means hateful. What do you Americans call that? You were telling me the other day. It's a pun — a kind of bitter pun."

The second exchange with Takako in English increased the tension in the room. It wasn't polite, in any case, I realized, for our hosts were obviously unable to follow what we were saying. It's *Nihongo* from now on, I resolved; and that's what I came here for anyway! To relieve the tension I circulated a pack of Luckies. "American cigarettes are really fine," said one of the newscasters. "But, remember the excellent American cigarettes we used to get in Shanghai before the war?" put in one of the other newscasters. "It seems to me that the quality has declined somewhat." "Possibly it's because you Americans had to distribute so many of them to your soldiers during the war," suggested Yamagiwa, and when I expressed surprise at the idea he added quickly: "But they're very good. Much better than Japanese cigarettes!"

Yamagiwa's last remark was the signal for one of the newsmen to pull some *Kinshi* cigarettes out of his pocket and insist that I try one. I had, of course, smoked Japanese cigarettes before and didn't like them; but I was anxious to keep things on an even keel, so I lit up the *Kinshi* and pretended to enjoy it. The conversation then switched to the subject of how long I had been overseas, and Takako, at my prompting, told the newscasters that when she first asked me where my home in the United States was, I said, "about twenty miles outside of Tokyo," thinking of the town on Long Island where my parents lived. "When I start confusing Tokyo with New York City," I moaned, as everyone laughed, "I think it's about time I headed for home!" Mention of New York led Yamagiwa to ask me about the *New York Times* and then to inquire whether I read Japanese newspapers. I said I read them occasionally, with the help of a dictionary, and then added, for the fun of it, that I got a big kick out of reading a new little Tokyo daily called *Mimpo*. "That's a radical paper," Yamagiwa said quickly. "It's not written in good Japanese. The best papers for you to read," he went on, almost as if lecturing me, "are the *Asahi Shimbun* and the *Nichinichi Shimbun*." "I think he likes *Mimpo* because of the cartoons," put in Takako, and went on to describe one we had seen that morning of a beggar seated by the roadside holding a little sign announcing: "Nothing under 60 *sen* accepted."

No one found the *Mimpo* cartoon more than mildly amusing, which I expect it wasn't, and the conversation took a serious turn. "What you do you think of the Russians?" Yamagiwa asked me. While I was thinking up an appropriate answer in *Nihongo*, he went on: "A lot of American soldiers tell us they hate the Russians. They like the Japanese much better." "That's strange," I said mildly. "Probably most of them, like me, have never known any Russians personally. I have a feeling I'd like them if I met any of them." Yamagiwa persisted, "I wasn't thinking so much of the Russian people. I meant the country as a whole. What do you think of the present state of relations between your country and the Soviet Union?" Here, Takako, noticing my mounting irritation, gave a little laugh and exclaimed: "I don't know why we Japanese worry so much about Russian-American relations these days. After all, we've got our hands full with our own problems right now."

Takako's words obviously stung Yamagiwa, but one of his colleagues quickly smoothed things over by bringing up the subject of American movies. Everyone brightened at the mention of movies and the newscasters quickly made a list of their film-star favorites, including Charlie Chaplin, Bette Davis, Deanna Durbin, and Mickey Mouse. Since a rumor, possibly government-inspired, had circulated in Japan during the war that Deanna Durbin had passed away, I took the opportunity to remark that Deanna was still going strong and, for all I knew, was working on a new picture. I went on to tell them something about the newer movie celebrities and amused everyone by trying to pronounce the name of Ingrid Bergman in the Japanese style (*I-nu-gu-ri-do Be-ru-gu-ma-nu*).

It was close to ten by the time we finished talking about movies, and as I fumbled for a match to relight my almost forgotten *Kinshi,* one of the newscasters, noting the time, excused himself by saying he had a program coming up. This was the signal for the group to break up, so I dropped the *Kinshi* into the ashtray, and Takako and I got up and prepared to leave. Yamagiwa insisted on walking us out to the hall, and as we stood there waiting for the elevator he suddenly exclaimed: "I almost forgot. I have a little book I want to give you to help you in your study of Japanese. Have you another moment to spare? You'll excuse us?" he said, turning to Takako. The book which he took from a shelf in the newscasters' room turned out to contain a list of difficult Japanese words, with pronunciations indicated in *hiragana* (the Japanese syllabary) beside them, apparently prepared for the use of radio broadcasters.

The vocabulary book was indeed a useful one, I could see at once, and I pressed some Luckies on Yamagiwa to show my gratitude for the gift. As we walked back to the elevator he remarked: "Miss Hirose is very pleasant. Where does she come from?" "Sasebo," I said, somewhat amused, for I had told him that when I introduced her. "Oh, yes," he said thoughtfully. "Her accent sounds like western Kyushu. Is that where you met her?" I explained that I had gotten to know her when I was stationed in Sasebo and having interviews with the mayor, for whom she was doing secretarial work. But I couldn't help adding: "Considering the fact that she has never been outside of Japan, it's remarkable how well she speaks English, isn't it?'' Yamagiwa nodded vaguely and then murmured apologies for the fact that he had forgotten so much of the *Eigo* he had learned at *Teidai*. Then, just before we joined Takako in front of the elevator, he slackened his pace, lowered his voice, and said in a confidential tone: ''You won't take offense if I give you a little advice about your study of Japanese, will you?'' I assured him I wouldn't, and he continued: ''You should, of course, as I said before, read the best newspapers; and, as I've told you, you hear the best Japanese when you listen to newscasts.'' He paused for a moment and finally got to the point. ''You probably noticed it yourself, Lieutenant Boller,'' he said, ''but, if not, I think I should tell you: Miss Hirose speaks very poor Japanese.'' I wanted to say, ''But she speaks pretty good English, doesn't she?''; but I didn't. I merely smiled, and when Takako and I boarded the elevator I cried: *''Ja, mata!''* (''See you again!'')

A few days later Takako returned to Sasebo and I never saw her again, though we corresponded for a while after I left Japan. By the time she returned to Sasebo all of my best Navy friends were beginning to receive travel orders and departing, one after another, for the States. By the end of December I was feeling lonely and deserted, weary from working all day and socializing in *Nihongo* all night, and anxious to get back to the States myself to see family and friends and re-enter civilian life. But my last excursion in Tokyo — on New Year's Eve, my birthday — was one of my pleasantest. I spent it at the home of a former Japanese pilot, about my age, whom I had met during the course of my work for USSBS. It was a large dinner party; not only did I meet my host's attractive young wife there for the first time, I also met his parents, some aunts and uncles, and, as I recall, his grandparents and some friends as well. We had *sake* and *sushi*, played games, and, best of all, had a great deal of lively talk all evening.

I was well-prepared for the *kaiwa*. Earlier that day I had looked up several common words in *Kenkyusha* (the Japanese-English dictionary the Navy had issued us), ferreted out possible puns, and, to my great glee, found that some of them fit beautifully into our talks that evening. My plays-upon-Japanese-words all produced considerable merriment, but I was aware of the fact that the host's wife remained still and expressionless throughout, even during my wildest sallies. She was being *hazukashii* (quiet and demure), the wifely custom in Japan those days, I knew, but in my democratizing fervor, I resolved not to leave the house that evening until I had wrested one laugh, even one tiny smile, from her. Toward the end of the evening I finally succeeded. When one of the guests, during a lull in the conversation, asked whether I knew where to get some *sumi* (charcoal), the phrase *sumi kara sumi made* (from corner to corner) flashed into my mind and I at once seized the opening. *"Sumi kara sumi made sumi wo sagashimasu!"* "From corner to corner I'll look for charcoal!"), I cried. At that, even the host's young wife broke into a laugh, almost in spite of herself, as everyone else roared with delight, and I left the party soon after exhilarated and triumphant.

And then suddenly it was all over. I returned to the States, left the Navy, returned to graduate school, took my doctorate, and began teaching history at SMU. For a year or two I tried to keep up with *Nihongo*, but the pressure of teaching forced me eventually to give it all up. Forty-five years later, when I returned to Japan with two friends — Jeff Barnard, a painter from St. Louis, and David Broiles, a Fort Worth lawyer — for a ten-day visit, I was mortified by my inability to read much of anything but *kana* (the syllabary) or to come up with any puns, even feeble ones, when I got into halting conversations in *Nihongo*.

One day we took the train to Hiroshima, visited the Peace Memorial Museum there, and were deeply moved by the exhibits of the havoc wrought by the *genshi bakudan* years earlier. To my surprise, one of the exhibits was a set of the leaflets which the prisoners on Guam and I had prepared in the spring and summer of 1945; and I couldn't help wondering how it would have been if we had been able to prepare leaflets about the *genshi bakudan* to drop beforehand.

Just before leaving Japan we visited the War Museum in Tokyo and made the rounds of the exhibits there: charts, maps, and pictures, as well as weapons, commemorating Japanese engagements, on land and sea, with American forces during World War II. There was no mention of Pearl Harbor; but all the major battles were presented in loving detail. There were also captions accompanying the displays (which I was able to decipher with the help of a pocket dictionary) lauding Japan's soldiers and sailors for their courage, dedication, and heroism in encounters with the enemy. And I realized again what I had known all along: I was one of the lucky servicemen who had been spared that side of the Japanese during World War II.

# 3

# Movie Music:
## The Sound of Silents

I FIRST became aware of film music one evening when I was about eight years old and living in Lancaster, New York. The film I watched in Lancaster's main theater was D. W. Griffith's *Isn't Life Wonderful?* (1924), an anti-war movie dealing with post-war Germany and containing a plea for brotherhood. But I remember nothing whatsoever about the film itself; it was the theme music, played recurrently by an organist holding forth at the mighty Wurlitzer, that caught my attention. The music that bewitched me that evening was Edwin MacDowell's "To a Wild Rose," I later learned, and I never went to the movies after that without hoping to hear more music as enchanting as that.

It wasn't until about 1926, however, when my parents moved to Watertown, New York, that I began attending movies regularly, and in short order I got to know what to expect in the town's five movie theaters which ranked in a descending order of opulence: the Avon (Wurlitzer organ and on occasion a small orchestra); the Olympic (Wurlitzer); the Palace (organ and piano); the Liberty (piano); the Strand (piano and drums); and the Victoria (piano). I heard a lot of junk in those theaters, of course, but also a great deal of classical music and some good popular music, too. I even enjoyed the "hurry" music (most of it composed, I eventually discovered, by J. S. Zamecnik) that went with the cops-and-robbers and chase scenes in the weekly serials.

In 1928, when Watertown's movie theaters, beginning with the Avon, began converting to sound, I felt a bit melancholy; it looked as though it was the end of my beloved movie music. It did come to an end, to be sure, for a time, but during the early thirties I began to notice background music in some of the "talkies" I attended. And then, suddenly, came *King Kong* (1933) and *The Lost Patrol* (1934) with full-scale musical scores written by Max Steiner, and I was hooked again. By 1934 I was a Max Steiner fan.

By 1934, too, I was playing music for films myself. A high school friend named Roger Marmon somehow came into possession of a 35-mm silent movie projector and some old silent feature films and, for the fun of it and also to make a little money, he conceived the idea of putting on shows for churches, granges, and civic groups in little towns in upstate New York that had no movie theaters and sharing box-office receipts with his sponsors. He knew that I played the piano (for my brother John's dramatic recitations) and the organ, too (for church services), and that I knew something about movie music, so he invited me one day to team up with him and play the piano for the films he intended to present. I accepted his offer eagerly, sent off to Sam Fox Music Publishers in New York for some of the old silent movie music, then still in print, and began working out my accompaniments, and trying them out on my younger sister, Vickie, who encouraged me to try making up some themes of my own. By the time Roger was ready to launch our little enterprise, he had added a new member to the team: "Miller the Mystic," a professional magician in his thirties who was out of work and eager to pick up a few extra dollars here and there. During the next few months the three of us traveled from town to town in the north country in the automobile Roger borrowed from his dad, devoting Saturday mornings to making future bookings and Saturday evenings to putting on our movie-and-magic shows. Roger arranged to print up advertisements for our shows to spread around the towns we visited, but he was an indifferent speller. One of his flyers went like this: "FUED WOMAN. MILLER THE MYSTIC. MUSIC BY PAUL BOLLER."

In some towns I played the harmonium, the little organ you pumped with your feet, and in others old upright pianos slightly out of tune. Once I even held forth an entire evening on a piano whose keys in the middle range were swollen from the cold and absolutely unmovable, forcing me to play all my music an octave higher than usual. But the audience didn't seem to mind and I was proud of my ability to meet any emergency. On occasion, I recall, I sneaked some of the Max Steiner background music I heard in Watertown's theaters into my accompaniments and this always seemed to go over big.

On at least one occasion, though, movie music led me astray. One day Watertown's leading funeral director, knowing that I played the organ as a substitute in churches around town, engaged me to play at a funeral for the handsome sum of one dollar. Stimulated by the opportunity to do something new and different, I carefully prepared the music I was to play at the beginning of the service. It did not, for some reason, occur to me that I was expected to play some of the old hymns. Instead, I riffled through my collection of Zamecnik mood music and selected the most doleful numbers I could find: "Sorrow," "Tragic Scene," "Remorse," "Despair." When I began playing my mournful music at the start of the funeral service, the family and friends of the deceased were sitting quietly and stolidly in the pews, reconciled, doubtless, to the departure of their loved one. But as I proceeded with my disconsolate Zamecnik, proud, again, of being equal to every exigency, I couldn't help overhearing sighs and moans from among the mourners, and though I assumed this was to be expected, I was nevertheless a little surprised by the vehemence of the grief. And then, to my astonishment, people began getting up and heading for the exit, weeping and wailing, and supporting each other as they shuffled out. Something was wrong, I realized, but I didn't realize how wrong until the funeral director came hurrying over, asked me to cease and desist, pressed a dollar into my hand, and bid me good day.

Years later I acquired a film collection of my own. In the sixties, when Super-8 films became available at reasonable prices, I acquired a Super-8 film projector and some old silent-film comedies — Chaplin, Keaton, Laurel and Hardy, Harold Lloyd — and prepared piano accompaniments to go with them when I ran them off at parties for friends. One day my friend Joe Frantz, University of Texas professor and president at the time of the Southern Historical Association, called from Austin to ask me to take part in the SHA sessions scheduled for the spring of 1978 in St. Louis. Joe knew I collected films and played for them and he wanted me to present some of them, with a piano accompaniment, for the SHA the night before formal sessions got under way. "Let me think about it, Joe," I responded. It didn't seem quite right to do nothing but put on a movie show for the SHA, and I finally decided to do some research on the history of music for films, present a paper on the subject to my fellow historians, and then demonstrate what it was like in the old days of silent movies by running off one of my old films and accompanying them at the piano. I spent several months on research, prepared my SHA paper, and then went to work on the film I planned to run off at the conference.

The film I picked for the SHA was Charlie Chaplin's *Easy Street* (1913), which was not only a good Chaplin comedy but also had a nice little story involving the Little Tramp (Chaplin), a beautiful young woman (Edna Purviance) for him to fall in love with, and a villain (Eric Campbell) for him to overcome. I devised themes of my own for the principals — a bouncy number in G for Chaplin, a sentimental waltz in F for Purviance, and a sinister theme in A-minor for Campbell — but decided to depend on Zamecnik's "agitato" music for the chase scenes. For the fun of it, I decided to emulate Max Steiner's technique of using sudden modulations for crucial screen happenings when I came to the end of the film. The final sequence in *Easy Street* shows Chaplin contentedly in control of things, with the villain at length tamed, and I

# Return Engagement

By Popular Demand

## Milmar Amusement Co.

Offers

A Complete Change of Program

---

Personal Appearance

# " Miller The Mystic "

The Friendly Man of Magic

Tricks -- Tricks -- Tricks

Entirely New - - - All Different

FUN FOR **ALL** FOR FUN

---

Also on the Screen

DOROTHY DREW IN

# " Accused "

With Charley Delany and Miss du Pont

A Thrill a Second - Count'em

It Sizzles = = = =It Pops

Music by Paul Boller, Jr.

---

# Felts Mills High School

Benefit Junior Class

Monday December 3,      7:30 P. M.

Adults 25c      Children 10c

*High school showbiz (author's collection).*

began playing the love music in F as the scene opened. But part way through the scene, Edna Purviance appears, and, as Chaplin hurries toward her, I used a couple of bridge chords to get me at once into the key of B-major, and then, as the two went into a clinch, I ended the movie playing the love theme in a triumphant B-major. My colleagues in the SHA seemed to enjoy the paper I delivered on film music (which appeared in an expanded form in *American Heritage,* August/ September 1985) and one man in the audience, a musician himself, told me he liked my F-to-B jump cut.

★ ★ ★ ★

"If I ever kill anyone," D. W. Griffith once exclaimed, "it won't be an actor but a musician." He had been arguing with Joseph Carl Breil, his collaborator on the score for *The Birth of a Nation.* Griffith wanted to change some of the notes in the Wagner music they were planning to use and Breil was outraged. "You can't tamper with Wagner!" he cried. "It's never been done!" But Griffith insisted that the music for his picture "wasn't primarily music." It was "music for motion pictures." He was perceptive in noting the difference between film music and music for the concert hall; nevertheless, like other filmmakers during the silent era, he was heavily dependent on Wagner and the other great masters for his musical scores.

Griffith's interest in music for motion pictures was almost as keen as his interest in other aspects of filmmaking. "Watch a film run in silence," he once said, "and then watch it again with eyes and ears. The music sets the mood for what your eye sees; it guides your emotions; it is the emotional framework for visual pictures." Griffith was the first American director to engage a professional musician like Breil to help prepare a complete score for a motion picture. He was also the first to include the musical director's name in the film credits. For the premiere of *Birth* in Los Angeles in February 1915 and in New York City the following month, he arranged for the Breil score to be performed by a symphony orchestra and for program notes to be distributed to audiences containing a list of the classical numbers utilized in the score. Musically, as well as artistically and technically, *The Birth of a Nation* was a major event in American film history. After *Birth,* musical scores arranged in advance for first-class feature pictures became customary in the United States. Music as a "cinematic ally" seemed finally to have arrived in America with Griffith.

Music for films did not, of course, begin with Griffith. There had been musical accompaniments for silent movies long before the talented Kentuckian entered the scene. From the very beginning, the association of music with films seemed natural and logical. Thomas A. Edison thought of music in connection with motion pictures from the outset. When he became interested in movies, he wanted to unite his kinetoscope with his phonograph and make grand opera available on film to everyone "for a dime." But early filmmakers like Edison were unable to synchronize sound and sight satisfactorily and the idea of sound pictures quickly died. Silent films became the rule (in vaudeville houses, penny arcades, nickelodeons, and, finally, in lavish "picture palaces"): first, short subjects depicting prize fights, horse races, cockfights, acrobatics, and the like; then short features like *The Great Train Robbery* (1903); and finally longer pictures like *Home Sweet Home* (1914), which Griffith made just before producing *The Birth of a Nation*. But all of these films, even the earliest little short subjects, had music of some kind going along with them.

It would be pleasant to report that the motivations for supplying the first movies with music were, like Griffith's, exclusively aesthetic. The facts are more pedestrian. One of the main reasons for music in the earliest film days was to drown out the noisy clatter of the projector, usually stationed in the midst of the audience, while the film was being run off. Then, after projectors were put in soundproof boxes, it was necessary to use music to drown out the noise of the audience; music, as Paul Kresh put it, kept ears busy and mouths from flapping. Without music, wrote Harvard psychologist

Hugo Münsterberg, "the one-sided engagement of the senses would produce an intolerable tension." Psychologically, according to Irwin Bazelon, "the silent film presented an interesting phenomenon: sitting in a dark theater, immersed in a soundless world, created an aura of unnatural stillness, broken only by a mechanical whirr and the sounds coming from the audience itself. Coughing, sneezing, rattling candy wrappers, popcorn munching, and a general restlessness filled the air, unrivaled by any vocal resistance from the silent screen. . . . Music was introduced to cover up the silence and effectively combat audience disturbance. The early filmmakers had no desire to allow external annoyances to compete for attention with their visual product: music was their panacea for encouraging audience empathy."

It was important, too, to provide continuity to what was taking place on the screen. Until theaters began using more than one projector, it was necessary for music to bridge reel changes and provide cohesiveness to the succession of scenes appearing on the screen. But music could do more than this. As films developed in length and in sophistication, it became clear that music was indispensable for conveying to audiences some of the basic emotions behind the scenes which they were witnessing. On the silent screen, it soon became clear, "music must take the place of the spoken word"; it was essential for emotional depth. There were moods and feelings and nuances and overtones in some of the better early films that simply did not come across to audiences without music; the facial expressions, physical movements, and printed titles appearing on the screen were not enough.

Silent movies, as Kurt Weill put it, needed music the way dry cereal needs cream. By itself, the screen was a pretty cold proposition, Aaron Copeland noted, and film music was "like a small flame put under the screen to help warm it. . . ." Writing for *Moving Picture World* in April 1916, Paul Everts Denton summed up the experience of the first generation of movie-makers: "Moving pictures and music are inseparable. This the public cannot deny. . . . *Music, while it may escape the attention of the spectator, has the strange and subtle influence of creating moods, and that is why it is so important in the presentation of the moving picture.*" Music, in short, was the "emotional dialogue" of the silent film. As MGM production head Irving Thalberg once put it frankly: "There never was a *silent* film. We'd finish a picture, show it in one of our projection rooms, and come out shattered. It would be awful. We'd have high hopes for the picture, work our heads off on it, and the result was always the same. Then we'd show it in a theatre, with a girl down in the pit, pounding away at a piano, and there would be all the difference in the world. Without that music there wouldn't have been a movie industry at all."

But the earliest film music was horrendous. It did little more than drown out the racket of projectors and audiences. Hand-organs, music boxes, and phonographs supplied music — many kinds of music — for the first films. Then exhibitors abandoned mechanical music and began hiring pianists (often any piano-player who happened to be around) to play during a show. This was a step upward; but only a short step. "Don't shoot the pianist; he's doing the best he can," people used to say; but his best was often not very good. He usually lacked professional training and he played whatever he happened to know during a film in utter disregard of what was taking place on the screen. After a while pianists began making some efforts to accommodate their music to the screen; but even then their accompaniments were "often incongruous, irrelevant, or downright inappropriate." According to Irwin Bazelon, "They doodled, vamped, and attempted to reflect (by trial and error) the mood and tempo of the action. They improvised musical effects, mangled chords, arpeggioed up and down the keyboard, and filled in many sequences by playing popular music interludes." One gets the impression that in the early days of films the sound effects — train whistles, fire bells, gunshots, and cannon fire — performed by men behind the screen were better than the music. The sound effects were so realistic at times that they frightened audiences out of the theater.

Sometimes movie pianists played the harmonium with one hand and the piano with the other; but frequently the right hand "knew not" what the left hand was doing and neither was aware of the screen. Organ music by itself also became popular in the early years of film, and the day would come when the "mighty Wurlitzer" with its four or five manuals and scores of exotic stops and sound effects became featured in the major movie houses of the nation. In the first years of film, however, organ accompaniments did as little for films as piano music did. Whether at the piano or at the organ, the film accompanist was completely indifferent, according to Kurt London, to what audiences were seeing on the screen; "he played anything he liked, and there was little or no connection between the music and the film it accompanied." Comedy was accompanied by Schumann's "Träumerei" and winter scenes by Mendelssohn's "Spring Song." It was not at all uncommon for lively music to be played for solemn scenes and for tragedy to be converted into farce by the use of inappropriate music. In one theater the music was so bad that when the heroine jumped into the water someone in the audience yelled: "Take the pianist with you, while you're about it!" Even orchestral music — first trios (violin, piano, cello), then small ensembles, and eventually sixty-piece orchestras — gave little support to the films at first. The conductor might shout "Romance in F" during the picture and if one of the instrumentalists made an error there would be a terrible discord and the conductor would scream: "No, you so and so. . . . You've got the wrong music! It's 'Romance in F,' by Rubenstein!" What Bazelon called "audience empathy" was likely to be minimal at this point.

Even when accompanists began taking their function more seriously, the music wasn't always good. Musical clichés became common in the early days: chase scenes always accompanied by Rossini's "William Tell Overture," night scenes by Beethoven's "Moonlight Sonata," sleep by "Rockabye Baby," winter by "Jingle Bells," and "blighted love" scenes by the tearjerker "Hearts and Flowers" (so overworked at first that it began to evoke laughter). Musical faux pas also continued to be frequent, even though accompanists were trying harder. In October 1909, a writer for the *New York*

*Daily Mirror* reported that he had recently seen a movie in which a pathetic scene showing a man mourning his dead wife was accompanied by the strains of "No Wedding Bells for Me!" "Bad judgment in the selection of music," he complained, "may ruin an exhibition as much as a good programme may help it." Max Winkler, one of the inventors of cue sheets for movie music, witnessed a similar musical incongruity in a film starring Alla Nazimova in 1912. In the film, *War Brides,* Nazimova played the part of a pregnant peasant woman who, at the high point of the film, threw herself in front of the king, hands raised to heaven, and cried (according to the screen title): "If you will not give us women the right to vote for or against war, I shall not bear a child for such a country." When the king coldly ignored her plea and swept on grandly past her, Nazimova drew a dagger and killed herself. Up to this point, according to Winkler, the pianist had been doing fairly well; but then, just as Nazimova drew her last breath, surrounded by the heart-broken members of her family, he began to play a lively old favorite entitled "You Made Me What I Am Today." When Winkler queried him about it afterward, the pianist exclaimed: "Why, I thought that was perfectly clear. Wasn't it the King's fault that she killed herself?" In an editorial on July 3, 1909, *Moving Picture World* summed up the grievances of producers, exhibitors, reviewers, and audiences about film music in its early years: "There is one head under which nearly every moving picture theater in New York City, in our opinion, is lamentably deficient," said the *World*. "We mean the music — the music that accompanies, illustrates, or which is supposed to harmonize with the pictures. . . . Half the pianists whom we have heard these last six months deserve to lose their jobs, for if they can play, they either won't or don't. The pianos should be either burnt or put into tune or replaced with better ones. But, better still, we think, is our advice, wherever practical, to engage a small orchestra of strings, with the addition of the piano and sound effects."

But orchestras per se didn't necessarily do any better. As late as 1921, when the epic film, *The Queen of Sheba,* was shown in Liverpool, Jim McCartney (father of the Beatles' Paul McCartney) was called in the last minute to conduct a small orchestra, and for the chariot race he chose "Thanks for the Buggy Ride" and for the queen's death, "Horsey Keep Your Tail Up."

The basic problem with early movie music, of course, was that musicians did not get to preview films before they played for them. This meant that they sat in the dark watching the screen and playing whatever came to mind at the spur of the moment. "It was a terrible predicament," Max Winkler recalled, "and so, usually, was the music." Compilations of music for films, which began appearing just before World War I, were of some help. Sam Fox began publishing volumes of classified "mood" music in 1913 and Carl Fischer and other music publishers were soon doing the same. In such collections (designed for orchestra as well as for piano and organ), the basic "moods" (love, hate, passion, joy, sorrow, anger, fury, fear, terror, tension) were listed and appropriate music supplied for each mood. The word, mood, was also loosely defined to include atmospheric music (seasonal, scenic, and national) as well as music fitting different kinds of physical action (chases, fire-fighting, storms at sea). Moods can be complicated things, even in silent films, and the basic moods were usually subdivided into additional categories and the subcategories themselves sometimes split further into subunits. Under the classification Dramatic Expression, for example, there might be four categories (Climax — Tension, Misterioso — Tension, Agitato — Climax, Appassionato), with each category being further subdivided. Climax, Appassionato, for example, was further broken down into Despair, Passionate Lament, Passionate Excitement, Jubilant, Victorious, and Bacchantic, with appropriate music for each. There were many kinds of "Hurry Music": for struggles, duels, mob or fire scenes, sword fights, great confusion, and general use. Probably never before in the history of the world had music been pigeonholed in such a fashion.

What kind of music? Just about every kind. The music included under each category in the film-music collections came from many sources: grand opera, light opera, symphonies, musical comedy, folk music, popular songs, jazz, ragtime, and (notably) piano music of the great masters of the nineteenth century. One of the most interesting compilations of music for films came out in 1924: *Motion Picture Moods for Pianists and Organists,* prepared by Erno Rapee, musical director at the Capitol Theater in New York. Rapee not only included an enormous number of musical selections (mostly classical) for fifty-two different moods, he also presented an index of all the moods on every page of his anthology so that pianists could quickly turn to any of the 694 pages in the book for the mood he needed. When in the thirties Erno Rapee's huge collection was remaindered for a couple of dollars a copy, the *New Yorker's* E. B. White, discussing the book, was struck by the fact that, by Rapee's reckoning, there were the same number of moods as there were cards in a deck and weeks in a year, that Grieg was "the movie pianist's best pal and surest bet," and that Mendelssohn was the "aeroplane man."

Even more useful for film musicians than collections of mood music were "cue sheets" containing suggestions for music for specific films. As early as 1909, Edison Company began sending out "Suggestions for Music" sheets with its films; for its one-reel *Frankenstein* (1910) — a "liberal adaptation of Mrs. Shelley's story, made to carefully eliminate all the actually repulsive situations" — Edison suggested music like "Melody in F," "Der Freischütz," "Annie Laurie," and *Lohengrin* to accompany the picture's twenty-five scenes. But fully developed cue sheets listing individual scenes in their proper sequence and indicating length, basic mood, and appropriate music for each did not become common until two or three years later. Max Winkler claimed to have invented them, but other film-music specialists — Schirmer's S.M. Berg, the "cue-sheet man," and Vitagraph Studio's Bert Ennis — conceived of the idea about the same time. Winkler drew up a plan for analyzing a film's musical needs and making a list of musical suggestions fitted with precision to the action on the screen. As he conceived it, a cue sheet would go something like this:

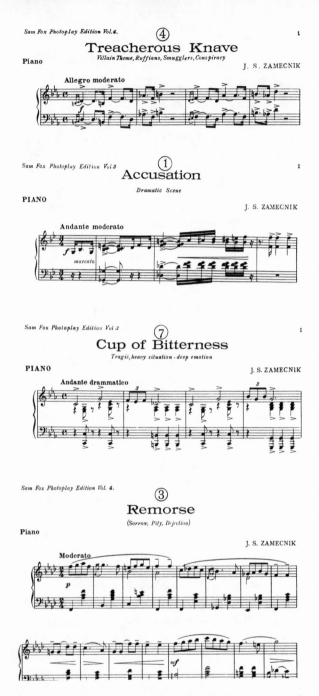

*Mood music (composite reproduction of original scores in author's collection).*

1. Opening — play Minuet No. 2 in G by Beethoven for ninety seconds until title on screen "Follow Me Dear."

2. Play "Dramatic Andante" by Vely for two minutes and ten seconds. Note: Play soft during scene where mother enters. Play Cue No. 2 until scene "Hero leaving room."

3. Play "Love Theme" by Lorenze — for one minute and twenty seconds. Note: Play soft and slow during conversation until title on screen "There they go."

4. Play "Stampede" by Simon for fifty-five seconds. Note: Play fast and decrease or increase speed of gallop in accordance with action on the screen.

Winkler sold his idea for musical cue sheets to Universal Film Company and was soon busily preparing cue sheets containing musical suggestions for every "scene, situation, character, action, emotion, nationality, emergency, windstorm, rainstorm and brainstorm, every dancer, vamp, cowboy, thief and gigolo, eskimo and zulu, emperor and streetwalker, colibri and elephant plus every printed title that flickered in the faces of the five-cent to twenty-five-cent audiences." Not surprisingly, cue sheets became enormously popular among pianists, organists, and orchestra leaders throughout the country. In large theaters, musical directors set about collecting and filing huge libraries of film music, and trade magazines inaugurated film-music columns in which they gave suggestions for forthcoming films.

With cue sheets, as with compilations, film musicians continued to raid — or, as some critics put it, "rape" — the works of the great masters. From Bach, Beethoven, Mendelssohn, Grieg, Tschaikovsky, and Wagner emerged Adagio Lamentosos, Sinister Misteriosos, Weird Moderatos, and Majestic Pomposos. Wagner's and Mendelssohn's wedding marches were used for divorces as well as marriages by "souring up the aisle," that is, playing them out of tune. Meyerbeer's "Coronation March," played slowly, accompanied criminals to the death room. Delibes' "Pizzicato Polka" was used for "sneaky" sequences by counting "one-two" between each pizzicato. And music featuring trombone solos invariably accompanied drunk scenes — "no other instrument," said Winkler, "could hiccup with such virtuosity." But the great masters didn't always have what it took and filmmakers started seeking original music, as well, for their productions. Music publishers began to assemble a group of movie-music specialists, among them Gaston Borch, Irénée Bergé, Maurice Baron, Hugo Riesenfeld, and the prolific J. S. Zamecnik, who turned out nine volumes of *Sam Fox Moving Picture Music* between 1913 and 1929 and was so adept at "hurries" and "agits" (*agitato*) that some of them were still being used in serials and newsreels in the thirties, long after music had gone onto the sound track. Before long, the American public was hearing huge quantities of Borch-Bergé-Zamecnik-Riesenfeld music in the movie theater.

From original mood music to original scores for whole films was only a small step. But it was not until 1915 that D. W. Griffith took it with his tremendously innovative (if distressingly racist) epic, *The Birth of a Nation*. For this film, Griffith (who had studied music in Louisville and New York) and Joseph Carl Breil, orchestra leader and composer, prepared the first "full orchestral score," constructed on symphonic lines, for an American film. Breil wrote some of the music himself, most notably, the love theme for the Little Colonel and Elsie Stoneman which, published separately as "The Perfect Song," eventually became the theme song for the "Amos and Andy" radio show. The score also made use of traditional American tunes like "Dixie" and "The Star-Spangled Banner" and, in addition, music from the great masters: Grieg's "In the Hall of the Mountain King" for scenes of the evacuation of Atlanta and Wagner's "Ride of the Valkyries" for the ride of the Klansmen in the last two reels. Elsewhere it utilized extracts from Massenet, Dukas, Suppé, Weber, Bellini, Smetana, Tschaikovsky, Hadyn, Verdi, Bizet, Offenbach, Mozart, Schumann, Flotow, Mahler, Rossini, Bach, Brahms, and Liszt. The cuing was precise and detailed throughout, and the score as a whole established standards for film music that influenced all subsequent filmmakers. Griffith's production has been called the "most discussed film and film musical score" of all time; and after its premiere at a legitimate theater on Broadway at two dollars a ticket in March 1915, film music acquired a prestige in this country that it had never before possessed.

After *The Birth of a Nation,* original scores for major productions became practically *de rigueur.* Joseph Breil did the score for Griffith's *Intolerance* the following year, and special music was prepared for all of the most famous Hollywood movies of the twenties: *Orphans of the Storm* (Louis F. Gottschalk and William Peters, 1922), *The Covered Wagon* (Hugo Riesenfeld, 1923), *Greed* (Leo Kampenski, 1924), *The Iron Horse* (Erno Rapee, 1924), *The Big Parade* (David Mendoza and William Axt, 1925), *Ben Hur* (Mendoza and Axt, 1926) and *Don Juan* (Mendoza and Axt, 1926).

There was even "original" music for the silent version of *La Boheme* (1926). Puccini's estate was in litigation when the film was being made, and his music was unavailable, so David Mendoza and William Axt did a substitute score that the critic George Jean Nathan liked even better than Puccini's. Most scores were prepared by film-music specialists, but occasionally American composers unconnected with films tried their hand at movie scores. Victor Herbert did music for *The Fall of a Nation* (1915), Sigmund Romberg for *Foolish Wives* (1922), Charles Wakefield Cadman for *The Rubaiyat of Omar Khayyam* (1922), and Mortimer Wilson for *The Thief of Baghdad* (1924). In Europe, serious composers did quite well by films: Camille Saint-Saëns composed music for *The Assassination of the Duke of Guise* (the first music written especially for a film) in 1908; Mikhail Ippolitov-Ivanov scored several Russian films before World War I; Pietro Mascagni did music for two Italian films during the war; in the twenties Arthur Honneger, Darius Milhaud, and Erik Satie scored French films, and Werner Haymann and Paul Hindemith composed music for films in Germany. But composers like these were not ordinarily attracted to films; the impossibility of developing musical ideas at length for movies and the evanescent character of films (and their music) prevented them from taking much interest in film music.

Music was utilized on movie sets as well as in theaters

during the silent era. One reason was to drown out the sound of the camera and noise from nearby sets. But its main purpose was to help put performers in the proper mood for the scenes they were doing. Griffith seems to have been the first to employ music on a set; he used it when filming *Judith of Bethulia* in 1913 to help Blanche Sweet in some highly emotional scenes. He also used a brass band to accompany battle scenes being filmed for *Intolerance*. But Griffith rarely used music on sets; he once said he would never employ an actor "who could not feel the role enough to weep at rehearsals." Like Griffith, Cecil B. DeMille also restricted the use of music on the set. He did arrange for Bizet music to be played during the filming of *Carmen* at the request of opera singer Geraldine Farrar, but most of the time he did without music because he found it too distracting. Others — directors like William Wellman and King Vidor — thought music was extremely useful for inducing the proper moods and so did many of the performers. Pola Negri insisted on soft passionate music for emotional scenes, Mary Pickford liked Charles Wakefield Cadman's "From the Land of the Sky Blue Water" and Massenet's "Elegy," John Gilbert chose "Moonlight and Roses," and Ben Lyon requested "My Buddy" ("ye gods, it was effective!"). Before long, pianos, portable organs, violins, and cellos were common sights on Hollywood sets. Maurice Torneur once saw a unit filming a chase from the back of a truck with another truck full of frantically playing musicians racing alongside it.

By the twenties, American film music had come a long way from its early hit-and-miss days. For the screening of Germany's expressionistic *The Cabinet of Dr. Caligeri* in New York in 1921, Capitol Theater manager S. L. Rothafel ("Roxy") and musical director Erno Rapee made use of the music of composers never heard (or heard of) before by mass audiences — Debussy, Strauss, Stravinsky, Prokofieff, and Schoenberg — and *Musical America* heartily endorsed Roxy's judgment that it was "the most daring musical achievement in the history of the American motion-picture theater." When *The Birth of a Nation* was revived at the Capitol a little later, the original score had come to seem too elementary and it was replaced by a more sophisticated one. "The art of musical presentation," explained Roxy, "has progressed so markedly during the seven years since *The Birth of a Nation* was first produced, that different standards and methods of adaptation have educated the public to new musical values. . . ."

By 1921, there were probably sixty theaters in the country with orchestras of thirty or more instruments; and there were hundreds with small orchestra combinations or large organs, and thousands with competent pianists conscientiously consulting mood-music collections and cue sheets. The largest theaters had huge libraries of film music and sizable staffs consisting of musical directors, conductors, associate conductors, concertmasters, vocal coaches, organists, and vocalists. Eugene Ormandy was assistant conductor at the Capitol Theater in New York and was permitted on occasion to conduct for newsreels; Jan Peerce was one of the Capitol's vocalists.

Meanwhile, throughout the twenties, compilations, encyclopedias, guides, and manuals of film music poured from the press. In 1925 Erno Rapee published an *Encyclopedia of Music for Pictures* listing even more moods than his collection of the previous year and offering advice on how to handle special problems: two characters with different musical themes appearing in the same scene; long and short flashbacks; and different kinds of villains (sneaky, boisterous, crafty, powerful, and evil-minded). Maurice Borodkin's 1928 *Guide to Motion Picture Music* was still more ambitious; it listed more than 6000 musical numbers and classified them into more than 150 different categories. In *Motion Picture Synchrony for Motion Picture Exhibitors, Organists and Pianists* (1925), Ernest Luz proposed something entirely new for film-music classification. He assigned different colors to the basic human moods and suggested attaching gum tabs of the appropriate color to all musical selections. "Always remember," he admonished, "that the Love Theme is White; the Villain's Theme is Red; the Vampire's Theme is Dark Green;

the Heavy Agitated Motif is Dark Blue; the Light or Hurried Suspense Motif is Light Blue; the Lullaby, Pastorale or Characteristic is Brown; the Regal is Purple."

In *Musical Accompaniment of Motion Pictures*, Edith Lang and George West suggested different keys for different moods: A-flat and E-flat suggested warmth or languor; E-flat minor and G minor fit moods of sorrow or grief; A and D major lent themselves to "brilliancy"; E minor suggested "clear skies" or "the ocean's wide expanse"; and the key of F was appropriate for scenes of a meditative or religious nature. "The key of C has nothing to commend it," they concluded, "except that after long wanderings through the rich realms of sharp or flat tonalities, it is most gratifying to hear the crisp and bright 'key of keys.'" Above all, they urged the player not to adhere slavishly to one key, especially the black keys, D-flat and G-flat.

May Meskimem Mills tried something different to help the overburdened accompanist. In her book on "photo-playing," she linked some of the major Hollywood stars with music of a certain kind. Constance Talmadge and Billie Burke, she reported, required "music of the dainty 4/4 Moderatos, with a broad and melodious theme." For Douglas Fairbanks, she recommended a "humorous, snappy, fast and furious style of music"; for Mary Pickford, the "old fashioned type of eccentric comedy" music; for Theda Bara, music which was "cold, sensual, emotional and heavy dramatic"; for Lillian Gish, a "demure, plaintive, and heavy dramatic" music; and for Mary Garden and Geraldine Farrar, music which was "intensely dramatic and of the grand opera style."

George Benyon, the most primly pedagogical of all the film-music instructors, predicted great things for accompanists who took picture-playing seriously: "It has been said that genius is the art of taking pains. Every theatre can have a genius if the leader so desires it. A genius in the orchestral pit means a full house, a full house means a successful business and a satisfied employer, and the last two mean a raise in salary. It pays to be a genius."

Benyon went on to forecast a great future for silent film

music: "The future holds a promise, stupendous in its magnitude, that picture music will rank favorably with grand opera and symphony." But while aspiring young film musicians were busily plowing through Benyon's manual and consulting Rapee's encyclopedia, motion-picture technicians were renewing their efforts to synchronize sound and sight and produce the kind of "talking pictures" that Edison had envisaged in the 1890s. By the mid-twenties they had succeeded in coupling projectors with sixteen-inch phonograph records with a fair degree of success. The fruits of their efforts, *Don Juan* (which opened in New York in August 1926 using a prerecorded musical accompaniment) and *The Jazz Singer* (which appeared the following year, containing a bit of song and dialogue), signaled the beginning of the end of the silent era. Playwright Robert E. Sherwood, for one, was glad of it. Reviewing *Don Juan*, he noted that "it will be possible in the future to dispense with orchestras and organists in movie theatres." He added: "Well, I for one will shed no tears. I'm tired of hearing 'Hearts and Flowers' during the views of the United States Cavalry riding to the rescue, and 'Horses — Horses — Horses' during tender love scenes."

Sherwood was harsh. But even so dedicated a film-music specialist as George Benyon warned that much of the mood music written especially for the screen "holds no great merit." He lamented the fact that Beethoven, Liszt, and Berlioz "lived too early to furnish picture music" and recommended using the great masters as much as possible. Indeed, many of the great masters took quite a beating for their posthumous contributions to movies. Much fine music came to sound hackneyed and silly through overuse in movie houses, and some of it remains impossible to listen to even today. There was a great deal of truth in the charge of critics that silent-film accompanists "raped" and "murdered" some of the great music of western civilization.

D. W. Griffith was thoughtful enough to know that there was a vast difference between concert music and film music. But even he failed to realize that changing notes in Wagner was no way to develop appropriate accompaniments for films. He was extremely proud of the fact that the score for *The Birth of a Nation* contained so many different classical selections, and his program notes gave the impression that he was presenting a concert as well as screening a film for the enjoyment of his audiences. Many people appreciated this double offering, but at least one critic had grave misgivings about it. "It is strange," wrote Carl Van Vechten, music critic for the *New York Times,* "but it has occurred to no one that the moving picture demands a *new* kind of music." Only with the advent of sound did the kind of music he was suggesting come into being.

In the thirties, as Hollywood freed itself from the conventions of the silent era, it began employing composers to write original music for its films, and, for the first time, music began to become an integral part of American moving pictures. The silent era produced nothing in the United States to compare with some of the most striking scores of the early sound era: Max Steiner's for *The Informer* (1935), for example, or Eric Wolfgang Korngold's for *The Adventures of Robin Hood* (1938), or Adolph Deutsch's for *The Maltese Falcon* (1941).

By the late thirties, the avant-garde composer George Antheil was commenting favorably in the pages of *Modern Music* on the "daring advances and startling newnesses" appearing in the scores of Hollywood's master craftsman Max Steiner, and distinguished composers like Aaron Copland and Virgil Thomson — as well as Antheil himself — were doing music for films that still continues to evoke interest. Even Charlie Chaplin, who stuck doggedly to silent films until 1940, made splendid use of the new opportunities for film music. Beginning with his first feature, *The Kid* (1921), Chaplin had distributed cue sheets with his pictures, but, like everyone else, he made use largely of established music. With sound now available to him, he began composing music of his own and, by carefully supervising the orchestration and conducting the recording himself, he made his scores for *City Lights* (1931) and *Modern Times* (1936) an essential and delightful part of his films as a whole.

In a way, then, Griffith, who had given film music such a big boost during the silent era, turned out to be right when he forecast its bright future. The more adventurous Hollywood composers, who were eagerly exploring the exciting new possibilities sound had opened up to them, may not have been doing exactly what Griffith had had in mind when he made his prediction. But they were trying to do what he always tried to do himself — advance motion pictures to a higher level of artistic achievement.

# 4

# The Bright Side of Calvinism:
## Those Coolidge Stories

I FIRST heard of Calvin Coolidge when I was seven years old. It was election night, November 4, 1924, when Coolidge beat John W. Davis, the Democratic candidate that year, by a large margin, and of course clobbered Progressive Party candidate Robert M. LaFollette, Republican senator from Wisconsin, who was running on a third-party ticket. My parents joined friends that night in a room in the Presbyterian church in Lancaster, New York (where my father was the minister), to listen to the returns over the radio. Meanwhile my sister Margaret and I joined the other kids that night in the Sunday School room to talk and play games. At one point, I recall, we all stood on chairs and began writing names on the blackboard. All our playmates wrote "COOLIDGE" in large letters, while Margaret and I wrote "LaFOLLETTE" in big letters too. Later, when my mother took us home, I expressed bewilderment over Coolidge's big victory over LaFollette. "Well, the good people, like Jesus, are always defeated," said my mother simply. My parents had voted for Eugene Debs in 1920, I later learned, and in 1928 they started voting for Norman Thomas. In 1952, when Thomas was no longer running for president, they voted for Adlai Stevenson.

I didn't learn much about Coolidge until I read William E.

Woodward's *A New American History* (1936), a debunking kind of book, when I was a college undergraduate majoring in English history. The section on Coolidge, which made much of the Vermonter's reputation as an "odd stick," was hilarious, I thought, and I reveled in the mirth I provoked when I read passages in Woodward about "Silent Cal" to my college friends. Years later I enjoyed reading up on Coolidge in some detail and writing a chapter about him for *Presidential Anecdotes* (1981). But if I had to do it over again, I would still write LaFollette rather than Coolidge in large letters on the blackboard.

★ ★ ★ ★

"Coolidge!" H. L. Mencken once snorted. "A remarkable man, a really *remarkable* man. Nero fiddled while Rome burned, but Coolidge only snores." Mencken thought Coolidge's record as president was "almost a blank. No one remembers anything that he did or anything that he said."

Mencken erred. Many of the things Coolidge did and said are remembered. Not his public policies, to be sure, for he was a commonplace president. ("The greatest man," someone joked, "ever to come from Plymouth Notch, Vermont.") Not his public addresses, either, for, though mostly well-written, they were filled with obviosities. But Coolidge's personal style — the stony silences, the droll remarks, the Yankee twang, the deadpan humor, the mischievous moments — tickled the fancy of his contemporaries and continued in legend to amuse and delight the American people long after both he and Mencken had departed from the scene. It is surprising, when you come to think of it, that the Sage of Baltimore, with his keen eye for American absurdities, missed the funny side of Calvin Coolidge. For it is as a humorist — albeit a prickly one — that Coolidge is chiefly remembered today. He was not a folksy storyteller like Abraham Lincoln; nor was he given to showbiz one-liners like Ronald Reagan. He was more of a one-worder, or even no-worder, than anything else. But in his own eccentric way he was something of a funnyman. Most of our presidents have been excessively solemn, especially about themselves, and some of them even mistook solemnity for seriousness. Coolidge was solemn, too, a great deal of the time, but frequently tongue lurked whimsically in cheek when he held forth in public.

The Coolidge persona fascinated the public from almost the beginning. Long before Coolidge became president upon Warren G. Harding's death in 1923, amusing stories about the Vermonter's terse putdowns, cagey leg-pulls, and enigmatic silences were beginning to accumulate, and while he was in the White House they increased rapidly in number and popularity. Some of the tales were contrived, but many of them were hilariously authentic. Coolidge knew about the stories and was quietly amused. "Intuition told him," according to one observer, "that humor . . . when employed in the right place was unequalled as an agent of success." Speaking at a Gridiron Club dinner in December 1923, Coolidge good-naturedly blamed the newsmen for all the stories about him. "They have undertaken to endow me with some characteristics and traits that I didn't altogether know I had," he declared. "But I have done the best I could to be perfectly fair with them and in public, to live up to those traits."

Coolidge did a good job of living up to the tales about him. He had a nice sense for the ridiculous, as his associates realized, and his humor was not, as Mencken charged, the "sad, necrotic kind." Richard L. Jervis, chief of the White House Secret Service detail, thought Coolidge had "the greatest sense of humor" of any of the seven presidents — from Theodore Roosevelt to Franklin D. Roosevelt — under whom he served. Coolidge was "half owl, half elf," said a man who was close to him during his presidency. Will Rogers, who knew about such things, once said that Coolidge "had more subtle humor than almost any public man I ever met." It was of course low-keyed. "He never smiled at his own jokes," reported Ira R. T. Smith, chief of the mails in the White House, "and if you wanted his respect, you never acted more than moderately amused. He didn't face you when he was making a joke, but he always cut his eyes around to see whether you caught it." Added Smith: "I usually found his jokes of a caliber that enabled me to restrain my laughter and we got along fine."

There are more tales, true and untrue, about Lincoln than about Coolidge, but there are plenty of stories about Coolidge, too, and certainly more stories about him than about any other president except Lincoln. The Coolidge stories tend, like the Lincoln stories, to fall into several fairly well-defined categories. In Coolidge's case, stories about his taciturnity are the most common, followed by tales about his parsimoniousness and about his propensity for physical inactivity. Coolidge was never as silent nor as solemn nor as stingy nor as sluggish as legend portrays him, but the exaggerations appearing in some of the tall tales about him are based on undoubted truths about his character, personality, and temperament. He was dour at times, to be sure, but he did in fact have a keen awareness of life's risibilities. There was unquestionably a bright side to "Calvinism" (as Mencken dubbed the Vermonter's narrow and crabbed outlook on life), and his contemporaries appreciated it.

The most popular Coolidge stories — as Coolidge himself realized — center on his close-mouthedness. Coolidge could of course talk fluently if he felt like it, but his taciturnity was indubitable, for he was a shy man, not good at all at what is called "small talk." Sometimes, to be sure, his reserve was a deliberate ploy — like Lincoln's homely little stories — designed to get people out of his office as quickly as possible. Soon after Coolidge became vice-president, Channing Cox, his successor as governor of Massachusetts, asked him how he had been able to see so many visitors every day when he was governor and yet always left the office at 5 P.M., while Cox himself often had to stay as late as 9 P.M. "Why the difference?" he asked. "You talk back," Coolidge told him. Coolidge never talked back, when faced by people he regarded as pests, for he wanted to get them out of the office as quickly as possible. Bernard Baruch once had a long conference with him in the White House and was so surprised by his talkativeness that he exclaimed just before leaving, "Everybody said you never say anything." "Well, Baruch," said Coolidge, "many times I say only 'yes' or 'no' to people and that is too much. It winds them up for twenty minutes more." In 1929, just before leaving the White House, Coolidge gave President-elect Herbert Hoover some advice. "You have to stand every day three or four hours for visitors," he remarked. "Nine-tenths of them want something they ought not to have. If you keep dead-still they will run down in three or four minutes. If you even cough or smile they will start up all over again." Coolidge did wonders with *paucis verbis*.

Still, Coolidge was basically a reserved person and frequently lapsed into stony silences even when he was with friends. "Cal don't say much," his grandfather once remarked. "No," agreed Cal's father. "He ain't gabby." The Coolidges "don't slop over," was the way Coolidge himself put it. When Grace Goodhue, a teacher in the Clarke Institute for the Deaf in Northampton, accepted Coolidge's proposal of marriage in 1905, she facetiously expressed the hope that "having taught the deaf to hear, she might perhaps cause the mute to speak." In the Massachusetts House of Representatives, to which Coolidge was elected in 1906, he made one of the shortest — and most effective — speeches ever made there. One afternoon, one of his colleagues, known for his long-windedness, got up and delivered a lengthy and tiresome speech in support of some measure and prefaced each of his arguments in favor of the bill with the words, "Mr. Speaker, it is. . . ." When he finished, Coolidge got up and announced: "Mr. Speaker: it is not," and sat down. Everyone laughed and the measure went down to defeat.

In 1918 Coolidge became governor of Massachusetts and his peculiarities were soon the talk of the town. His long silences, in particular, puzzled people who worked with him and even dismayed his friends. One day a Massachusetts businessman boarded a train to discuss a matter of importance with him, but in one hundred miles of conversation, from Boston to Springfield, he reported, all Coolidge said was, "Yes," seven

times, and "Good Day," when he got off the train at Springfield. In 1919, when Coolidge stood for five hours on a platform in Boston with the governors of the five other New
England states reviewing the famous Yankee Division returning from Europe at the end of World War I, he made only one
remark the entire time to the governor of New Hampshire
who stood next to him: "Governor, I think you will find that
if you put one foot on the rail and lean in my position a while
and then change to the other foot, you will find it will rest
you." Reflected the New Hampshire governor afterward: "I
do not, and cannot now, comprehend a man who could stand
five hours and have nothing else to say."

Even with friends Coolidge sometimes remained mute.
One day he was scheduled to speak in a town about thirty
miles inland from Boston and a friend volunteered to ride out
there with him. But on the way out Coolidge said nary a
word to him, and on the return trip said nothing until they
neared the seacoast, whereupon he ventured: "It is cooler
here." Frank Stearns, Boston businessman who was probably his best friend, dined frequently with Coolidge when the
latter was governor, but he once figured out that during
those four years the total conversation they had probably
didn't amount to more than three or four hours — about an
hour of talk a year. Soon after Coolidge received the Republican nomination for vice-president he invited Stearns to take
a ride with him, and the latter joined him for a long drive
along the north shore and into the hills of Massachusetts.
When Stearns entered the car, Coolidge said, "How d'ye
do?" and when it got dark he said, "Guess it's time to turn
back." That was the extent of his sociability. After he became
vice-president he had to attend numerous luncheons, din-
ners, and receptions, but most of the time all he ever said on
those occasions was "Hello" and "Goodbye." Washington
hostesses called him "the still-life of the party" and joked that
if he ever uttered ten words the Washington Monument
would become Secretary of the Navy. "I guess going to all
those parties must bore you," Alice Roosevelt Longworth
once remarked. "Why do you go?" "Well," said Coolidge,

"a man must eat." Apparently he couldn't eat and talk at the same time.

Coolidge's prolonged silences produced many amusing stories, but the pithy remarks he made when he did choose to speak produced even better ones. Once, according to an unauthenticated yarn, he was having his hair cut in a small Vermont barbershop in which there was only one chair. The town doctor entered, sat down to wait, and said, "Cal, did you take the pills I gave you?" Coolidge said nothing for a minute or two and then answered: "Nope!" A little later the doctor asked, "Are you feeling any better?" Another long silence and then: "Yup!" His haircut finished, Coolidge started to leave, when the barber timidly asked, "Aren't you forgetting something, Mr. Coolidge?" A bit sheepishly Coolidge cried: "I'm sorry; I forgot to pay you. I was so busy gossiping with the doctor it just slipped my mind."

The barbershop story may be a fake, but Coolidge's preference for short, if not small, talk was real enough. When he returned to Northampton (where he had practiced law for years and served as mayor) for the first time after becoming governor, an elderly gentleman who hadn't kept up with the news said to him when they met on the street, "How d'ye do, Mr. Coolidge. I ain't seen ye about lately." "No," said Coolidge, "I've been out of town." Once, after he became president, a famous architect visited the White House and went on at great length about the architectural beauty of the executive mansion. Coolidge listened to him for some time in silence, and then finally said shortly: "Suits me."

One day a friend called on him at the White House, and after they shook hands, the story goes, Coolidge turned and motioned the man to follow him. So the friend followed him into the hall, up a flight of stairs, and into a room where Coolidge unlocked a door, shoved it open, flipped on a light, and stepped back. The friend peered in and found himself confronted by a painting of the president which was so bad that he couldn't think of anything whatever to say. There was a moment of embarrassed silence. Then Coolidge announced, "That's what I think too," flipped off the light,

*Silent "Cal" (courtesy of the Calvin Coolidge Memorial Foundation, Inc., Plymouth Notch, Vermont).*

and led his friend downstairs. "Hello, Chatterbox!" cried General Clarence Edwards when he ran into Coolidge on the street one day. "Well, General," returned Coolidge (aware that Edwards was in trouble for some remarks he made) "I've found out that what I don't say doesn't get me into half as much trouble as what you do say."

Coolidge delivered some fairly lengthy speeches during his many years of public life, but on occasion he could be breathtakingly brief. Once, when he was vice-president, he presided at the laying of a cornerstone for a public building, and did only the minimum. He turned the customary spadeful of earth and then stepped back as the workmen laid the stone. When the workmen finished, the crowd looked expectantly at Coolidge, but he said nothing. After a minute or two the master of ceremonies asked for a few words. Coolidge thought for a moment — the long and pregnant pause was his speciality — and then, pointing to the spadeful of earth he had thrown up, murmured, "There's — a — mighty fine fishworm," and walked off to his waiting limousine.

Sometimes, though, when he was president, he said even less than that in public. Once, when he was returning from an American Legion convention in Omaha, his train stopped for coal and water at a small town near St. Louis. A large crowd gathered to see the president. Colonel Edmund W. Starling, chief of the White House Secret Service, went into the private car to tell him about the people gathered outside. He found Coolidge seated on a big lounge, his elbows on the table, his hands cupped about his chin, fast asleep. Starling tapped him on the shoulder and said, "Mr. President, there are about twenty-five hundred people waiting to see you." Without a word, Coolidge got up, smoothed his hair, straightened his jacket, and followed Starling out to the observation platform. Once there, he gave the people crowding around the train his "official" smile and they applauded heartily. Then Mrs. Coolidge stepped out on the platform and the people gave her a big ovation. After that the local master of ceremonies shouted: "Now, you folks keep quiet. I want absolute silence. The president is going to address us."

The crowd became still. "All right," said the man, turning to Coolidge, "Mr. President, you may speak now." Just then the train began to move away. There was a hiss of air as the brakes were released and the party rolled gently out of the station. Coolidge, still smiling, raised his hand to the crowd and said: "Goodbye."

It was a waste of time trying to pry remarks out of Coolidge when he was in a quiescent mood. When he toured the stunning tropical garden on the Dupont estate in Delaware one afternoon, he said nothing until he passed a plant on the way out and exclaimed: "Bananas!" Traveling with a friend from Andover to Northampton (a distance of a hundred miles), he was completely silent until they reached their destination and then said, "Pleasant ride, wasn't it?"

At one White House luncheon he sat gloomily in silence, even though an Amherst College classmate and his wife were his special guests. His friend's wife sat on his right and all through the meal tried hard to engage him in conversation but finally gave up. Then, suddenly, in the midst of a long, dead silence that had everyone feeling uncomfortable, Coolidge picked up a dish of olives and, holding it toward the woman, said, "Will you have an olive?" "Oh, you little chatterbox!" exclaimed the woman, and even Coolidge smiled as the company broke into laughter.

Just before he left the White House, according to a popular, but probably spurious story, his Vermont neighbors decided to recognize his devotion to the old-fashioned farm by giving him a hand-made rake. They made the presentation an elaborate ceremonial occasion. The orator who presented the rake dwelt at length on the qualities of the hickory wood from which the rake was made. "Hickory," he said, "like the president, is sturdy, strong, resilient, unbroken." Then he handed the rake to Coolidge and the audience settled back for his speech of acknowledgement. Coolidge turned the rake over, looked at it carefully, and then said: "Ash." End of ceremony.

Sometimes, though, Coolidge was a bit more talkative. A society woman was placed next to him at a dinner party, and as she said down, according to Mrs. Coolidge, she exclaimed: "You must talk to me, Mr. Coolidge. I made a bet today that I could get more than two words out of you." Said Coolidge: "You lose."

Coolidge's terse remarks delighted people. They seemed to prove that you could hit the nail right on the head when you avoided verbosity. Once, according to a popular taciturnity tale, a Baptist preacher dined with the Coolidges before leading a revival service and ate almost nothing, saying that abstinence improved his preaching. After hearing him preach, Coolidge told his wife: "Might as well have et." On another occasion, when he was at a dinner party, he listened for some time to a discussion of the morality of playing golf on Sunday and said nothing. Finally his hostess asked him his opinion and he declared: "I had a grandmother. She was a Baptist. She didn't."

But the most famous example of what might be called "Coolidge laconics" had to do with a Sunday sermon. One Sunday, according to this story, Mrs. Coolidge was unable to attend church so President Coolidge went alone. When he returned, she asked whether he had enjoyed the sermon. "Yes," he said. "And what was it about?" asked his wife. "Sin," he said. "But what did he say?" persisted Mrs. Coolidge. "He was against it," said Coolidge. After this story began making the rounds, Mrs. Coolidge said it was such a good story that "it is almost a pity to refute it." And Coolidge himself remarked that it would be funnier if it were true.

If Coolidge was stingy with words he was thrifty with worldly goods, too, and his penuriousness produced almost as many tales as his pauciloquy. When it came to frugality, many of the Coolidge stories were both funny and true, for the Vermonter believed deeply in living within one's means. One of the best stories depicted him as a somewhat grudging host. After he was elected governor of Massachusetts, according to a tale that has many versions, an old friend of the family named Bill called at the Adams House (the dingy place where Coolidge rented rooms for a dollar a day) to say that he wanted to be the first newspaper correspondent to congratulate the governor-elect. A relative of the Coolidges let Bill in the room and explained that Coolidge would be ready in a few minutes. Coolidge soon appeared and after he had greeted his visitor, his hospitable relative said, "Cal, aren't you going to give Bill a drink?" At this, Coolidge fished out a fistful of keys from his pocket, deliberately selected two of them, opened a closet door with one, and a trunk inside the closet with the other. He then raised the lid of the trunk, lifted out the top tray, set it down on the floor behind him, extracted a bottle from the depths of the trunk, poured a modest drink, carefully recorked the bottle, replaced it in the trunk, put the tray back in place, locked the trunk, and locked the closet door. A few minutes later another newspaperman, Jim, arrived to congratulate the governor-elect too. Jim, Bill, and Cal chatted for a moment and then Coolidge's relative asked Cal if he wasn't forgetting Jim. Again Coolidge went through the routine of procuring the bottle from the trunk. Carefully he filled a glass, handed it to Jim, and, as he recorked the bottle, explained: "Bill's had his."

Coolidge was not a generous giver (except when it came to clothes for his wife), but he always tried to do the right thing. One day he walked up to the desk of Chief of Mails Ira Smith and handed him a box of cigars. "Have some tobaccah," he said. Then he walked on down to the desk of Nelson Webster, the disbursing officer, and gave him some cigars too. Afterward Smith and Webster compared notes and they found that Coolidge had taken the trouble to find out how much each of them paid for his cigars. Webster smoked twenty-five-centers and got twenty-five-cent cigars from Coolidge; Smith smoked ten-centers and that's what he got. Both boxes, however, came from the large number of cigars sent as gifts to the president from admiring citizens which he stacked up in his study. One day New Jersey Senator Joseph Frelinghuysen was a guest at the executive mansion and during the evening as he sat chatting with his host, he mentioned that he had had some fine Havana cigars made especially for the president. Unfortunately, he added, there had been some delay in securing the lithographed bands bearing the initials, "C. C.," to put around them. "Well, Joe," said Coolidge, "you know I don't smoke the bands."

Probably the best cigars Coolidge ever received were a gift of the wealthy engineer John Hays Hammond. Hammond knew that Coolidge was a good judge of cigars and he once sent him a box of particularly fine ones and received a nice note of appreciation from the president. The next time he was in the White House he found Coolidge smoking a cigar which had the familiar aroma of Hammond's own brand. As Hammond sat down, Coolidge opened a drawer in his desk, picked out a box of cigars, and held it out to the engineer. Hammond leaned over and eyed it critically. One glance convinced him that Coolidge had taken literally the remark of Woodrow Wilson's vice-president: "What this country needs is a good five-cent cigar." So he smiled and said politely: "No, thank-you." Coolidge grinned a bit sheepishly at this, dipped into his desk again, and this time came up with Hammond's gift box. "Come to think of it, you sent me these," he said. "Try one." Hammond gratefully accepted one.

Hammond did better with Coolidge than *New York Times* writer Arthur Krock did. Krock was talking to Coolidge in the White House one day and suddenly the president pulled out a box of fine Havana cigars. "Those are excellent, Mr. President," remarked Krock. "Those are very fine cigars, aren't they?" "Yes, they are," nodded Coolidge, and he lit one and put the box back in his desk. "You smoke, too, don't you?" he said as he puffed away. "Yes, I do," murmured Krock. And that was the end of that.

Coolidge was as careful about his money as he was about his cigars. When he was a young man, it was said, a friend tried to borrow five dollars from him but was turned down. Many years later the friend was taking a tour of the White House and ran into the president. Again he tried to borrow five dollars and again he was turned down. His eyes wide with admiration, he is said to have exclaimed: "Well, I got to say one thing for you, Cal. Success hasn't changed you one bit!" But if Coolidge didn't like to lend money, he was also cautious about where he deposited it, according to a story told by Jimmy Reynolds, former treasurer of the Republican National Committee. Not long after relinquishing his post as RNC treasurer, Reynolds was elected vice-president of a Washington bank and went to see Coolidge to tell him about his good fortune. "Mr. President," he said, "you know the success I had in securing funds for the Republican Party. I did not ask for any recognition or thanks at the time and I do not ask for any now. But it would do me an enormous amount of good and be a feather in my cap if you would become a depositer in my bank. Will you do it?" Coolidge puffed away at his cigar and after several minutes of silence finally said: "Couldn't you make me an honorary depositer?" In the end, though, Coolidge did make a deposit in the bank. Some time later he was strolling past the bank with an old Boston friend and they suddenly heard a terrific noise inside the bank. "What in hell is that noise?" cried the friend. "That deposit of mine drawing interest," said Coolidge calmly.

Coolidge thoroughly enjoyed the way he received his first paycheck in the White House. A messenger from the Treasury Department delivered it to him in person and made something of a ceremony out of it. "Call again," Coolidge told him as he was leaving. There were many more such paychecks, of course, but Coolidge continued to watch his nickels and dimes carefully. One afternoon he took Colonel Starling up to his room before taking a walk and while he changed clothes Starling began looking through the new *Collier's* he had just bought. "I gave somebody a nickel one afternoon to buy a *Collier's,*" said Coolidge, looking at the magazine, "and I didn't get my nickel back." "It wasn't I," protested Starling. "I don't know who it was," whined Coolidge, "but somebody owes me a nickel." "I don't owe you a nickel," persisted Starling. "I didn't say you did," returned Coolidge. "I don't know who he was, but he didn't give me back my nickel." "Well," repeated Starling, "it wasn't I." "Well," said Coolidge gloomily, "I'm not going to do anything about it. But he kept my nickel. He didn't give it back to me." He was glum by the time he was ready for the walk.

Coolidge enjoyed his afternoon walks with Starling though the conversations were never lively. Sometimes, when they returned to the White House, Coolidge took his Secret Service guard out to the butler's pantry and made two sandwiches of Vermont cheese, one for himself and one for Starling. He always cut the cheese carefully, measuring the sandwiches, one against the other, and if they weren't exactly the same size, he shaved off some of the cheese on one of the sandwiches to make them come out even. Then he gave one to Starling and they sat down to eat them. The cheese, Starling reported, was as strong as a billygoat. One day Coolidge exclaimed: "I'll bet no other President of the United States ever made cheese sandwiches for you." "No," said Starling. "It's a great honor." Added Coolidge morosely: "I have to furnish the cheese too."

Coolidge not only enjoyed between-meal snacks; he also loved to sleep, and thereby hangs many a tale. He went to bed at ten and got up between seven and nine o'clock; in the afternoon, moreover, he always took a nap lasting an hour or so and sometimes even longer. Coolidge's ideal day, scoffed Mencken, was "one on which nothing whatever happens." One afternoon a member of the White House staff had to wake him up because of a matter of some urgency. When he opened his eyes, Coolidge grinned and asked: "Is the country still here?" He once told an associate that it was in the national interest for him to take long afternoon naps because while a president was sleeping he couldn't be getting the country into mischief. One evening, when he went to the theater to see the Marx brothers in *Animal Crackers,* Groucho spied him in the audience and cried: "Isn't it past your bedtime, Calvin?"

Coolidge didn't attend the theater often. He had few diversions, in fact, and was also one of the least athletic of all our presidents. Once someone asked him, "What part did you take in college athletics?" "I held the stakes," he replied.

"What is your hobby?" a woman asked him one day. "Holding office," he drawled.

Asked how he got his exercise, he once explained, "Having my picture taken." In a speech to the Gridiron Club in 1923, however, he had the newspeople in stitches by describing how he pushed the wrong button on the mechanical horse he had just acquired, thus producing paces, trots, and gallops all at the same time and almost breaking his neck. "Mr. Coolidge's genius for inactivity is developed to a very high point," observed *New York World* columnist Walter Lippmann. "It is far from being an indolent inactivity. It is a grim, determined, alert inactivity which keeps Mr. Coolidge occupied constantly. Nobody has ever worked harder at inactivity, with such force of character, with such unremitting attention to detail, with such conscientious devotion to the task." Lippmann linked Coolidge's physical languor to his laissez-faire social philosophy. "Inactivity is a political philosophy and a party program with Mr. Coolidge," he declared, "and nobody should mistake his unflinching adherence to it for a soft and easy desire to let things slide. Mr. Coolidge's inactivity is not merely the absence of activity. It is on the contrary a steady application to the task of neutralizing and thwarting political activity wherever there are signs of life."

For years, about the only exercise Coolidge took was walking. When he was in the White House he got in the habit of taking long walks with Starling just about every day. Under Starling's prodding, however, he finally took up fishing, but he was rather formal about it at first. He wore gloves while holding the rod and made the Secret Service men bait the hook (much to their indignation) and take off any fish he caught. Eventually, though, he became an ardent fisherman. One day he lost a fish he had been playing with and exclaimed: "Damn!" Then he turned to Starling with a shy smile and said, "Guess I'm a real fisherman now. I cussed." One of his favorite angling places was the River Brule in Wisconsin. One day a newspaperman asked him how many fish there were in the river. Coolidge said the waters were estimated to contain about 45,000 trout. "I haven't caught them all yet," he added, "but I've intimidated them."

Coolidge's droll way of putting things endeared him to people who would otherwise have thought him a dreadful bore. Once, when he was President of the Massachusetts Senate, two senators got into an angry debate and finally one of them told the other to go to hell. Furious, the latter called on Coolidge as presiding officer to do something about it. "I've looked up the law, Senator," Coolidge told him, "and you don't have to go there." Right after he became vice-president, he received a dinner invitation from a resident of Washington and called his secretary to ask him if he knew the gentleman. The secretary said he did not and he added that he couldn't find the man's name listed in the Social Register. "No conclusion can be drawn from that," drawled Coolidge. "I've been in it myself only half an hour." Coolidge disliked snobs and never felt completely at ease with Boston Brahmins like Senator Henry Cabot Lodge, who, in fact, looked down on the Coolidges as a bit on the vulgar side. Sometimes Coolidge excused himself and left the room when he saw a society woman approaching him in the White House receiving line. At one White House reception a woman rushed up to him and announced: "Mr. President, I'm from Boston!" "You'll never get over it," Coolidge told her. He was teasing, but he also meant it.

Coolidge had his barbed side. When people got on his nerves he usually made clear his irritation sooner or later. One of his pet peeves was a Smith College professor who had spent eight years as a missionary in Palestine and liked to hold forth at length on his experiences there. One afternoon the Coolidges were sitting on the porch of their house in Northampton when the talkative professor came by for a visit and was soon going on at great length about his work as a missionary. Mrs. Coolidge's mother was fascinated, but Coolidge was irked by the interruption and bored by the harangue, so he finally got up and went into the house. Later, when Mrs. Coolidge began praising the former missionary, Coolidge murmured from behind his newspaper: "He's used to talking to the heathen." He was similarly put off by the woman who took the opportunity at a White House luncheon to run down an American ambassador whom Coolidge admired. While she was denouncing the man as uncouth, uncultured, and lacking in respect for the customs and traditions of the country to which he was assigned, Coolidge's old black cat Tige sauntered into the room and began lazily rubbing itself against the table leg. Coolidge turned to the person on his right and in a voice quite audible to the talkative woman on his left exclaimed: "This is the third time that cat has stopped at this table." Illinois Congresswoman Ruth Hanna McCormick also rubbed him the wrong way by her persistent efforts to secure a Federal judgeship for a prominent Chicagoan of Polish descent. As part of her campaign of persuasion, Mrs. McCormick arranged for some Chicago Polish-Americans to call on the president at the White House. Coolidge's secretary ushered them into the president's office and they stood there in awkward silence for a couple of minutes while Coolidge, his eyes fixed intently on the floor, said nothing. Finally Coolidge ventured: "Mighty fine carpet there." With relief and expectation the visitors smiled and nodded their heads. "New one — cost a lot of money," Coolidge went on. To this the Chicagoans smiled even more and again nodded their heads. "She wore out the old one, trying to get you a judge," said Coolidge, abruptly bringing the interview to an end.

But if Coolidge could be testy, he could also be mischievous. According to his son John, he enjoyed teasing people who assumed that he was always aloof and dignified. Soon after he became president he stepped out of his office one day and pressed an alarm button summoning all the guards to their posts and then hurried back into his office before they could find out who sounded the alarm. On another occasion he pushed all the bells on his desk summoning members of his White House staff and then hid in a closet as they gathered in his office. When Kansas editor William Allen White and his wife joined the Coolidges for a party one afternoon on the presidential yacht, the *Mayflower*, they were surprised to learn that "Silent Cal" had his pixieish side. Coolidge arrived on the wharf to greet them, White recalled, and some cameramen at once closed in to take pictures of the party. One photographer, a moving-picture man, arranged them carefully for a silent newsreel sequence, and then instructed: "Look pleasant, and for Heaven's sake, say something — anything, good morning, or howdy do!" To which Coolidge remarked dryly as he assumed his stage face: "That man gets more conversation out of me than all Congress!" To the surprise — and dismay — of Coolidge's friends, he once permitted himself to be photographed wearing a cowboy uniform given him while the summer White House was in the Black Hills of South Dakota. "But I don't see why you object," said Coolidge. "The people here have sent me this costume, and they wouldn't have sent it unless they expected me to put it on. Why shouldn't I have my picture taken with it on to please them?" One of his friends explained, "It's making people laugh." "Well," said Coolidge, "it's good for people to laugh."

People smiled rather than laughed at Coolidge's whimsey, for it was always quite restrained. One day Everett Sanders, White House secretary, told him, "Mr. President, the attorney-general has just arrived," and Coolidge, amused by the cabinet official's almost pathological timidity about taking up his time, exclaimed: "I suppose he is clamoring to get in!" Once when Sanders sent Coolidge some material with a note saying, "Would it not be well for me to send a copy of this letter to the Senator to allay his fears?" Coolidge scribbled below: "No, let him tremble." On one occasion a large delegation arrived to be photographed with the president on the White House lawn, with the explicit understanding that Coolidge would not make a speech, but the head of the organization, to Sanders' dismay, assured the group that the president was going to address them. When Sanders went in to tell Coolidge how many times he had informed the man that there was to be no speech, Coolidge gave a little smile as he started out and said: "If they have not understood, I will elaborate on what you said by saying nothing."

On a cross-country tour not long before he left the White House, Coolidge was scheduled to make a speech at an Indian reservation, and thereby hangs a possibly spurious tale. When he arrived, he noticed that the audience seemed dispirited. "What's wrong?" he asked the tribal chief. "It's the drought," explained the chief. "We've never had one so bad. Our rainmakers have prayed, but it hasn't helped. Soon the fields will lie in waste." "I know," said Coolidge sympathetically. "That's one of the reasons I'm here. When I return to Washington, I'm going to see what can be done about it." No sooner had he uttered those words than the heavens opened wide and the rain came pouring down. Thoroughly drenched, Coolidge looked up at the sky and muttered: "I said, 'When I get back to Washington!'"

Another cute-comment tale — also probably apocryphal — has to do with the White House renovation during Coolidge's presidency. One day, according to this story, when the White House was undergoing repairs, Coolidge went up to the attic where the architect and the contractor were examining the roof rafters and girders. When the architect saw the president, he began calling his attention to the bad condition of the timbers and went on to explain that they had been charred by the fire British soldiers set when they invaded Washington during the War of 1812. They must be replaced, he told Coolidge, but he wanted to know whether it should be done with wood or with the more expensive steel beams. Coolidge is said to have examined the charred wood carefully and then turned to the architect and exclaimed: "All right. Put in the steel beams and send the bill to the King of England!"

Even more improbable is the story about the smart remark Coolidge is supposed to have made when he and his wife were taking a tour of a farm run by the Department of Agriculture. At one point, according to the story, Mrs. Coolidge stopped to observe the chicken coops, and asked her guide how often the rooster there performed his sexual duties each day. "Oh, dozens of times," said the guide. Mrs. Coolidge is supposed to have raised her eyebrows, deeply

impressed, and exclaimed: "Please tell that to the president!"
A little later, the story goes, when Coolidge himself came to
look at the chicken coops and observed the rooster, he was
informed of his wife's remark. "Same hen every time?" he is
said to have asked. "Oh, no, sir," said the guide. "A different
one each time." Coolidge nodded and said: "Please tell that
to Mrs. Coolidge." The story continues to circulate, but is
entirely out of character for both Coolidge and his wife. The
Coolidges teased each other on occasion but never, so far as
we know, in that fashion.

In 1929 Coolidge left the White House and spent his remaining years quietly in Northampton, but Coolidgiana
continued to accumulate. One day a reporter visited the
former president and sat on the porch with him to talk and
smoke. While they were chatting, a farm wagon passed the
house and the man in it waved his whip and cried: "How 'ye,
Cal?" "How 'ye, Zack?" replied Coolidge. The wagon rattled on and disappeared around the corner. "Zack Brewer,"
explained Coolidge. "Cousin of mine. Haven't seen him —
must be twenty years!" About this time some alumni of
Amherst College, who were in Madrid for a conference, decided to have a reunion of Amherst men in Spain and sent
Coolidge, class of 1895, a cable asking him to send a message
to be read at the class dinner. To make sure that the former
president realized he could say as much as he pleased, they
made it clear that there would be no cable charges on his
message. Sixty-five people attended the dinner, and when, at
the climax of the evening, Coolidge's name was announced,
there was a burst of applause. The master of ceremonies then
read the message: "Greetings. Calvin Coolidge."

The stories kept coming until the end. At a 1932 luncheon
party in the Coolidge home, it was reported, guests began
discussing the question of whether the United States should
extend diplomatic recognition to the Soviet Union, and when
things got a bit heated, Mrs. Coolidge tactfully tried to
change the subject. Indicating two containers, she announced: "One is French dressing and the other is Russian."
Piped up her husband: "I'll take the one that isn't red." In

October 1932, Coolidge came out of retirement to make a speech in New York City's Madison Square Garden on behalf of Herbert Hoover in his campaign for re-election. Afterward a woman, it is said, rushed up to him and exclaimed: "Oh, Mr. Coolidge, what a wonderful address! I stood up all through it!" "So did I," said Coolidge.

Coolidge had enjoyed being president, but he was happy in retirement. Soon after he left the White House he was asked to fill out a card to accompany the payment of his annual dues to the National Press Club. He filled in his name and address, and then, on the line provided for "Occupation," he wrote, "Retired." After a moment's thought he wrote on the line labelled, "Remarks," the following comment: "Glad of it." About this time the President of Amherst College retired and Coolidge's name was mentioned as a possible successor. But Coolidge was utterly uninterested. Told by the head of the Amherst Alumni Society that he led the list of men being considered for the post, Coolidge shook his head emphatically. "Easier to control Congress than a college faculty," he explained. Just before the 1932 election, actor Otis Skinner's wife told the former chief executive: "Oh, Mr. Coolidge, I wish it were you that we were going to vote for in November. It would be the end of this horrible depression." "It would be the beginning of mine," said Coolidge.

Historians don't rate Coolidge highly, nor should they; at best he was one of our many run-of-the-mill presidents. He was lucky enough to leave the White House before the Great Depression hit the nation, and it is hard to believe that he would have done any better in the crisis than Herbert Hoover ("the Wundah Boy," as Coolidge sarcastically called him) did. His knowledge and experience of the world was far less than Hoover's; Michigan's Republican Senator James Couzens once told him point blank that he had "a Northampton viewpoint, instead of a national viewpoint." In an essay about Coolidge appearing in 1931, Gamaliel Bradford declared that "it can hardly be said that Calvin Coolidge had much to do with the twentieth century."

To Coolidge's credit he was aware of his limitations. "I hear talk of nominating me for 1936," he told New York publisher Henry L. Stoddard shortly before his death in 1933. "That cannot be. There is no way I can decline something not yet offered, but I am embarrassed by the discussion of my name." He went on to explain why. "We are in a new era to which I do not belong," he said, "and it would not be possible for me to adjust myself in it."

Today if one visits the Coolidge room of the Forbes Library in Northampton, he is informed that "the voice of Calvin Coolidge can be heard by pressing the button." But when the button is pressed there is complete silence. Coolidge would have enjoyed that, and perhaps even have appreciated the irony.

# 5

# Purlings and Platitudes:
## H. L. Mencken's Americana

WHEN I heard H. L. Mencken speak one afternoon during my undergraduate days at Yale in the late 1930s, I was a bit disappointed. He omitted a formal lecture for one thing, and for another opened the meeting up to questions from the audience without even making any preliminary remarks. Still, I enjoyed his witty answers to questions and recall chortling over his statement that Gertrude Stein "hasn't got any ideas, and she can't express them."

Mencken was only partly right about Stein, of course, but then he was only partly right about a lot of things and downright wrong about many things too. Franklin Roosevelt was surely far abler than Mencken was ever willing to concede; and even William Jennings Bryan, whom Mencken despised, was unquestionably wiser than HLM in detecting the absurdities of social Darwinism. But Mencken was right on target when it came to a number of important issues, and his blasts at humbug, hypocrisy, sanctimoniousness, and patrioteering seem to me as exhilarating to read today as they were in his lifetime. His championship of free speech and expression was important, too, and I was delighted when I learned recently that in 1936 he had teamed up with Texas Congressman Maury Maverick, a feisty New Deal Democrat, in framing a bill (which attracted little support) making it a felony for any public official to violate the Constitution and especially the Bill of Rights. The *Chicago Tribune's* Mike Royko probably comes closer to HLM than anyone else writing in America today in his ability to puncture the pretensions of the new crop of pests clamoring for attention — the oracularly wise, aggressively virtuous, and vehemently compassionate — without neglecting the old pests, still with us, that Mencken loved to assault.

Mencken's "Americana" first appeared in the *Smart Set* intermittently and then became a regular feature of *American Mercury* in the 1920s. In 1920, the *New Republic* started a somewhat similar column called "The Bandwagon" which presented weekly reports on the silly statements and bizarre goings-on of the Great, the Near-Great, and the Not-So-Great. And in 1978, the *Progressive* came up with a monthly page entitled "No Comment," which, like "The Band-wagon," took on the rich, the powerful, and the prestigious as its main target. Mencken, by contrast, took on the masses as well as the classes. But he was tickled by anything absurd. The *New Yorker's* fillers at the bottom of the page — the How's That Again Department, the Clouded Crystal Ball, the Remarks We Wish We Had Never Heard — are very much in the Mencken style, too, and were possibly inspired by Mencken's "Americana."

Every Mencken reader has his favorite quotation, and mine is probably (it's hard to pick just one) his description of War-ren Gamaliel Harding's prose. President Harding, wrote Mencken on March 7, 1921, right after the inauguration, "writes the worst English that I have ever encountered. It reminds me of a string of wet sponges; it reminds me of tattered washing on the line; it reminds me of stale bean soup, of college yells, of dogs barking idiotically through endless nights. It is so bad that a sort of grandeur creeps into it. It drags itself out of the dark abysm (I was about to write abscess!) of pish, and crawls insanely up the topmost pinnacle of posh. It is rumble and bumble. It is flap and doodle. It is balder and dash."

Still, one can't help thinking, Harding at least wrote most

of his own stuff and he was one of the last presidents to do so. And he made at least one word, normalcy (he mispronounced "normality") popular. But who would really want to go "back to normalcy," as the 1920 Harding campaign slogan urged, after reading Mencken? Efforts to do so in the 1980s, in fact, proved calamitous for the nation's economy.

★ ★ ★ ★

H. L. Mencken's heyday was the 1920s. His was "one of the loudest voices," it was said, "whose noise combined to make the Roaring Twenties roar." In November 1920, we are told, he cast his vote for Warren Gamaliel Harding and then sat back to enjoy the fun. "No other such complete and dreadful nitwit," he was soon saying, "is to be found in the pages of American history."

Mencken was not, of course, unknown to the American reading public before the twenties. He had already published several books, including his study of the American language, and they had won considerable attention. His lively book reviews for the *Smart Set* had also attracted much interest. But it was in the pages of the *American Mercury* (founded in 1924) that Mencken's name became a byword among college-educated Americans. Not only did the high level of material, much of it satirical, appearing in the *Mercury* under Mencken's editorship attract favorable comment, but Mencken's own special contributions to each issue also won a host of admiring readers, especially on college campuses: editorials, book reviews, and, above all, the monthly department which he called "Americana." Mencken's "Americana" columns make absorbing reading today. Not only do they reveal — by the principle of selection governing choice of material each month — the bent of Mencken's own mind; they are also a treasure trove of data portraying many of the actions and passions of the American people during the Roaring Twenties.

In 1914, after Mencken became one of the editors of *Smart Set*, he began gathering excerpts from foolish speeches, sermons, and books and presenting them for the amusement of his readers under such titles as "The Purling of the Platitudinarians" and "More Purlings." In 1922, he began calling them "Americana." In 1924, the popular department was transferred to the *Mercury*. In his preface to a collection of items culled from the *Mercury* for 1925, Mencken explained that his purpose in assembling "Americana" was "to make the enlightened minority of Americans familiar, by documentary evidence, with what is going on in the minds of the masses — the great herd of undifferentiated, good-humored, goose-stepping, superstitious, sentimental, credulous, striving, romantic, American people. Some of the ideas cherished by that herd are obviously insane. Many others stand in sharp opposition to everything that civilized men regard as decorous and for the common weal. But it must be obvious that no headway can be made in opposing and changing those ideas until it is known clearly what they are."

To assemble his material, Mencken scanned hundreds of newspapers, magazines, pamphlets, and books, looking for preposterous statements, spectacular idiocies, and shocking barbarities in the life of what he liked to call the "American booboisie" in every part of the country. The items were always arranged alphabetically by states and frequently preceded by genially ironic comments by Mencken. Sometimes, having traversed the continent from Alabama to Wyoming, he appended clippings from abroad under the heading of "In Partibus Infidelium"; but his major interest was in Americana. Though it lingered until 1933, the department was at its best from 1924 to 1929 — the very years when the *Mercury* was at its best and when Mencken was at the peak of his influence. For insight into what has been called the "Era of Wonderful Nonsense," Mencken's "Americana" for those five years is well-nigh indispensable.

Some of the items pounced on by Mencken were merely funny: reports of chewing-gum parties, long-distance spitting matches, rolling-pin contests, Bible-reading marathons, crossword puzzle church services, PTA debates on whether a sewing machine is more beneficial to a family than a cow, sermons preached from a casket or while the minister was standing on his head, and the marriage arranged by a Lion's Club to take place in a cage with a couple of lionesses as witnesses. Quotations from pompous eulogies of such conspicuous non-heroes as Warren Harding and Calvin Coolidge were also used by Mencken as instances of American silliness. And he zealously followed the "progress of the higher learning": the addition to the curricula of our colleges of courses in meat packing, yell leading, swine husbandry, crossword puzzles, janitor engineering, embalming, charm, and the theory and practice of milk condensing.

But Mencken was frequently making a serious critical point about the United States in his monthly roundup of news. He was a master of what may be called "quotemanship," that is, the use of quotations for polemical purposes. There are several ways, it may be noted, of manipulating quotations to prove a particular point. One is by quoting a person out of context. Another is by quoting your opponent to prove your own point. Still another is to confront a person with a statement he has made in the past which contradicts his present point of view. A fourth method — and this was Mencken's — is to quote a statement that is so intrinsically absurd that it self-evidently refutes itself. Mencken specialized in what we may call the "fatuous quote." By simply reproducing, in all its stark simplicity — and inanity — what someone had said, he automatically discredited the opinion expressed. Mencken, in short, utilized quotations for satirical purposes; his "Americana" contained a great deal of criticism by quotation.

There was no month in which Mencken omitted items having to do with organized religion in the United States. Religion, particularly fundamentalism, was a favorite whipping boy of his. During the twenties, he was endlessly entertained by efforts of pious people to Americanize Christianity — in particular, to reconcile Christ and mammon. Judging from hundreds of items appearing in "Americana," Americans outdid themselves in the twenties to prove the validity of Max Weber's thesis about the special affinity of Protestantism for capitalism. In a salesmanship course at the

YMCA in Dallas, for example, a speaker insisted that salesmanship dated back to Biblical times. "Among other
things," according to the *Dallas Times-Herald* "he said that
Christ Himself sold Christianity to His disciples and His disciples sold it to others, and that it had been so well sold that
nobody else had ever been able to sell any other form of
religion." A speaker in Pasadena called Jesus "the world's
supreme salesman." A speaker in Omaha called Jesus "the
greatest Sales Manager of all time." At the University of
Arkansas, a lecturer in an insurance class declared: "Joseph,
the lad who wore the coat of fifty-seven varieties of color,
was the world's first life insurance agent." Joseph, he added,
"provided during seven years of plenty for the following
seven lean years. The writing of life insurance . . . is next in
importance to the preaching of the gospel." "Cain and Abel
were probably the first realtors," according to a writer in the
*Des Moines Tribune.* "Development of real estate in Florida
had its historic precedent many thousand years before
Christ," said a former commissioner of agriculture in Florida. "In fact, it is mentioned in the Book of Genesis, being
one of the first acts recorded in Holy Writ." In the opinion of
an Iowa minister, "God was the first advertising man. . . . He
was the first publicity man." "He blazed the way in outdoor
advertising," said a Denver preacher. "The world is His bill-
board," affirmed a Florida minister. "Publicity is of divine
origin," announced a Kiwanis speaker in California. "The
first distinct publicity in the history of the world came when
the Creator first spanned the heavens with the rainbow. . . .
This is the Almighty's illustrated advertisement, in colors, of
His pledge to mankind." A booklet entitled "Moses, Per-
suader of Men," declared that Moses was "one of the greatest
salesmen and real estate promoters that ever lived. Read how
he conducted the Promised Land project. . . ." "Next to
Christ," said a speaker to a Kiwanis Club in Wisconsin,
"Moses was the greatest of all salesmen. He sold a line of
goods that he could not show to his customers, and kept sold
himself for thirty-eight years on a line he had never seen
himself." In an Oklahoma newspaper appeared this state-

ment: "As a businessman, Christ stands at the head of the class. . . . Christ seemed to have understood His business relation with His Father from childhood. . . . He talked much of profit and loss, and counting the cost of things. . . . He believed in money and organized His church on a business basis, equipped with a secretary and treasurer." In South Carolina, a Greenville speaker's proud boast was that "The records reveal that Christ started the Greenville Chamber of Commerce." In New York, a speaker summed it all up: "Christ was the author and founder of big business. . . . God was the wealthiest big businessman of all time."

If Mencken (together with his readers) was immensely entertained by simple-minded efforts like these to combine profit and piety, he was equally titillated by the endeavor to make Christ a good joiner. "If Jesus Christ was on earth today," said a Los Angeles preacher, "He would be a Shriner." "Jesus Christ," said a Rotarian speaker in Chicago, "is the greatest Rotarian." "There was one 100% Rotarian," according to a speaker before a Rotary Club in Delaware. "He lived 2000 years ago. He was Jesus of Nazareth." A speaker in Oregon made the same point: "Jesus Christ was the first and the only perfect Rotarian." But a speaker in California insisted that the "first president of the Lions International was Jesus Christ. I quote you from the Bible: He was the 'Lion of the tribe of Judah.'" And a Kiwanis speaker in Mississippi declared: "God was the first Kiwanian."

The effort to prove that Christianity was the sportsman's as well as the businessman's and the clubman's religion was another source of mirth for Mencken. "Football," he quoted Bishop William Manning of New York as affirming, "is one of the highest forms of spiritual exercise." "Jesus," said a Baptist minister in Philadelphia, "would have made a good quarterback on a football team." "Our Master," said a Minnesota minister, "spent much time in recreation. Christ Jesus was an expert recreator." A sports writer for the *Atlanta Journal* described Christ as "the Greatest Sportsman Who ever lived." "Baseball," a Kiwanis speaker assured a Pennsylvania audience, "will be taught in Heaven." "St. Paul," said a Philadelphia minister, "was the sports writer of the New Testament." In a Hollywood newspaper appeared this announcement of a series of sermons on "The Great Athletes of the Bible":

Samson — The World's Strong Man
Jacob — The Great Wrestler
Enoch — The Long Distance Walker
David — The Pinch Hitter
Saul — The Man Who Fumbled the Ball
Daniel — The Athlete Who Kept Fit — and How
Jesus — The World Champion

"God," said an Ohio clergyman simply, "is a regular fellow."

If Mencken, as a "true unbeliever," took special pleasure in reporting the crudities in American religion, he also enjoyed picking up items illustrating the vulgarity of the masses in America in cultural matters in general. Often he simply reprinted mawkish and inane poems appearing in daily newspapers to prove his point. Frequently he made reports on the popularity of such lowbrow novelists as Zane Grey or sentimental poets like Edgar Guest to demonstrate the deplorable taste of Americans in literary matters. In May 1925, for example, the League of American Penwomen in Knoxville picked Gene Stratton Porter as its favorite modern novelist. A Missouri newspaper selected the following as "the cream of current literature": Rupert Hughes, Irvin S. Cobb, and Harold Bell Wright. "Michael Arlen," someone wrote the *Chicago Tribune* to say, "is greater than Shakespeare." The *Haldeman-Julius Weekly* listed the favorite authors in Kansas as follows: Zane Grey, James Oliver Curwood, Harold Bell Wright, Gene Stratton Porter, and Mary Roberts Rinehart. Students at Kansas Teachers' College voted, in the order named, *The Keeper of the Bees* and *Ben Hur* as their favorite books and Hamlin Garland, Gene Stratton Porter, Dickens, Margaret Hill McCarter, Shakespeare, and Harold Bell Wright as their favorite authors, in the order named. "Close up the churches and schools," said the *Portland* (Oregon) *Lariat,* "burn up every volume of Shakespeare . . . but let

Eddie Guest write on and on; let his songs that bring smiles, then tears, be sung in every household and our nation will not go wrong." "Who makes American literature?" asked the *Camden* (New York) *Courier*. "Not the Lowells and the Longfellows. Not the Mark Twains, even — or the Sinclair Lewises. The characteristic literature of this nation is not poetry or the novel, not the essay or the volume of philosophy. It is the Book of Business that grips and holds our people. Thus a great writer on current business, like Roger Babson, may truly be called a maker of American literature today." Mencken especially enjoyed reporting on the activities of literary societies in the United States: the Shakespeare Club in Kansas, discussing Eddie Guest; the Browning Literary Society in Ohio, hearing a paper on the origin of baseball and a rendition of "Casey at the Bat"; and the Shakespeare Club in Florida, studying Henry Ford's life, hearing an Irving Berlin song, and then listening to "Turkey in the Straw" on the violin.

Most Americans, Mencken thought, were hostile to high culture. An Arkansas minister, he noted, criticized members of a music club for wasting their time studying grand opera, which, he said, "no one can understand, and if they did, it would do them no good." A member of the staff of the Curtis publications said this: "Rockefeller's beneficence to humanity may be understood and be appreciated by everybody. Brahms contributed something to the few, and bored, and still bores, millions of others stiff." A candidate for mayor in Cedar Rapids, Iowa, exclaimed: "Do we want a generation of artists? . . . When I went to school we had none of these highfalutin ideas. We learned how to read, write, and spell. There was no painting of pictures. And we got along just as well." Along with cultural ignorance there was also, Mencken thought, a deep current of anti-intellectualism in American life. "I don't think we want a public library in Milburn," he quoted a speaker in New Jersey as saying. "They are nothing but hot beds of Anarchism and Communism." "Read the Bible," said a Georgia legislator. "It teaches you how to act. Read the hymn book. It contains the

*HLM: the Sage of Baltimore (courtesy of the Enoch Pratt Free Library, Baltimore).*

finest poetry ever written. Read the almanac. It shows you
how to figure out what the weather will be. There isn't another book that is necessary for anyone to read, and therefore
I am opposed to all libraries." "Be on your guard when a
Ph.D. is around," warned a Baptist magazine in Memphis.
"In nine cases out of ten they are infested with the germs of
rationalism."

Mencken saw this anti-intellectualism particularly evident
in the fundamentalist campaign against the teaching of evolution in public schools. Both before and after the Scopes trial
of 1925, he presented many quotes having to do with the
anti-evolution movement. "The theory of evolution," said a
Baptist publication in Memphis, "has contributed more to
the disintegration and downfall of organized government
than any other agency." "The World War," in the opinion of
an Atlanta preacher, "was directly due to the teaching of
evolution." In New York, hot-gospeler Billy Sunday delivered himself of these remarks: "If anyone wants to teach that
God-forsaken, hell-born, bastard theory of evolution, then
let him go out and let him be supported by men who believe
that blasted theory and not expect the Christian people of this
country to pay for the teaching of a rotten, stinking professor
who gets up there and teaches our children to forsake God
and makes our schools a clearing-house for their God-forsaken dirty politics." According to a newspaper report, Senator Tom Heflin "startled disciples of Darwin by pointing
out that not a single monkey, gorilla or chimpanzee in zoo-
logical gardens in hundreds of years has produced an off-
spring that developed into a human being. He claimed that
his citation was absolute proof that the theory of evolution
was fallacious."

Mencken was inclined to blame the Puritan tradition for
most of the shortcomings he detected in American life. By its
distrust of beauty and its antagonism to freethinking, Puri-
tanism was, he thought, a major source of cultural and intellectual mediocrity in the United States. It was also responsible for the extreme prudishness (which Mencken took joy
in reporting) that was so widespread in the land. To puritanic

Americans in the twenties, Mencken observed, dancing was beyond the pale. According to a Methodist minister in Washington, D.C., "Dancing is a divorce-feeder. It is heathen, animalistic, and damnable. It results in spiritual paralysis. It degrades womanhood and manhood. Now is the time to say plainly that it is one of the most pernicious of all modern customs." "Dance halls," said a Baptist paper in Louisiana, "are ticket-offices to Hell. The dance-hall has always been the handmaid of the brothel and the saloon. Innocence can not endure in dance-halls, where the atmosphere is heavy with sensual music, and men and women seem to be held together with adhesive tape. If girls would dance with girls and men with men the movement against dance-halls would not be necessary." A men's Bible class in West Virginia condemned the local "Y" for sponsoring a dance, pointing out that dancing was "a thing and practice that will reach to the highest pinnacle known to man and pluck the brightest jewels in all the land and drag them down to degradation and shame and finally to a devil's hell." Mixed bathing seemed equally iniquitous to the puritanic. A Baptist paper in Louisiana complained: "Decent people no longer find lake and sea-shore a place of rest and relaxation. Modern bathing suits make modest men and women feel like hiding their faces in shame. Again and again, I have been told in different parts of Louisiana, that the present day swimming-pool is a menace to the morals of the young. Mixed bathing must be abolished." The human body, after all, was to be seen as little as possible. A Kansas high school specified that uniforms of basketball players "be such as not to expose their nakedness, that the trousers of the boys come to the knee and that the hose likewise come to the knee." In West Virginia, teachers in one of the school districts had to sign a pledge to wear dresses "reaching from their Adam's apple to their ankles." In Salt Lake City, there was an outcry against a man who dressed the model of a woman in a store window. In Baton Rouge, the display of artificial legs in a show window was condemned as "a menace to public morality" and a prominent clubwoman purchased and burned them.

There were, of course, the inevitable blue laws which Mencken reported with relish. The North Carolina legislature, he noted, considered a measure for prohibiting flirting on college campuses. In Wisconsin, a man and his wife were fined for kissing in a parked automobile. A girl in Waterbury, Connecticut, was arrested and charged with "being in danger of falling into vice." A law in Washington, D.C., banned "immoral music." Mencken also kept his readers posted on the Sabbatarian movement: the ban on pitching horseshoes on Sunday in Pomona, Kansas; the outlawing of Sunday golf, billiards, and dominoes in Alabama; the denunciation of Sunday newspapers as one of the "most pernicious forms of Sabbath desecration."

But the Eighteenth Amendment was Mencken's special peeve. He regarded Prohibition as an outrageous intrusion by government into the private lives of citizens, and he included many items in the "Americana" columns showing how the rights and liberties of individuals were flagrantly violated by Prohibition enforcement officers. He also reproduced with pleasure the most idiotic statements he could track down uttered by defenders of Prohibition. The president of the Georgia WCTU: "When the Bible speaks favorably of wine, it means unfermented wine. When it speaks unfavorably of wine, it means fermented wine." An army officer speaking to the New Jersey Anti-Saloon League: "The Kaiser was drunk when he ordered mobilization of the German Army in 1914 and therefore liquor was one of the main causes of the World War." A Baptist minister in Tennessee: "Prohibition was first enforced in the Garden of Eden." A Washington preacher: "Any man who drinks liquor either in public or in private is an anarchist."

The use of tobacco was almost as bad as drinking, and a WCTU chapter in Kansas resolved that "Passages in Mother Goose which mention tobacco or alcoholic beverages should not be read by children. . . ." Even the taking of aspirin tablets — the Rhode Island WCTU put on an "anti-aspirin play" — was regarded as morally heinous by the super-puritanic. As for lovemaking by young people: "Petting," announced a Baptist minister in Boston, "is adultery." "Spooning," according to a California preacher, "is the vilest form of degeneracy known to mankind, it is dirty, it is nasty, it is filthy. . . ." An El Paso minister solemnly explained that a "girl's natural impulse at the touch of a man is revulsion."

Mencken's opposition to puritanic restraints was accompanied by an immense devotion to freedom of expression in the United States. Mencken was a staunch civil libertarian; he believed in wide boundaries for the expression of opinions, written and oral, including opinions with which he personally was in total disagreement. In "Americana" he presented many items dealing with the suppression of free speech in the twenties. Often he cited, without comment, incidents of civil-liberty violations taken from the bulletin of the American Civil Liberties Union. Although he had nothing but amused contempt for radicals, he believed they had the right to air their views and he cited many instances in which this right was denied them. A sixteen-year-old boy, he reported, was beaten up by policemen for attending a radical meeting in Chicago. In New York a man who mentioned his constitutional rights so irritated a policeman and later a magistrate that he was fined $5.00. A man who criticized Woodrow Wilson was arrested and deported to Canada. A California newspaper urged the death penalty for persons with radical ideas. The *Houston Chronicle* declared: "Granting the right of free speech, why should it be exercised at times and under circumstances which irritate people?"

Incidents of academic-freedom violations also caught Mencken's attention. He noted that a history instructor at Baylor University lost his job because he didn't believe in Noah's Ark; a citizens' committee in Florida sought to ban "obscene, vile, and vicious" books by Freud, Shaw, Russell, and Upton Sinclair from college libraries in the state. In an Atlanta paper Mencken came across this editorial suggestion: "Instead of censoring school books so severely, we should censor school teachers. Many a man or woman who is a good teacher should never be permitted to teach."

Another target of Mencken's was "100% Americanism."

He was amused by a resolution adopted in Reading, Pennsylvania, opposing the erection of a monument to the memory of Columbus on the ground that such an honor should be reserved for those "who are native heroes and sons of the soil of America." In Pittsburgh, the Minute Men of America also opposed erecting a statue of Columbus in the city: "This is America, and as Americans we should be ruled by no foreign government, people, race, sect, creed or color. There is no halfway stop on this subject. You either are an American or you are not. Columbus did not discover America." Mencken had a lot of fun with the WASPs. He quoted a writer for the *Dearborn Independent:* "The Bible is an Anglo-Saxon book and foretells Anglo-Saxon destiny, and strange as it may seem to those who learn of it for the first time, the destiny of Anglo-Saxondom is the destiny of the world." He also excerpted an editorial from the *American Standard* which denounced grand opera as "foreign to the decent and Christian spirit of the United States." The Metropolitan Opera House, said the *Standard,* was "the most thoroughly foreign institution in this country. Standing at the back of the house and surveying an operatic audience, one can scarcely find an Anglo-Saxon face. Jews and Italians predominate, with a liberal proportion of Germans, Slavs, and miscellaneous dregs of the Mediterranean and Levantine races." Mencken once listed the names of Rhode Islanders (the majority obviously non-Anglo-Saxon) who had died in World War I and entitled the item: "100% American Rhode Islanders"; on another occasion, he named the members of Arturo Toscanini's orchestra and explained ironically: "footnote on the Anglo-Saxon as artist." From a Spokane newspaper he extracted a clipping about a Japanese boy who headed his high school class, and observed: "One reason why the Pacific Coast 100% Americans are convinced that the Japs are an inferior people and incapable of true civilization."

The theme of 100% Americanism led Mencken inevitably to the Ku Klux Klan, and during the twenties he filled "Americana" with lengthy quotations illustrating the barbarity of that organization. In Birmingham, Alabama, he noted that the KKK, with the approval of local police, raided three Chinese restaurants and told diners to "stop patronizing these Chinese joints unless you are looking for some serious trouble. There are plenty of good 100% American cafés in town." Mencken found the *American Standard* (a Klan organ in New York) a rich source for imbecilities. He quoted its editorial stating that "Roman Catholicism does not belong to the white race." He also quoted the editor's praise of Warren G. Harding for having been "awake to a large extent on the Roman Catholic question." The editor denied that Harding (who died of a heart attack in 1923) had been poisoned by food; he had been "poisoned mentally, *a victim to the telepathic practice of Jesuit adepts.*" In a Pennsylvania paper Mencken found this advertisement: "Milk from a Holstein cow; Protestants only." His comment: "counter offensive against the Pope." As "evidence of the effects of the KKK campaign of education," Mencken reported that in an Indiana town the rumor spread that the Pope was planning to reside there incognito until moving to Washington and that he was arriving on the evening train; more than 1,500 people waited at the station for him.

The most poignant of all the material contained in the *Mercury* had to do with the American black. Just about every month Mencken included, usually without comment, news stories revealing the callous contempt with which the blacks were regarded by whites and the cruel and barbaric treatment they frequently received. Clippings about the black appearing in "Americana" were always outrageous and often hair-raising. When, for example, the president of a black college in South Carolina appeared before a legislative committee, he wore a finely tailored suit. "This fact," according to a Greenville newspaper, "stirred an unexpected prejudice against him in the minds of the legislators, but it was quickly removed when he told them that the suit had been fashioned by students of his college who were learning the tailoring trade." The *San Antonio News* had an item about a black man sentenced to five years for stealing a dollar and a white man given two years for killing a woman. When President

Hoover's wife entertained the wife of a black Congressman at a White House tea party, a writer in a Georgia newspaper urged that the White House be boycotted until the Hoovers left it and then be blown up. Reports of violence and brutality against blacks appeared regularly in "Americana." In Jackson, Mississippi, a black "who was taken from officers last night by a party of masked men, was returned here today from Clinton, where he was found after his release from his captors, who performed an operation on him." In Plymouth, North Carolina, a black was taken from his barbershop and branded with the letters KKK. In the *Chattanooga News* appeared this headline: "Negro Resists Arrest. Funeral Tomorrow." In Alabama, a sixty-year-old black was taken out of his bed and beaten to death by a mob. His offense? "Some school children had become frightened at seeing him walk along the road." In Pickens, Mississippi, an eighteen-year-old black girl was shot by a mob searching for her brother; the brother was said to have borrowed fifty cents from a white man and refused to pay ten cents interest. In Bishop, Texas, the automobile of a black doctor collided with a car occupied by whites; his hands and feet were promptly cut off by the whites and then he was burned to death. From Vicksburg, Mississippi, came this report: "The Negro was hauled up five feet but slipped back. The sight of the nude body rising from the crowd increased the excitement. 'Shoot him,' someone called out. 'No, no,' came the answer, 'let him die slow.' Seeing that he was merely suffering discomfort, the men below began to jerk his legs. Others smeared kerosene upon the body, while others prepared a bonfire below. The Negro assumed an attitude of prayer, raising his hands, palms together. The whole affair was witnessed by many ladies who followed the mob from the jail, and by others who joined in on the terraces nearby." The impact of items like these can be appreciated only if it is recalled that they appeared cheek by jowl with statements like the following from the *Los Angeles Times:* "There has never been a greater nor higher civilization than that which now stands proudly upon the soil of the United States. . . . There is nowhere on earth a more Christian civilization with the precepts of love, charity and generosity to mankind underlying its official and social life."

Mencken's "Americana" naturally came in for much criticism. His selections, it was charged, were one-sided and didn't give a fair picture of what the United States was like. *Dial* magazine said that "'Americana' is not America." Fred L. Pattee called the department "monthly rakings . . . from the entire press of America, with everything winnowed out save those scraps that tend to belittle our civilization." In *McNaught's Monthly* (which got even with Mencken by instituting a department called "Intelligentsia" made up of silly passages from highbrow writers), K. V. Hoffman declared in March 1925: "His 'Americana' is a collection of fanaticisms, bigotry, and inane stupidities, culled from our hastily and poorly-written press, but no fair-minded person could call it a true reflection of American life and thought." In 1927, the *Saturday Evening Post* began presenting Americana of its own, depicting the basic decency and generosity of the American people.

Mencken's choice of material was undoubtedly one-sided. He did not pretend to be objective; his aim in life, he once said, was to combat "chiefly by ridicule, American piety, stupidity, tin-pot morality, cheap chauvinism in all their forms." In the "Americana" columns of the *American Mercury* he succeeded brilliantly in his aim. To the extent that the things satirized in "Americana" are no longer taken seriously or approved of by most Americans, Mencken surely deserves some of the credit for the improvement. He performed an invaluable function as a social critic in his chronicling of things American in the twenties.

It would be a mistake, however, to regard Mencken as a reformer. He despised reformers as much as he did Babbitts and fundamentalists; he thought they were chasing butterflies. He was too pessimistic to believe that the masses of men were capable of any real progress. He had no faith in popular government; his contempt for democracy was as profound as, say, that of the John Birch Society — chiefly because he thought democracy was always producing nutty ideas and silly societies. (Had he lived into the late 1950s, he would not have been at all surprised at the rise to national prominence of such triumphs of mindlessness as the Birchers.) But if Mencken rejected democracy, he did champion a point of view which is essential to democratic society. Mencken, quite simply, insisted on civilized procedures in human relations; cultivated people, he made it clear, just did not think and act as did the people whose antics he recorded in "Americana." They did not join Klans, engage in patrioteering, support censorship and blue laws, or participate in lynchings. But most people, Mencken thought, were hopeless; they simply could not get along without their Klans, their censorship drives, and their witch hunts. Only a "civilized minority" was capable of behaving decently and intelligently. Mencken's preference for minority rule was clearly a form of elitism; and Mencken, unfortunately, ignored the fact that privileged elites (intellectual or otherwise) have never been known especially for their tolerance, their forbearance, or even their infallible judgments. If Mencken's associate, Charles Angoff, is to be believed, Mencken's views, expressed in private, contained almost as much ignorance, prejudice, and vulgarity as those of the *boobus Americanus* whom he ridiculed in the *Mercury*; and his public statements on social issues after the twenties, we know, became increasingly narrow, shrill, and uninformed.

Mencken's preferred minority, one has no doubt, would have its own special set of absurdities if it came to run the show. Was it not George Orwell who said that there was no idea so absurd but that some intellectual could be found subscribing to it? Democracy certainly has many of the failings that HLM attributed to it, but it does have the great virtue of attempting to check and balance the absurdities that all of us possess to some degree.

Still, for all his wrong-headedness, Mencken unquestionably furthered the civilizing process in the United States and helped elevate the quality of American life. Democracy, as Thomas Jefferson realized, can work only if its citizens are educated and enlightened. Mencken, by his satire, surely helped enlighten the American people and thus, without particularly intending it, helped advance American democracy. There is no period in which the United States does not sorely need its Menckens.

# 6

# The Quotatious
## Lyndon B. Johnson

"**B**Y necessity," announced Ralph Waldo Emerson, "by proclivity, and by delight, we all quote." He was right. We all like to quote; we all make use of apt quotations on occasion. Quotations help us to clarify or emphasize or expand on a point we are trying to make. As Montaigne put it: "I quote others only the better to express myself." There is nothing like quoting an impeccable authority to back up an argument we are making. It is even better if we get a good quotation from one of our opponents in order to prove the very point we are making. "A great man," Emerson declared, "quotes bravely."

There are a lot of brave quoters in this world. Years ago I made a systematic study of the art of quotation and quickly discovered that citing an esteemed authority was only one way in which people made use of quotations to underline a point they were making. Some people, I found, liked to use statements from the opposition to bolster their own position; they also enjoyed discrediting their opponents by quoting remarks they had made in the past that turned out to be either egregiously imperceptive or hilariously fatuous in the light of later events. Less scrupulous quoters, I also learned, cheerfully quoted people they disliked out of context; and sometimes, to strengthen their own positions, made up quotable statements of their own and attributed them to famous authorities. I was struck by the number of phony Washington and Lincoln quotes (and, until the Cold War ended, fake Lenin and Stalin quotes) circulating in this country. The upshot of my researches was a book published in 1967 entitled *Quotemanship: The Use and Abuse of Quotations for Polemical and Other Purposes* in which I examined the various ways writers, reporters, newspaper columnists, advertisers, publicists, and politicians made use of quotations, both legitimately and illegitimately, to back up their arguments and bolster the opinions they were expressing. Years later political scientist John George (the University of Central Oklahoma in Edmond) and I teamed up to do a book devoted entirely to spurious quotations: *They Never Said It: A Book of Fake Quotes, Misquotes, and Misleading Attributions* (1989).

In *Quotemanship,* I was particularly interested in public figures, and I placed special emphasis on how American presidents used quotations in their speeches, official proclamations, and press conferences. Some presidents, I discovered, liked to quote and others didn't. Until Franklin D. Roosevelt, however, our presidents were not in the habit of doing much quoting. But FDR, it was clear, enjoyed using apt quotes in his speeches, and after FDR, it became customary for presidents to use choice quotations in their public pronouncements. This was particularly true of John F. Kennedy and Lyndon B. Johnson. President Kennedy's speech adviser, Theodore Sorensen, kept a copy of Bartlett's *Familiar Quotations* handy because JFK liked to lace his speeches with lively quotes from esteemed authorities. But President Johnson, I learned, liked to use quotations in speeches even more than JFK did. He was, it seems, forever quoting during informal encounters with friends and associates as well as on public occasions. The following essay is a light-hearted look at the quotational style LBJ developed while in the White House — aided and abetted, of course, by speech advisors and ghost writers.

★ ★ ★ ★

Lyndon B. Johnson was without question the quotingest president ever to occupy the White House. He made constant use of quotations in his public speeches. More than just about any other president, he liked to intersperse his public pronouncements — messages to Congress, addresses to the American people, even informal chats with visitors to the White House — with carefully chosen quotations from the opinions of recognized authorities. Compared to LBJ, previous chief executives did very little with the art of quotation.

Some observers belittled LBJ's quoting skills. "In 37 years," huffed liberal columnist Murray Kempton in the pages of the *New Republic,* "we have advanced from a president who quoted nothing that he had not read on a 50-cent piece [Warren G. Harding] to a president who quotes what he reads on the backs of books in somebody else's library." A writer (pen named "Pyrrho") for the conservative *National Review* was similarly unimpressed. "Lyndon Johnson," he wrote, "never seems to find the right word, and yet all the words he uses seem to fit him. What is remarkable is that so many can be said and yet none remarkable. Even the conventional quotations drawn from the texts of civilization tend to seem out of context or marred by their utterance."

Kempton and Pyrrho were unduly harsh. The fact is that Johnson on occasion displayed real quotemanship, that is, genuine skill in the use of quotations to press home a particular point. He seems to have derived pleasure from quoting some highly regarded authority to reinforce the points he was making in public, and he frequently sent his speech advisers off on a diligent search for appropriate citations. This was particularly true during the early years of his presidency when he was seeking popular support for the measures he sponsored for developing the country into a Great Society.

In his State of the Union Message to Congress on January 4, 1965, Johnson told the American people that the United States, in its relations with other nations, would follow the example of Andrew Jackson, who once said: "I intend to ask for nothing that is not clearly right and to submit to nothing that is wrong." He also reiterated Jackson's promise that "the honor of my country shall never be stained by an apology from me for the statement of truth or the performance of duty." When he presented his Health Message to Congress a few days later, he started off with a quote from Thomas Jefferson, who, as the *New Republic* observed, was "almost as quotable as the Bible." In his Education Message on January 12, he began with a phrase from the Northwest Ordinance of 1787, included quotes from Thomas Carlyle and from Mirabeau B. Lamar, second president of the Republic of Texas and "the father of Texas education," and, in a nice touch, invoked the authority of the late Senator Robert A. Taft of Ohio ("Mr. Republican"), who had once declared that the Federal government had obligations "in the field of education, as in the fields of health, relief and medical care." His Immigration Message of January 13 quoted Walt Whitman, his Defense Message on January 18 began and ended with quotes from George Washington, his Inaugural Address ended with a scriptural allusion, his February 2 message on home rule for the District of Columbia quoted James Madison, and his February 8 message on natural beauty cited Thomas Jefferson. In April he delivered a speech on foreign policy at San Marcos, Texas, filled with echoes of famous American quotations: "Liberty has only one price and that is eternal vigilance"; "Freedom shall not perish from the earth"; "Speak softly but firmly." And so it went. Later messages to Congress and addresses to the American people during 1965 quoted Aristotle, Henry Clay, Felix Frankfurter, Patrick Henry, the Declaration of Independence, the Bible, Rachel Carson, and, of course, Jefferson.

During 1966 Johnson continued to make use of tried-and-true sources — Jefferson, Lincoln, Madison, Webster — but he also experimented with new authorities. In a special message to Congress in January on improving the nation's cities, he told the legislators what Thomas Wolfe had written: "To every man his chance — to every man, regardless of his birth, his shining, golden opportunity — to every man the right to live, to work, to be himself, and to become whatever thing his manhood and his vision can combine to make

him — this . . . is the promise of America." In a message on
conservation and pollution on February 23, he included
words from Albert Schweitzer; and in a speech in New York
the same day he appealed to the words of two famous Re-
publicans of yesteryear — Wendell Willkie and John Foster
Dulles — for vindication of his policy in Vietnam. In 1966,
he also cited words of wisdom from such diverse sources as
Louis Pasteur, John Jay, William Wordsworth, Thomas
Macaulay, Leonardo da Vinci, and Will Rogers.

But President Johnson did not confine his quoting to public occasions. He also carried quotes around with him, ready
for instant use, and at times he seemed to wear his quotes on
his sleeve. Stung by criticisms of his actions in Vietnam in the
spring of 1965, he got in the habit of pulling out of his pocket
and reading to reporters some quotations from a letter he had
received from former President Dwight D. Eisenhower: "If
there is any who opposes the President in his conduct of our
foreign affairs, he should send his views on a confidential
basis to the Administration; none of us should try to divide
the support that citizens owe to their head of state in critical
international situations." Whatever one thinks of the Eisenhower statement (and even *Time* was quick to point out that
Ike had himself been severely critical of Harry Truman's conduct of foreign affairs during the 1952 campaign), the appeal
by a Democratic president to the authority of an enormously
popular former Republican president was surely a neat bit of
quotemanship. To link Eisenhower, moreover, with his own
military build-up in South Vietnam during 1965, Johnson
also began carrying around a letter which Eisenhower had
written to South Vietnamese Premier Ngo Dinh Diem in
October 1954, promising aid to South Vietnam, and quoting
from it whenever the opportunity arose. When Eisenhower
protested that he was "not talking about military programs,
but foreign aid" in his letters to Diem, there was talk of a rift
between Johnson and Eisenhower over Vietnam policy. But
Ike's subsequent announcement that he supported the president fully in Vietnam laid this talk to rest. Evidently
Johnson's quotes were in the right place after all.

Soon after his re-election in 1964, Johnson decided to Americanize the war in Vietnam and he started carrying a copy of the Tonkin Gulf resolution around with him so he could quote from it whenever people raised questions about the legal basis for his intervention in Vietnam. The resolution, adopted by Congress in August 1964, supported "the determination of the President to take all necessary measures to repel any armed aggression" in Southeast Asia. Not only did LBJ quote the resolution time and again, he also quoted what John F. Kennedy said in 1963, two months before his assassination: "We want the war to be won, the Communists to be contained and the Americans to go home." And he also quoted popular historian Bruce Catton. In a conference with congressional leaders in February 1966, Johnson expressed irritation at Arkansas Senator J. William Fulbright's suggestion that he consult with the Senate Foreign Relations Committee before ending a temporary bombing truce in Vietnam, picked up a copy of *Never Call Retreat,* the last volume of Bruce Catton's Civil War trilogy, and read a passage to the congressmen describing how Abraham Lincoln responded to a demand by a group of senators that he reshape his cabinet according to their specifications in order to assure greater harmony. "Mr. Lincoln had no intention of doing this," declared Johnson. "He had told a friend that all of the responsibilities belong to that unhappy wretch Abraham Lincoln," and as he tried to meet those responsibilities, the last thing he needed or wanted was a contrived or enforced harmony." Catton's publisher, Doubleday, thereupon placed an advertisement in the *New York Times Book Review* calling attention to the fact that the president had quoted from Catton's book.

But Senator Fulbright remained defiant. On May 5, 1966, he made a speech in which he warned the United States against displaying the "arrogance of power" in its conduct of foreign affairs. LBJ tried to respond good-naturedly. Meeting Fulbright in a diplomatic reception receiving line a few days later, he all but hugged his arch critic (according to *Time* on May 13) and told Mrs. Fulbright: "I read Bill's speech on the arrogance of power and I analyzed it." Then he twitted the Senator: "You don't have to worry about the arrogance of power when you get notes like this from our cook Zephyr." Pulling a slip of paper from his pocket, Johnson read the Fulbrights the following: "Mr. President, you have been my boss for a number of years, and you always tell me you want to lose weight, and yet you never do very much to help yourself. Now I am going to be your boss for a change. Eat what I put in front of you and don't ask for any more and don't complain. Zephyr." Looking at Lady Bird with a mock frown, Johnson declared: "Now if arrogance of power is any-where, it's in the kitchen." Fulbright was amused by the quotational put-down, but continued to criticize the president's Vietnam policy in speeches in the Senate.

To defend his foreign policy, President Johnson took to quoting an old Roman consul. In a brief talk to some eight hundred top-ranking military officers and defense department officials and their wives at a White House reception in the spring of 1965, Johnson recalled that "a friend of mine, observing some of my problems, recently sent me for my desk a quotation from a Roman consul back in 168 B.C." The consul was Aemilius Paulus; he was speaking to the Roman Senate which had picked him to lead Rome's legions in the Macedonian War and then had heaped criticism on him for his conduct of the war. Said Paulus (and Johnson quoted): "I am not one of those who think that commanders ought at no time to receive advice: on the contrary, I should deem that man the standard of his own single judgment." But, as Johnson told the assemblage, Paulus went on to say that if anyone wished to give him some free advice, "let him come with me into Macedonia. He shall be furnished with a ship, a horse, a tent, even his traveling charges shall be defrayed. But if he thinks this too much trouble, and prefers the repose of city life to the toils of war, let him not, on land, assume the office of pilot." Henry R. Luce's *Time,* a warm supporter of the Johnson administration's policy in Vietnam, rather liked the quote. "Johnson's choice of quotations," observed the newsweekly, "was rather enlightening in view of the criticism he has been getting from campus and column-writing armchair generals about his conduct of the Vietnamese and the Dominican crises." (Those supporting Johnson's foreign policy, on campus or in newspaper columns, were not, of course, armchair generals.)

The Paulus quote was one of three which hung in frames above President Johnson's desk in the small auxiliary room adjoining the oval office where LBJ worked late at night. The other two consisted of quotations from Edmund Burke and from Abraham Lincoln, both dealing with the thick skin required by men holding public offices. The Lincoln quote, framed and presented to LBJ by Lady Bird Johnson as a Christmas present in 1964, had this to say: "If I were to return, much less answer, all the attacks on me, this shop might well be closed for any other business. I do the very best I know how — the very best I can, and I mean to keep doing so until the end. If the end brings me out all right, what is said against me won't amount to anything. If the end brings me out wrong, 10 angels swearing I was right would make no difference." The Burke statement reads as follows: "Those who would carry on the great public schemes must be proof against the most fatiguing delays, the most mortifying disappointments, the most shocking insults and, worst of all, the presumptuous judgment of the ignorant upon their design." In October 1965, when President Johnson entered the Naval Hospital at Bethesda for a cholecystectomy (gallbladder removal), he took a framed copy of the Burke quotation with him and had it put on the wall of his hospital room.

Paulus, Lincoln, and Burke seem to have comforted President Johnson, but his favorite source for apt quotations was the Bible. Perhaps no other president filled his public addresses with so many excerpts from the scriptures. Where President Kennedy liked to quote Jefferson or some political philosopher in his speeches, Johnson preferred biblical allusions. Bill D. Moyers, his press secretary for a time and then his special assistant, was a big help to the president in plucking phrases from the Bible for use in speeches. An ordained

Baptist minister, Moyers knew his Bible well and he was able to supply his boss with appropriate quotations on demand. But Moyers told the editors of the *Christian Century,* a non-denominational Protestant weekly, that he could not take full credit for biblical citations in Johnson's speeches; Richard Goodwin, a "brilliant young Jew" on the White House staff, Moyers told them, was the Old Testament expert who saw to it that the Old Testament received equal time with the New. In addition to Moyers and Goodwin, Billy Graham, the popular evangelist, also located biblical references for the president. It was Graham, not Moyers or Goodwin, who suggested that Johnson end his inaugural address on January 20, 1965, with a quote from King Solomon's prayer upon his accession to the throne of Israel: "Give me new wisdom and knowledge that I may go out and come in before this people: for who can judge this, thy people, that is so great?"

On September 16, 1964, when Johnson spoke in Seattle about the longings of the United States for peace, he said that the American people hoped to see the following biblical prophecy fulfilled: "The morning stars sang together, and all the sons of God shouted for joy." Speaking on another occasion of the United States' determination to fight communism in Asia, Johnson utilized this phrase from the Bible: "Hitherto shalt thou come, but no further." When he signed a $280 million program of medical research at the National Institutes of Health in Bethesda, Maryland, in August 1965, he quoted Acts 8:5-7 on curing the palsied and the lame and promised that "this bill will accomplish the miracles of which today we only dream." When making extemporaneous remarks, as well as when delivering formal addresses, Johnson liked to cite scriptures. "There will be many complaints spoken of us," he said, when talking about the Alliance for Progress to a group of ambassadors to the Organization of American States in 1964, "but we must, in the words of the prophet, 'mount up on the wings of eagles, run and not grow weary.'" During the course of an off-the-cuff talk to Peace Corps alumni in August 1965, he picked up a piece of paper from his desk and read from Second Peter: "and besides this,

*LBJ (courtesy of the Lyndon Baines Johnson Library, Austin).*

giving all diligence, add to your faith virtue; and to your virtue knowledge; and to your knowledge temperance; and to your temperance patience; and to your patience godliness; and to godliness brotherly kindness; and to brotherly kindness love."

President Johnson did, to be sure, get quotes from many other sources than the Bible. On occasion he cited Churchill, Lord Acton, Franklin Roosevelt, Robert E. Lee (both Johnson and his wife, campaigning in the South in 1964, quoted Lee on the necessity for reconciliation after the Civil War) and, of course, a lot of Jefferson. He once even quoted comedian Fred Allen when he referred to a "conference" as "a gathering of important people who singly do nothing but together decide that nothing can be done." And he did not overlook Ralph Waldo Emerson. In a speech before the National Education Association at Madison Square Garden in New York on July 2, 1965, he made use of the following sentence from Emerson's *Society and Solitude* (1870): "The true test of a civilization is, not the consensus, nor the size of cities, not the crops, but the kind of man that the country turns out." (So much, apparently, for LBJ's beloved consensus.)

But the Bible — "the good book," as LBJ liked to call it — was Johnson's favorite source. And the quotation he apparently liked best of all — one to which he continually referred and one, according to some observers, that formed the basis of his political style — was from Isaiah 1:18: "Come now, and let us reason together."

It was a former senator, as Johnson told it, who first called his attention to the Isaiah quote. In his early days as a politician, according to Johnson, he once got into a fight with the head of a power company who wouldn't let him build a little REA (Rural Electrification Administration) line in his country district in Texas. LBJ finally told the man to go to hell. But an ex-senator who overheard the exchange reminded Johnson that "telling a man to go to hell and then making him go is two different propositions." Explaining, the former senator said: "First of all, it is hot down there and the average fellow doesn't want to go, and when you tell him he has to go, he just bristles up and he is a lot less likely to go than if you hadn't told him anything. What you better do is get out the good book that your mama used to read to you and go back to the prophet Isaiah and read what he said. He said, 'Come now, let us reason together.'" After that episode (which LBJ told and retold with many variations), the Isaiah quote became Johnson's favorite. (In a footnote to a book on JFK identifying the Isaiah reference, historian Arthur Schlesinger, Jr., added: "L.B.J. *passim.*")

Johnson believed that reasoning together, in the spirit of Isaiah, until a consensus was reached was the best way to run a government. If the Democratic slogan during the 1964 presidential campaign was, "All the way with LBJ," the motto of the Johnson administration, reporters suggested, was, "All the Way with Isaiah!" When a steel strike seemed imminent in August 1965, Johnson called industry officials and union leaders to the White House and told them: "Come now, let us reason together. That's why I have brought you here." And reason they did, until a settlement was reached. A few months later, when machinists struck at five airlines, Johnson's special assistant, Bill Moyers, told newsmen that the president hoped the airlines and the union would "reason together." And again reason prevailed. Johnson's critics noted, however, that the president had a tendency to regard disagreement with his views as falling into the category of the "unreasonable." They also reminded him of the two verses that come a little later in the Bible after the Isaiah quote: "If ye be willing and obedient, ye shall eat the good of the land . . . but if ye refuse and rebel, ye shall be devoured by the sword, for the Lord hath spoken." "Surely by now," commented *Chicago Sun-Times* reporter Carleton Kent, after quoting the entire passage, "the reader will have realized that, particularly with a tough old bird like Isaiah, one runs a risk in lifting verses out of context."

On at least one occasion, Johnson's quoting habits led him astray. On August 4, 1965, Johnson was scheduled to give an address to about nine thousand college students who were spending the summer in Washington working in various government departments and agencies. Because poet Robert

Lowell was popular with young people, one of the members of Johnson's staff thought it would be a good idea to quote the Pulitzer Prize-winning poet to the students. Lowell, moreover, had offended LBJ in June, when he turned down an invitation to attend the White House Festival of the Arts because of his objection to the president's policy in Vietnam, and it was suggested that Johnson could perform a neat ploy if he introduced a quote from Lowell in his address. The White House staff member who conceived the idea had read a good deal of Lowell, but he had difficulty in locating an appropriate quotation for the occasion. Several other White House aides joined the search and someone finally came up with what was regarded as a suitable line. In his speech to the students, then, Johnson declared at one point: "Robert Lowell, the poet, doesn't like everything around here. But I like one of his lines where he wrote: 'For the world which seems to lie out before us like a land of dreams.' Well, in this great age, and it is a great age — the world does seem to lie before us like a land of dreams."

Unfortunately for Johnson's efforts to make peace with the pacifist poet and bring him amicably into the great consensus, the passage quoted was not from Robert Lowell but from Matthew Arnold. It was a line from Arnold's "Dover Beach" which Lowell had utilized himself to introduce one of his own poems, thus misleading LBJ's quote-hunters. The dark view of things taken by Arnold, moreover, bore little resemblance to the president's own exuberant optimism. Arnold had written:

> Ah, love, let us be true
> To one another for the world, which seems
> To lie before us like a land of dreams,
> So various, so beautiful, so new,
> Hath really neither joy, nor love, nor light,
> Nor certitude, nor peace, nor help for pain;
> And we are here as on a darkling plain
> Swept with confused alarms of struggle and flight
> Where ignorant armies clash by night.

The *New York Herald Tribune,* noting that the hopeful line quoted by Johnson was expressly nullified by the rest of the stanza, had a couple of quotes of its own for the president. "I think, sir," the *Tribune* quoted a great Oxford scholar as having said, "you will find it a very good practice always to verify your references." The editors also reminded the president of the words of Isaac D'Israeli: "The art of quotation requires delicacy." In the opinion of the *Tribune,* Johnson's misattributed and misapplied quote "was, on its minor scale, a truly monumental booboo. And we suggest that the most appropriate penalty for the person guilty of leaving Mr. Johnson on his darkling plain would be a sound spanking with a naked shingle until his edges were drear indeed."

On August 12, 1965, President Johnson held a ceremony in the Rose Garden, honoring the memory of Herbert Hoover, to which he had invited leading Republican notables. Not all of them could participate in the president's newest effort to broaden the consensus, but Senate Minority Leader Everett Dirksen of Illinois was at hand, and when it came time for him to speak he couldn't resist teasing the president about the Lowell fiasco. Among other things, Dirksen recalled that when he introduced former President Hoover at a Republican national convention some years before, he had chosen some lines written by James Russell Lowell (from whom Robert Lowell was descended) to describe him. Dirksen thereupon quoted the lines correctly and from memory. Commenting on Dirksen's performance, columnist Mary McGrory wrote admiringly in the *New York Post:* "Dirksen has a delicate sense of one-upmanship, which he displayed flawlessly. . . . Having observed with the rest of the world the president's hapless attempt to extend the olive branch to poet Robert Lowell, the country's most conspicuous holdout to consensus, Sen. Dirksen chose another poet named Lowell — James Russell Lowell — as a source of quotation. It was a small point, but it was the only one scored at the ceremonies in the Rose Garden."

LBJ let Senator Dirksen win that one; he came up with no counterquotes. As time passed, in fact, he seems to have lost his passion for quoting notable authorities in speeches and during interviews. There were occasional references to Jefferson, Jackson, and Lincoln in later addresses, to be sure, and even a novelty or two: quotes from Martin Luther and Sir Isaac Newton. But there was a marked decline in the number of erudite citations appearing in LBJ's public utterances after 1967. There were no more appeals to Isaiah and sweet reasonableness. There were few scriptural references, for that matter, in Johnson's last years in the White House. Perhaps this was because Bill Moyers departed Washington in 1967 for newspaper work in New York. Or perhaps it was because Johnson himself was coming to be widely — and unpleasantly — quoted by critics of his Vietnam policy.

The Johnson quotes were embarrassing. During 1965 and 1966, as LBJ gradually increased U.S. military involvement in the Vietnamese civil war, his anti-war opponents began searching the record, digging up the anti-interventionist promises LBJ had made during his campaign for reelection in 1964, and confronting him with his own words in their speeches, articles, editorials, pamphlets and books. "We are not going North and we are not going South," the *Progressive* quoted him as having announced in New Hampshire in September 1964. "Losing 190 lives in the period we have been out there is bad, but it is not like the 190,000 that we might lose the first month, if we escalated the war." In another campaign speech, the *New Republic* noted, LBJ had exclaimed (in an obvious reference to the hawkish Arizona Senator Barry M. Goldwater, his Republican opponent): "Some others are eager to enlarge the conflict. They call on us to supply American boys to do the job that Asian boys should do. They ask us to take reckless action [such as bombing North Vietnam]. . . . Such action would offer no solution at all to the real problems of Viet Nam."

The Johnson quotes kept coming. Oregon Senator Wayne Morse, leading opponent of LBJ's Vietnam policy, reminded people of another Johnson statement made in August 1964: "I have had advice to load our planes with bombs and to drop them on certain areas that I think would enlarge the war and result in our committing a good many American boys to fighting a war that I think ought to be fought by the boys of Asia to help protect their own land. And for that reason, I haven't chosen to enlarge the war." Walter Lippmann, the venerable newspaper and magazine columnist, also went after the president with awkward quotes from the past. Right after Johnson announced defiantly in a speech in Omaha that the American people had "voted me a majority for the presidency of this country" in 1964 to make major foreign-policy decisions, Lippmann reminded him (in a *Newsweek* column) of what the president had told the people on September 25, 1964: "There are those that say you ought to go north and drop bombs, to try to wipe out the supply lines, and they think that would escalate the war. We don't want to get involved in a nation with 700 million people [China] and get tied down in a land war in Asia." LBJ's Omaha speech prompted the *Progressive* to come up with still another Johnson quote from the 1964 campaign: "We are not about to send American boys nine or ten thousand miles away from home to do what Asian boys should be doing for themselves."

The betrayed-promises quotes unquestionably damaged the Johnson presidency; they destroyed Johnson's credibility and helped discredit his administration. LBJ was deeply hurt by the mounting opposition to his Vietnam policy, especially on college campuses around the country, where anti-Vietnam demonstrations became common, and on at least one occasion he came up with a Jefferson quote about students by way of response. In a commencement address at Texas Christian University on May 29, 1968, he utilized a lengthy quotation from a letter President Jefferson wrote in 1808 recommending that public officials resolutely ignore their student critics. "Keep aloof," wrote Jefferson, "from such youthful critics, as you would from the infected subjects of yellow fever or pestilence. Consider yourself, when with them, as among the patients of Bedlam, needing medical more than moral counsel. Be a listener only, keep within yourself . . . the habit of silence, especially on politics. In the fevered state of our country, no good can ever result from any attempt to set one of these fiery zealots to rights, either in fact or principle. They are determined as to the facts they will believe, and the opinions on which they will act. Get by them, therefore, as you would by an angry bull; it is not for a man of sense to dispute the road with such an animal."

The Jefferson quote may have given Johnson some comfort, but it scarcely stilled his critics, youthful or otherwise. In the end, the Johnson presidency, which had begun so promisingly with the Great Society, went down to defeat with the Vietnam War. If it had not been for Vietnam, said Averell Harriman, Democratic bigwig, after LBJ's death, Johnson "would have been the greatest president ever." In retirement, LBJ was reported to have said of the Vietnam War: "The kids were right. I blew it." And on another occasion he mused: "I knew from the start that if I left the woman I really loved — the Great Society — in order to fight that bitch of a war . . . then I would lose everything at home. All my hopes . . . my dreams. . . ."

Perhaps Johnson abandoned Isaiah too soon; and perhaps, too, he picked the wrong quotes as guidelines. What if he had taken to heart some of the quotes his critics liked to cite from General Matthew B. Ridgway (former army chief of staff) and General David Shoup (former commandant of the Marine Corps) warning against embroilment in Vietnam? Or a quote from General Douglas MacArthur's stern warning to the Senate Defense Appropriations Subcommittee in August 1962: "Gentlemen, let me warn you of one thing. Keep your foot soldiers out of the jungles of Southeast Asia"?

Should not quotations enlighten as well as reassure?

# 7

# History and War:
## Beard and Batault

**W**HEN I began graduate work in history in the fall of
1939, Charles A. Beard was known as "the dean of American
historians." The first seminar paper I did in graduate school
was on Beard, and I still recall the excitement I felt while
getting to know his books and articles on American history.
I found his *Economic Interpretation of the Constitution of the
United States* (1913) spunky and iconoclastic and admired *The
Rise of American Civilization* (1927, and later editions), which
he wrote with his wife Mary, for its stately prose and for the
way it not only sought out basic tendencies in the development of this country but also put our country in the larger
context of world history. I devoured *America in Midpassage*
(1939) a sequel to *Rise of American Civilization*, which came
out while I was working on my paper, and enjoyed both its
anti-war bias and its friendliness to the New Deal.

Beard was still identified with the economic interpretation
of history when I was in school, but he was already beginning to emphasize the power of ideas as well as economic
interests in shaping human events. He was becoming absorbed, too, in what used to be called the "philosophy of
history" and bewildering many of his colleagues with his talk
of objective history as "a noble dream" and his assertion that
writing history was essentially "an act of faith." But I was

fascinated by all these elements in his thinking, though my main interest was intellectual history (I studied under Ralph Henry Gabriel at Yale), and I was also attracted to the anti-interventionist opinions he had about American foreign policy. After I completed my paper, I took the bus to New Milford, Connecticut, and spent a wonderful afternoon with him talking about Washington, Lincoln, Wilson, and FDR, and about the importance of staying out of the war in Europe.

Beard was not alone in his anti-interventionist views, of course. The 1930s was an anti-war decade — without question the most strongly anti-war period in the nation's entire history — and probably most Americans shared Beard's outlook when World War II broke out in the fall of 1939. With the fall of France in the summer of 1940, however, increasing numbers of Americans came to support FDR's policy of aiding Britain in its struggle with the Nazi barbarians, even if it meant risking war. Beard loved Britain, where he had studied as a young man, but he remained adamantly anti-interventionist until Pearl Harbor, even going to Washington in the spring of 1941 to testify before Congress against the Lend-Lease Bill. When we entered the war, he gave it his critical support, but after the war he published two books charging that FDR had duplicitously taken the country into war and thus set dangerous precedents for the future. That ended him in the historical profession. His colleagues savaged his books and many of his former admirers dismissed him as a cranky and outdated "old isolationist."

The dismissal was undeserved. Beard may have been wrong in opposing U.S. entry into World War II, but he was certainly right about many of the criticisms he made of U.S. foreign policy in the twentieth century. "Had Americans read and taken Charles A. Beard seriously years ago," wrote historian Ronald Radosh during the Vietnam War, "perhaps the nation we have inherited from the bipartisan cold warriors might have been different." Perhaps so; perhaps not. The Cold War ended in 1989, but in 1990 the United States sent thousands of troops to the Middle East in its latest crusade to "check aggression" and establish "lasting peace" in the world.

The following essay, which appeared in the *French-American Review* in the spring of 1979, is a study of what Beard had to say about the role of war in history and an effort to discover what seems to me to be still compelling about Beard's philosophy of war. I have translated the passages from Georges Batault that originally appeared in French.

★ ★ ★ ★

Shortly before the United States entered World War I, historian Charles A. Beard told one of his classes at Columbia University, with tears in his eyes, that he had reached the conclusion that it was impossible for the United States to avoid entering the war against Germany. For Beard, who had attended a Quaker academy as a boy, this could not have been an easy position to take. Not long after the United States went to war, he resigned his professorship at Columbia to protest the administration's firing of two of his colleagues on the faculty — H. W. L. Dana and J. M. Cattell — for their refusal to support the war. Only a few years before, in a textbook entitled *Contemporary American History* (1914), he had included the sardonic remark: "contrary to their assertions on formal occasions, the American people enjoy war beyond measure, if the plain facts of history are allowed to speak." Beard himself didn't enjoy war. But here he was supporting American intervention on the side of the Allies in the most terrible of wars up to that time.

World War I turned out to be the only war that Beard ever supported wholeheartedly. Although as a young man he had imbibed enough of the popular enthusiasm for the Spanish-American War to think of volunteering, he never defended that particular war as an adult. He always looked upon it as a gigantic aberration on America's part. It was, from Beard's point of view, a war for empire, and almost from the beginning of his political life he was a devout anti-imperialist, as were many of the early twentieth-century Progressives with whom he was associated. World War I, however, seemed different. By 1917, Beard had convinced himself that German militarism was such a threat to humane values throughout the world that the United States had no alternative but to join the Allies in exterminating it. He lamented the thought that the United States must take up arms, but he saw no other choice for the country in 1917; and throughout the war he gave the Wilson administration his loyal support, though deploring its practice of silencing critics on the domestic front. When the war ended, he was disillusioned by many of the settlements made at Versailles, as were his colleagues on the *New Republic* (founded in 1914 as an organ of the progressivism which Beard espoused); but for many years he did not recant his belief that in 1917 American intervention had been both necessary and justified. His first post-war book on foreign affairs — *Cross Currents in Europe Today* (1922) — took the need for American participation in World War I for granted.

In 1921, the editors of the *New Republic* sent Beard a book on war to review. It was written by Georges Batault, a free-lance writer, published in Paris in 1919, and entitled *La Guerre Absolue* (subtitled *Essai de Philosophie de L'Histoire*). Batault's thesis was simple enough. He took perpetual warfare for granted. War, in fact, from Batault's point of view, was a kind of law of history. It was the one constant in the affairs of men and nations. "War," he wrote, "has always been considered a calamity, though a temporary and accidental one, but careful study seems to show that under diverse forms war is the most fundamental law in the evolution of societies." There had been thousands of wars before modern times, but democracy, industry, and nationalism in Batault's view made war total and all-embracing. The French Revolution gave citizens the ballot but also made them conscripts. The industrial revolution transformed war from a limited activity into a major human undertaking. And nationalism enlisted the passions of entire peoples in war. Born in the French Revolution and the wars of the Empire, then taken over and perfected by Germany, total war had come to be natural, inevitable, and inescapable in the world at large. Peace was simply a breathing spell between wars; in times of peace human beings prepared for war (the armed peace). Preparations for war and the waging of war itself were fundamental in shaping the structure and ethos of societies. "War," he wrote, "is necessarily the first need and concern of the State and the most important of its enterprises." Karl Marx was wrong. Economics was not the basic determinant in society. It was war which determined the social and political structure, as well as the intellectual life of nations. Though deploring his findings, Batault presented military determinism in its starkest form. "In the life of societies," he wrote, "war plays a preëminent role, molding them, designing them in her image, and imposing the forms of evolution on them and the laws of development. War is the most universal social phenomenon, the most important, and the most tragic; it is the fundamental phenomenon in every society. It is in war, the most absolute manifestation of force, that antagonistic human ideals confront each other and establish their ascendancy. Meanwhile war always appears in human eyes as an accidental phenomenon; when it comes it naturally terrifies us, but it shouldn't astonish us, for it is not an accident; it is the rule. War repels us; it seems criminal and without excuse. But IT IS. It is a basic fact of life." Elsewhere Batault wrote: "War does not tend to decline or disappear; on the contrary, it continually extends its domain, becoming more powerful, in all its manifestations, and more and more absolute."

Batault's general conclusion was that "the human race marches inevitably toward a new kind of barbarism." His vision of things was a far cry from the brave new world that Woodrow Wilson had envisaged when he took the United States into the First World War. Batault had little to say about America's role in that war, but his assumption was that the United States was subject to the same law of war that governed the other nations of the world.

Beard's review of *La Guerre Absolue* appeared in the *New Republic* for September 21, 1921. Beard spent most of his review summarizing Batault's thesis in detail. And then, at the very end, he exclaimed: "Hold, enough! It was dreadful to read such things in obscure and mystic German with its verbs a mile away. It is like crucifixion to read them in the clear, steel-cut, deadly precise language of a Frenchman. We know he cannot be right, because our hearts tell us so." Yet Batault continued to haunt Beard for years. In his introduction to a collection of essays entitled *Whither Mankind: A Panorama of Modern Civilization* (1928), he took up the question of whether the world was advancing to a better state of affairs or whether it was sinking into decadence. He cited Batault along with Oswald Spengler as an exponent of the latter point of view, but he himself took a more hopeful line. "Probably terrible wars will arise and prove costly in blood and treasure, but it is a strain upon the speculative faculties to conceive of any conflict that could destroy the population and mechanical equipment of the Western world so extensively that human vitality and science could not restore economic prosperity and even improve upon the previous order. According to J. S. Mill, the whole mechanical outfit of a capitalist country can be reproduced in about ten years. Hence the prospect of repeated and costly wars in the future need not lead us to the pessimistic view that suicide is to be the fate of modern civilization."

In *The American Leviathan: The Republic in the Machine Age*, written with his son William and appearing in 1930, Beard referred only in passing to "the dreadful phenomenon of war," but in *The Open Door at Home*, published five years later, he again faced squarely the question posed by Batault: is war a primordial force, independent of national policy and will? He emphasized the fact that although most Americans were unaware of it, the view that war was an invariable in history, for which nations must always be prepared, was not at all uncommon among military experts. "Any number of citations could be marshalled," he said, "to show that war is widely considered as an absolute and unavoidable phenomenon of history; and it is highly probable that most military and naval men in the United States operate on a profound

*Charles A. Beard (courtesy of the De Pauw University Archives and Special Collections, Greencastle, Indiana).*

belief in that formula. They doubtless hold, with Georges Batault, that *la guerre est la loi la plus generale de l'evolution des societes humaines"* ("War is the most general law in the evolution of human societies"). Beard went on to say that Batault's proposition could not be proven by any knowledge or method open to the human mind and, for the first time, he challenged its validity at length. "It is a generalization," he declared, "presumed to rest on human experience. It is a belief, a conviction, a prophecy; it is not a statement that can be verified, as a generalized law in physics can be verified. It can be described and repeated endlessly, but it cannot be authenticated to the satisfaction of anybody who has respect for exactness of thought, for it is a fundamental finding of exact science that an invincible law can arise only where there is an isolated sequence of occurrences arranged in fact in a deterministic order. No sequence can be found in human affairs to support the proposition that war is a primordial force, independent of policy, operating under its own momentum as a process under its own law. The very idea does violence to all that is known of the nature of history. It is an abstraction in words, satisfactory to those to whom it is satisfactory, but unsupported by knowledge of history as actual occurrences." Wars, as realities, Beard insisted, have always been associated with the purposes and policies of the leaders, governments, and ruling classes of nations. It was Beard's objective in writing *The Open Door at Home*, in fact, to outline for the governing elite in the United States a workable program for remaining at peace when the next war broke out in Europe.

Beard's views were called "isolationist" by those who believed that the United States could not remain aloof from the developing conflict in Europe in the late 1930s; as "interventionists," they insisted that if war broke out in Europe the United States would inevitably be drawn into it. Beard looked upon the interventionist view as a kind of Bataultian fatalism and he argued strenuously that whatever happened abroad the United States could remain at peace if she chose to do so. *America in Midpassage*, a lengthy study of America in the 1920s and 1930s, written with his wife Mary, appeared in 1939, and in it, Beard devoted extensive space to his anti-war views on foreign policy. Again he took up the thesis presented by Batault many years earlier: was war an independent factor in history transcending the desires and purposes of men and women? In *America in Midpassage*, Beard did not dismiss Batault's theory as summarily as he had in his previous writings. There was, he acknowledged, a fundamental "blood lust" in human beings which sought satisfaction in conflict; there was, he said, a "dark and convulsive urge to physical combat, which had manifested itself in endless wars, domestic and foreign, from the dawn of history, for one cause, or another cause, or for no cause at all. . . ." How potent this urge was in America Beard did not pretend to know, but he thought it was evident that it "quivered beneath the surface of things" even during peacetime and found outlets in lynchings and other forms of domestic violence in the United States. Yet on the whole he was extremely doubtful whether the mass of people, decently employed in the works of peace, ever lusted for war, and he thought it was significant that national governments were forced to resort to conscription in order to build up the "monster armies" of the modern world. In the United States, moreover, Beard noted, militarism "as a regular way of life" had never captivated the American people. And yet, despite these doubts about the validity of Batault's thesis, Beard was forced to admit that there were many men in America, military and civilian alike, "who deemed war forever inevitable and who were propelled by passionate emotions to choose 'the next enemy' and to bend propaganda toward war against that foe, when neither national peril nor national advantage was involved in the process."

Of course, Americans favoring intervention on the side of the Allies in 1939 thought that Beard was posing the question unfairly. Their insistence that the United States must aid England and France against Nazi Germany was not, from their point of view, another manifestation of the law of *la guerre absolue;* it was the result of their reasoned conviction that at this point in history America's national interest was bound up with the fortunes of France and England.

Despite Beard's strenuous efforts to keep America out of war — he appeared before a Congressional committee in 1940 to oppose a conscription law and he wrote articles and a popular book setting forth his anti-interventionist views — the United States entered World War II after the attack on Pearl Harbor. In *The American Spirit: A Study of the Idea of Civilization in the United States* (1942), the first book that Beard, with his wife, published after the United States went to war, he seemed, in his great disappointment at how things turned out, to yield, for the first time, to Batault's view of history. After analyzing the different ways in which Americans, from the earliest days of the republic until the 1930s, had conceived of civilization, Beard ended the book on a somber note. "Despite the mutability of things human," he wrote, "there is one invariable in the history of men and women. This is war. And inasmuch as the efficiency of war in spreading death and destruction depends upon some degree of civilization, it follows that, subject to the law of thermodynamics, if there be one, the future of civilization in the United States has at least this much assurance." And in the index to *The American Spirit* appeared this entry: "War, invariable in human history." Yet Beard had surrendered only momentarily to Batault's view of war. In *The Republic* (appearing two years later), a discussion in the form of conversations between Beard and his friends of the fundamental principles of the U.S. Constitution, Beard reiterated the view he had first put forth sixteen years earlier in *Whither Mankind* as to the durability of modern civilization. If *The American Spirit* had ended lugubriously, *The Republic* concluded with a note of hope. "I have confidence," wrote Beard in the last chapter, "in the tenacity of civilization, always in conflict with its foe, barbarism, and I hold to the conviction that it will not be extinguished on the earth. . . . I do not expect the United States ever to be as well-ordered as a Sunday School. Still less do I expect the world of nations ever to be as ordered as a Sunday School. The universe does not seem to be 'planned that way.' But civilization in the United States, I believe, will continue for long centuries to come."

After World War II, Beard published two books (one of them just before his death in September 1948) attempting to prove that the Roosevelt administration, frequently by devious methods, had led the American people unnecessarily into the Second World War. Franklin Roosevelt, in short, not *la guerre absolue,* was for Beard the basic cause of America's war from 1941 to 1945. Beard had never been able to accept Batault's doctrine for long; his anti-war predilections were too powerful for that. Still, his vast knowledge of the past, particularly of the American past, forced him to recognize the fact that mighty nations like the United States never seem to remain long at peace. As he put it in his chapter on foreign policy in *The Republic:* "In my opinion . . . there has been a decline in the sheer love of war among many nations. A lot of people in every country become sick of war after they have been in it for two or three years; but the great nations seem to like a war every generation or two. At least they seem to like it enough to get into it." Beard wavered much of the time, as historian Bernard Borning has pointed out, between the assumption that statesmen have it within their power to bring on or prevent wars and his belief that war was, as Batault maintained, an inescapable force in history. He regarded permanent peace — what might be called *la paix absolue* — as a chimerical goal, and for that reason he was severely critical of Wilsonian internationalism. But he never doubted that a realistic view of America's national interest would enable her to avoid unnecessary clashes with other nations.

Beard had his last say about war in a December 1947 address to the American Political Science Association in Washington, D.C. Toward the end of a discussion of "neglected aspects" of American political science, he made three points about the subject that had absorbed so much of his energy ever since World War I. He first called attention to the large number of wars that the United States had waged during its relatively brief national existence and he challenged the popular notion that Americans were a "peace-loving" people. He went on to deplore the fact that in American scholarly circles war was treated as an exceptional factor in human affairs rather than as "a primary datum of American political history, marked by some of the certainty that characterizes death and taxes. . . ." And he concluded by ridiculing the belief, widespread among American policy-makers, historians, and foreign-affairs writers, that war was "a wicked practice forced upon us, much to our indignation, by aggressive foreigners and then waged by us only for enduring peace, world democracy, and the rights of oppressed people." For Beard, it is clear, Batault had proved one point: that *la paix absolue* was an illusory goal. Furthermore, if war was inevitable, as Batault insisted, then, from Beard's point of view American foreign policy — with its emphasis on checking aggression wherever it took place, co-operating with "peace-loving" nations like itself in upholding law and order, and fighting to achieve "permanent peace" in the world — was a case of egregious folly. But Beard found fault with America's policy of "world pacification," as he called it, not merely because he thought it flouted Bataultian premises; he also criticized it because he thought it was too grandiose. World pacification, he warned, entailed continual intervention by the United States in conflicts all over the world, and American intervention was likely to turn local quarrels into large-scale clashes. In its quest for permanent peace in the world, he said, the United States would probably find itself waging "perpetual war for perpetual peace." A less ambitious foreign policy — one stressing national interest rather than world peace as its objective and eschewing unlimited intervention in the affairs of other nations — might produce fewer and less costly wars for America and for the world at large.

Beard, in short, was never a wholehearted Bataultian; it was simply impossible for him to bow to the inevitable when it came to war. He utilized Batault for purposes of criticism rather than from a deep personal conviction. He died lamenting the fact that global tensions were just as acute after World War II as they had been before the war, but he saw nothing inescapable about the situation. His hope was that his books on foreign policy might encourage the American people to demand that their leaders formulate more modest goals in world affairs than they had been pursuing since the late 1930s and thus diminish the likelihood of future wars for the United States and for other nations. Peace, he thought, was always a real possibility for the American people if they pursued it seriously and realistically. Despite occasional moments of pessimism, Beard could not bring himself to subscribe to the fatalism pervading Batault's view of history. For Beard, *la guerre* was never *absolue,* as it was for Batault; it was always a conscious and deliberate choice of the American governing elite.

# 8

# Hiroshima and the American Left:
## August 1945

For some Americans, August 6, 1945, not December 7, 1941, is "a day that will live in infamy." Since the late 1970s thousands of "peaceniks," as they are called, have been gathering in towns and cities throughout the land on "Hiroshima Day" to atone for the dropping of atomic bombs on Japan and to renew their dedication to the cause of world peace.

The Hiroshima memorialists are mainly leftists, young and old, who reject the opinion of mainline historians that the use of atomic bombs brought the war with Japan to a speedy end and thus saved thousands of American and Japanese lives. They take as established fact the "revisionist" thesis of historians like Gar Alperovitz who contend that the war with Japan was virtually over by the summer of 1945 and that Japan would have surrendered in August without the dropping of atomic bombs on Hiroshima and Nagasaki. If that was indeed true, why, then, did the Truman administration authorize the dropping of the bombs? To intimidate the Soviet Union, the revisionists contend, so that the United States could have its way in eastern Europe after the war. According to Alperovitz, "a combat demonstration was needed to convince the Russians to accept the American plan for a stable peace, and the crucial point of this effort was the need for agreement on the main questions in dispute: the American proposals for Central and Eastern Europe." Political scientist Michael Walzer put it more bluntly: "The bombing of Hiroshima was an act of terrorism; its purpose was political, not military."

My own reaction to the news of Hiroshima (like my reaction to word of the Japanese attack on Pearl Harbor and President Kennedy's assassination) remains deeply enshrined in my memory. I was in the Navy, stationed in the Marianas, at the time, and overwhelmed by the news. "The announcement of the new atomic bomb left me more depressed than anything else," I wrote home on August 8. "The prospects for the future look a little terrifying. I hope no more use of it is made in this war."

My initial depression soon gave way to irritation over the way some American leftists on the home front persisted in calling for "unconditional surrender" (which meant deposing the Japanese emperor and trying him as a war criminal), which, I was convinced, meant continued Japanese resistance, more bloody fighting, and probably more atomic bombs. I was greatly relieved, I recall, when the Truman administration decided to follow the advice of old-time conservatives like Joseph Grew (former ambassador to Japan), rather than that of leftists like Owen Lattimore, and junk the unconditional-surrender policy, let Japan keep its emperor, and thus enable her to surrender at once.

After the war ended, the United States Strategic Bombing Survey (USSBS) came to the conclusion that dropping the atomic bombs had been unnecessary. "Japan would have surrendered even if the atomic bombs had not been dropped," concluded the multi-volumned USSBS report in December 1945, "even if Russia had not entered the war and even if no invasion had been planned or contemplated." Whether this was simply hindsight, as mainline historians contend, or whether U.S. officials knew that Japan was collapsing, as the revisionists insist, but dropped the bombs anyway to scare Russia, continues to be hotly argued, especially whenever "Hiroshima Day" rolls around each year.

My own feeling is that the war had become so brutal by the summer of 1945 (the B-29 fire-bombing of Tokyo in March was as devastating as the Hiroshima bomb) that, for most people, using atomic bombs didn't seem particularly barbaric at the time. At any rate, the overwhelming majority of American liberals and radicals took Hiroshima and Nagasaki quite comfortably in their stride in August 1945. Some even gloated about it.

The following essay, first published in the *International Social Science Review* (Winter 1982), is an examination of opinions about the atomic bombing in leftist circles in the United States at the time of Hiroshima. I had a basic question in mind when I began my study: if dropping the atomic bombs was primarily an act of hostility toward the Soviet Union, how did leftist groups friendly to Russia in 1945 react to the attack on Hiroshima and Nagasaki? My findings, based on research in the magazines, journals, and newspapers of the major leftist groups in this country were surprising. The strongest defenders of the atomic bombings, I discovered, were the groups friendliest to Stalinist Russia, and the bitterest critics of the Bomb were anti-Stalinist liberals and radicals. The pro-Soviets also supported and the anti-Stalinists condemned a harsh unconditional-surrender policy toward Japan. History, for many people, I know, is supposed to be straightforward and retrodictable, but it rarely is. More often it is replete with ironies.

Responses to the essay were gratifying. Historians Arthur Schlesinger, Jr., and Robert A. Divine sent appreciative letters about it, and George Kennan called it "a well-deserved correction of opinionated people at both ends of the political spectrum." One of the most interesting reactions came from the late William Appleman Williams, prominent leftist historian, in a letter to me dated March 16, 1982. Williams was the executive officer of an LSM (Landing Ship, Mines) at the time of Hiroshima, he told me, and getting ready for an invasion of Japan. Having worked their way around from the Solomons to the Philippines to Borneo to the Marianas and on to Okinawa, he said, his men had the feeling they had used up their luck. "So the first response to the bomb was sheer relief — no more banging the bow into the beach in the face of a noisy unwelcome. Great elation. We even broke out the beer in gross violation of standard operating procedure. But the next day, and for at least another two days, there was an eerie quiet and unease aboard the ship. The enormity of what had been done cut forever into our minds and souls. I have never forgotten that palpable sense of regret and horror." In his letter Williams took exception to Paul Fussell's insistence ("Thank God for the Atom Bomb," *New Republic,* August 26-29, 1981) that combat troops naturally applauded the Bomb because they knew they would have been blown to pieces if an invasion of Japan had been necessary. "The amphibious corps was the Navy's equivalent of being an infantryman," said Williams, "and the response was quite different than the one Fussell has written about so many times."

From Victor Navasky, editor of the *Nation,* a leftist weekly (which had warmly supported the bombing of Hiroshima in 1945) came a query; he was "curious," he said, "about what you think is the contemporary significance of your documented findings on the attitudes of liberals and conservatives back then." It was a fair question; and I can only say that in addition to trying to set the record straight, a prime duty of historians, I was also trying to suggest a little less self-righteous dogmatism and a bit more humility when it comes to writing about the past and in making pronouncements on serious public issues.

★ ★ ★ ★

In *Atomic Diplomacy: Hiroshima and Potsdam* (1965), Gar Alperovitz first developed in scholarly detail the thesis that the United States dropped atomic bombs on Japan in August 1945 mainly to intimidate the Soviet Union and strengthen America's hand in Europe. Since the late 1960s, Alperovitz's thesis has, in popular form, become something like conventional wisdom in leftist circles in this country. An article for the *Progressive* in August 1980, for example, states flatly that

Japan was ready to surrender before Hiroshima but that the Truman administration engaged in "atomic diplomacy," that is, refused to "assure the Japanese that their emperor might stay on his throne after a surrender" until it had dropped bombs to impress the Russians. A year later Yale's Kai Erikson made the same point. Reviewing a book on Hiroshima and Nagasaki for the *New York Times* in August 1981, he took it for granted that Japan was so far gone by the late summer of 1945 that "the bombings were staged to impress the Soviets (and anyone else who might matter in the postwar world) with America's new muscle."

Not all historians accept that thesis. Specialists in American foreign policy, in fact, still disagree violently over the question of whether Japan would have surrendered in August 1945 without the use of atomic bombs. But with a large number of liberals and radicals in this country today the issue is regarded as settled: Japan was defeated before Hiroshima and the United States was engaging in "atomic diplomacy" against Russia when it bombed the two Japanese cities. The charge is of course a horrendous one; it places the United States, for cold and calculated brutality, in the same category as Nazi Germany. But the charge is also breathtakingly *ex post facto*. It certainly was not made by American leftists in August 1945. Not that the Left took a monolithic view of the matter. American leftists were as split in 1945 as they are today, and there were widely varying reactions to Hiroshima and Nagasaki in the different journals of opinion which they sponsored. But no one on the Left, not even the *Daily Worker*, talked of "atomic diplomacy" in 1945.

Ironically, those liberals and radicals who were harshest in their criticism of Stalinist Russia were also severest in their condemnation of the United States for having used atomic bombs on Japan. It is worth taking a close look at the record. At the very least it shows us that "ideological correctness" is extremely difficult to maintain for long in this unruly world of ours. It reminds us, too, of how thoroughly climates of opinion change from one generation to another and how faulty the human memory can be. And we can also learn, from studying the records of the past, something about the precariousness of expounding one's views on crucial issues with too much assurance at any given time.

It is useful to begin with the Stalinist Left: that segment of American leftist opinion associated with the American Communist Party and its two major organs, the *Daily Worker* and the *New Masses*. During and after World War II, American Stalinists were extremely protective of the good name of Soviet Russia. They identified her with the forces of peace and progress, were ultra-sensitive to any criticisms, even the mildest, of Soviet policy, and were continually inveighing against the "forces of reaction," which they thought were trying to sow the seeds of dissension between the United States and Russsia. But the record is clear: if the United States government was engaging in "atomic diplomacy" in 1945, those ever-alert American Stalinists were quite unaware of it. They looked upon the use of atomic bombs on Japan as right, justified, and necessary. And they insisted on "unconditional surrender," with no concessions whatever to Japan regarding the retention of the emperor, to the very end of the war.

The *Daily Worker* carried its first front-page headline about Hiroshima on August 7: "Atomic Bomb Hits Japan. Equals 10,000 Tons of TNT." It then went on to quote President Truman's announcement that Japan had rejected the Potsdam surrender ultimatum and Secretary of War Henry Stimson's assurance that the bombing "should prove a tremendous aid in shortening the war against Japan." On page twelve it also quoted with approval Truman's warning to Japan: "We are now prepared to obliterate more rapidly and completely every productive enterprise the Japanese have above ground in any city. We shall destroy their docks, their factories, and their communications. Let there be no mistake; we shall completely destroy Japan's power to make war."

The following day the *Daily Worker* presented more details about the Hiroshima bombing on its front page; but it also featured three stories which it thought would be of special interest to its readers. The first emphasized the fact that two French communists (Frédéric Joliet-Curie and Paul Langevin) had pioneered in the development of atomic energy; the second pointed out that Jewish scientists, who had been hounded out of Nazi Germany as "racial inferiors," had made major contributions to "this epochal discovery"; and the third exulted in the fact that "American Labor Contributed Its Share in Creating the Atom Bomb."

The *Worker* had no misgivings about Hiroshima. In a piece entitled "A New Epoch in Warfare," on August 8, the paper's military analyst ("A Veteran Commander") vigorously defended the bomb. "We are lucky," he said, "we have found The Thing and are able to speed the war against the Japanese before the enemy can devise countermeasures. Thank God for that." And he added: "So let us not greet our atomic device with a shudder, but with the elation and admiration which the genius of man deserves." Apparently the average American agreed with the *Worker*. An informal poll of New Yorkers by the *Worker's* Louise Mitchell revealed that although the people interviewed were awed by the thought of atomic power, they were convinced that it would shorten the war and eventually have "unlimited benefits for all the world."

On the same day as the poll the editors of the *Worker* ran a piece titled, "Challenge to Humanity," in which they presented their first reaction to the atomic bomb. "Today," they wrote, "humanity must stand back from itself for a moment and look at what this unique animal — the human being — can accomplish. A tremendous new weapon has been created for us in this war, created on the foundations of scientific progress and accelerated by the needs of war. What the actual effect on Japan will be, it is too early to say. . . . But it is certainly necessary to add a note of caution to all the speculations pouring forth on the radio and in the press. And that is very simply: the war is not over. The war will not be over until the conditions have been created for changing the social structure of our Japanese enemy, eliminating the war makers, punishing the emperor, unleashing the powers of democracy in all of Asia. Let's not forget that. The war is not over here at home, even though a vast new weapon has been created.

**179**

*Hiroshima: two views of the destruction (both courtesy of the National Archives, Washington, D.C.).*

Production for victory is still necessary in all fields as well as in the field of atomic bombs." The editors thought the United States could be justly proud of its work on the bomb; but they reminded their readers that "the underlying scientific work was international." For that reason, William Z. Foster, national chairman of the Communist Party, thought that control of the atomic bomb should eventually be vested in the United Nations Security Council.

For the *Worker*, the news of Nagasaki two days later was dwarfed by the almost simultaneous entry of Soviet Russia into the war against Japan. "This is the Payoff," exulted the *Worker's* Veteran Commander on August 9. "The atomic bomb hit Japan on the 'head' with a terrific impact. But aside from its 'head,' Japan still has a mighty big 'belly' on the continent of Asia. This 'belly' is practically immune to atomic bombs, at least at this stage of their development, because the mines, factories, bean fields and garrisons of Manchuria are so scattered that it would take a lot of atomic bombs to blast them. This is the strategic role of the Soviet Union: to rip the Japanese 'belly' while Japan is being hit on the 'head' from the air." Reminding his readers that "Japan's army is virtually intact," the Veteran Commander insisted that Russia's entry into the war would "save many lives."

Like the Veteran Commander, Communist Party leader Foster thought Russia's invasion of Manchuria the big event of the Pacific War. "Three days ago," he was quoted as saying, "Japan suffered the great shock of the first atomic bomb; now it staggers under the still heavier blow of the Soviet declaration of war." In an editorial on "The Soviet War Declaration," the *Worker* took the same line. " The atom bomb which shattered a Japanese city last Sunday has been followed by a political and military bombshell of even deeper significance: the Soviet declaration of war on Japan."

There was little room for Nagasaki in the pages of the *Worker*. The front-page headline for August 10 revealed the paper's priorities: "Soviet 14 mi. in Manchuria. Atom Raid Levels Nagasaki." In his column for that day, the Veteran Commander mentioned Nagasaki only in passing; his main focus was on Russian progress in Manchuria. "We have learned how to split the uranium atom," another writer, Joseph Starobin, explained, "but Generalissimo Stalin is currently splitting the Japanese armies in Manchuria." The *Worker* scoffed at the suggestion that Russia had entered the war because of the atomic bomb; her entry, the editors pointed out, had been decided on months earlier. And when, on August 15, it was able to announce the end of the war, the *Worker* assured its readers that it was not the atomic bomb, but Russia's entry into the war, that forced Japan to quit. The editors quoted Major General Claire Chennault and Lord Louis Mountbatten on that point.

During the final days of the war, the editors of the *Worker* insisted forcefully on adhering to Franklin Roosevelt's unconditional-surrender policy. They were adamantly opposed to any concessions to Japan regarding the emperor. The emperor, for the *Worker*, was a war criminal; to retain him on the throne would defeat the democratic purposes for which the United States had fought the war. The editors were harsh in their criticism of Americans who were "anxious for a compromise peace with Japan, which would leave its fascist structure intact." They continually warned against Joseph Grew, former ambassador to Japan and State Department undersecretary, who, the *Worker* noted, was "closely associated with those who would like to maintain Hirohito as a ruling power in Japan."

Joseph Grew's replacement by Dean Acheson, known for his tough attitude toward Japan, brought cheer to the hearts of the *Worker's* editors; Acheson, no doubt, would abandon Grew's "soft" policy. When Rhode Island's Democratic Senator Theodore F. Green urged dumping Emperor Hirohito, the *Worker* quoted him approvingly. The editors also reported that a majority of people polled by a *Worker* reporter in New York City regarded Hirohito as a war criminal who had to be punished. And on August 11, they featured a telegram sent to President Truman by several organizations opposing any concessions to Japan regarding the emperor:

"Surrender of principles now would make the theme of unconditional surrender a mockery."

The telegram to President Truman was signed by representatives of five organizations which the *Worker* regarded as
impeccably progressive: the National Lawyers Guild, Americans United for World Organization, the American Veterans
Committee, Friends of Democracy, and the Independent Citizens Committee of the Arts, Sciences, and Professions. But
their efforts were in vain. In the end, to the disappointment of
the *Worker*, the Truman administration decided to let the
emperor remain on the throne, though subject to the orders
of General Douglas MacArthur who was to head the American occupation of Japan. The editors of the *Worker* continued
to regard Hirohito as a war criminal, but they now suggested
that the Japanese people be permitted to decide his fate, perhaps by referendum.

Not surprisingly, *New Masses*, a Stalinist biweekly published in New York, expressed the same views as those contained in the *Daily Worker*. In its two issues for August 1945,
*New Masses* explained that Russian entry into the war was
more important than the atomic bomb in forcing Japan's
capitulation; that Russia had promised to enter the war long
before Hiroshima; that the atomic bomb was a "symbol of
the great potentialities that can be released once the energies
of the people are fully tapped"; that atomic energy should be
brought under international control through the Security
Council of the United Nations; and that the Emperor of
Japan had played a major role in bringing on the war and
must be made to admit his war guilt.

Like the *Daily Worker*, the *New Masses* was irked by suggestions that the atomic bomb was the critical factor in bringing about Japan's defeat. The editors lambasted the Japanese
government, Winston Churchill, the Hearst press, air generals
"with juvenile outlooks on world affairs," and "proud scientists" for expressing such an opinion. In a column on
"Strategy That Licked Japan," Colonel T., the magazine's
military expert, recapitulated the march of events after Pearl

Harbor in order to make clear to everybody concerned what the real determining factor of victory had been. When, in his chronological summary, he reached July 5, 1945, the day that Admiral William Halsey's Third Fleet campaign against the Japanese mainland commenced, he had this to say: "The rampage lasted almost three weeks, during which an incredible number of enemy ships and planes were destroyed. The great campaign was drawing to a close when the atomic bomb exploded on Hiroshima on August 6. But the Japanese were not giving up yet. On August 9 the Soviet Union entered the fray, having undertaken at Yalta . . . to enter the war against Japan ninety days after the collapse of Germany. The 'note' was met 'fully and on time.' Japan sued for peace."

If the Stalinist Left in America stressed unconditional surrender in August 1945, approved the use of atomic bombs, and emphasized the primacy of the Soviet Union in forcing Japan's surrender, what about the non-Stalinist Left? With the non-Stalinists we enter on difficult terrain. Non-Stalinist liberals and radicals in the United States were even more seriously divided in 1945 than they are today. At the time of Hiroshima the non-Stalinist Left contained, *inter alios:* Soviet sympathizers and Soviet critics, prewar hawks and prewar doves, liberal Protestants and Catholics with an antiwar bias, and liberal Protestants who had been hawkish before the war. It also contained a scattering of socialists, pacifists, anarchists, and Trotskyists. It is not possible here to take account of every minute shade of difference in the outlooks of American liberals and radicals at the time of Hiroshima. But it is possible to show that, by and large, the friendlier American leftists were to the Soviet Union and the more hawkish they were in supporting the war, the more they tended to favor unconditional surrender and applaud the use of atomic bombs. It was left to frankly anti-Stalinist liberals and radicals to condemn the United States for resorting to atomic bombs in August 1945.

Let's begin with the Soviet sympathizers. In 1945, pacifist-anarchist Dwight Macdonald wrote contemptuously of the "perpetual fogs, caused by the warm winds of the liberal

Gulf Stream coming in contact with the Soviet glacier."
When he wrote this passage he was thinking, he said, of "the
region inhabited by a few hundred thousand regular readers
of the *New Republic,* the *Nation,* and *PM."* His bias, as an
ex-Trotskyist, was anti-Stalinist as well as antiwar, and he
may well have overstated his point. Still, he was correct in
detecting a similarity of outlook on most issues in the three
leading liberal publications of the day. Some journalists, in
fact, wrote pieces for both the *Nation* and the *New Republic,*
liberal weeklies, and for *PM,* New York City's daily afternoon paper as well.

Macdonald was also right in noting the friendliness of the
*Nation,* the *New Republic,* and *PM* to Stalinist Russia at this
time. Eager to promote good relations between the United
States and the Soviet Union during and after the war, the
editors of the three liberal publications found it difficult, in
fact almost impossible, to bring themselves to criticize Soviet
policy in any serious sense. Not only were they convinced
that the Soviet Union represented a progressive socialist society with an impeccable antifascist outlook, they were also
afraid that criticism of Stalinism would play into the hands of
anti-Soviet reactionaries in the United States.

The editors of the *Nation,* the *New Republic,* and *PM* were
not really "fellow travelers." They did not follow the Stalinist
line. Before Pearl Harbor, indeed, they had favored U.S.
intervention in the war in Europe at a time when American
Stalinists, hewing to the Nazi-Soviet Pact line (August
1939 – June 1941), were vehemently expounding an anti-interventionist point of view. Still, at the time of Hiroshima,
their sympathies for the Soviet Union were open and undis-
guised. It is not surprising, then, that their reactions to world
events, beginning with Hiroshima, were remarkably similar
to those of the Stalinist press. Like the Stalinists after Hitler's
invasion of Russia in June 1941, the non-Stalinist liberals
were militant in their support of the war effort. They looked
with impatience, even disdain, on what the *New Republic's*
Bruce Bliven called "the hang-back boys," that is, pre-war
anti-interventionists like Norman Thomas, Oswald Garrison

Villard, and Charles Beard who supported the war but with-out the kind of millenial fervor they themselves felt.

To say that the *Nation*, the *New Republic*, and *PM* sup-ported the bombing of Hiroshima and Nagasaki is to under-state the matter. All three publications took for granted, from the beginning, the necessity and desirability of the bombings. Only when some Americans expressed misgivings about the bombs did they feel obliged to move on to a positive defense.

On August 31, in its first comment on Hiroshima, the *New Republic* identified the city as "an important base of the Jap-anese army" and pointed out that the Potsdam ultimatum of July 25 demanding immediate surrender was intended "to spare the Japanese people from utter destruction." But the "Japanese leaders rejected the offer," wrote the editors, "and they and their followers must now take the consequences. The new bomb . . . embodies 'a harnessing of the basic power of the universe,' as the president said. It may open the way for 'an entirely new concept of force and power.' Let us hope that its first result may be to bring the Japanese to their senses and cause them to end the war whose dreadful consequences to themselves are so greatly enhanced."

By the time the *New Republic* went to press the following week, Japan had surrendered and the war was over. In an editorial, "Military Review," on August 20, the editors an-nounced that the atomic bomb had "made certain the early collapse of the Japanese Empire," and went on to discuss the military implications of atomic power. And in a long essay on "The Bomb and the Future" for the same issue of the jour-nal, staff writer Bruce Bliven explored these implications in some detail. "Just what part the atomic bomb played in Ja-pan's plea for peace we do not yet know," he acknowledged. "Even before the first one was dropped on Hiroshima, it seemed certain that the Japanese could not hold out very much longer. The entry of Russia into the war would itself have been enough to bring the final act of the drama appre-ciably nearer. Yet the atomic bomb must have been an im-portant factor. The Japanese knew the terrible results it had brought on Hiroshima and Nagasaki, and the dreadful potentialities it carried for other cities and even for the armies in the field."

Bliven had no regrets about the use of the bombs. "Every American," he declared, "is glad to see the end of the war with Japan, which was certainly accelerated by the use of the atomic bomb." And he added: "They probably had mixed feelings about the Japanese civilians — men, women, and children — who were wiped out in a fraction of a second, 100,000 or 150,000 each time, in Hiroshima and Nagasaki. However strong the humanitarian impulse to pity those poor victims, it is complicated by the realization that the loss of these lives, by hastening the end of the war, probably in the long run saved many more lives by helping to compel Japan's fanatical rulers to capitulate. The general sadness, I believe, comes less from the application of the atomic bomb in the Japanese war than with thoughts of its future use elsewhere and specifically against ourselves and our children."

In an editorial on August 27, the *New Republic* discussed the morality of the bombings at some length. "The first use of the atomic bomb against a hostile population," the editors noted, "has, in spite of its stunning success as a weapon of war, brought forth expressions of guilt and horror from many parts of the world." It was, they admitted, "indeed difficult to justify use of an extreme form of the kind of weapon which hitherto has proved to us the cruelty of our enemies." But while it may have been difficult, it was not impossible. "In terms of logic," continued the editors, "it is easier to answer the contention that any new weapon is so much worse than any other that it ought not to be sanctioned. The individual victim is no better off if he is maimed or killed by a shell, a bullet, a bayonet, or even by a sword, an arrow, or a caveman's club, than if he is disintegrated or seared by an explosion of 'the Manhattan engineering project.' It is objected that such a weapon cannot be loosed without murdering thousands of non–combatants, including women and children. The same objection, however, applied with equal force to the strategic bombing of enemy cities. To admit all this is not to grant that the hesitation and fears about the atomic bomb are groundless. They are, however, futile as long as they are confined to an attempt to exclude some methods of warfare as opposed to others. As many have recognized, the eradication of Hiroshima is a dramatic proof, not that we must or can fail to use the utmost destructive power available to us when we wage war, but rather that mankind can no longer afford to wage war." The editorial concluded by pointing out that the peaceful potential of atomic energy was a tremendous challenge to human ingenuity and that with atomic power it might be possible some day "to abolish material want for all men and for all time."

What about lingering radioactivity in the bombed cities? The *New Republic* minimized the problem. In a piece appearing in September, the editors scoffed at charges by the Japanese that the bombs dropped on Hiroshima and Nagasaki had impregnated the soil with radioactivity that would continue to be harmful to life for a long period of time. Pointing out that American scientists had denied the allegation and that scientist Dr. Frank Thone had reported that plants were already growing in the blasted ruins of the two cities, the editors sarcastically proposed a way of settling the dispute: "If radioactivity is present in the soil, such plants will be marked by an unusual number of spots and mutations. Here is the ideal job for Emperor Hirohito, an amateur geneticist, after we are through with him — which, one trusts, will be soon. Let him go to Hiroshima, sit among the ruins, and watch the mutations grow."

No more than the *New Republic* did the *Nation* agonize over the bombing of Hiroshima and Nagasaki. According to editor Freda Kirchway, "The bomb that hurried Russia into the Far Eastern war a week ahead of schedule and drove Japan to surrender has accomplished the specific job for which it was created. From the point of view of military strategy, $2,000,000 (the cost of the bomb and the cost of nine days of war) was never better spent. The suffering, the wholesale slaughter it entailed, have been outweighed by its spectacular successs; Allied leaders can rightly claim that the loss of life on both sides would have been many times greater if the atomic bomb had not been used and Japan had gone on fighting. There is no answer to this argument."

Kirchway went on to propose internationalizing atomic energy, either through the United Nations or through a world government, to which each nation would surrender an important part of its sovereignty. British scientist J. D. Bernal, in a special essay on atomic power for the *Nation,* echoed Kirchway's views. The "immediate effects" of the bombs, "however horrible," he said, "have been decisive in ending the war"; but it was now necessary to work for the international control of atomic energy. Reports of Japanese criticisms of atomic bombings annoyed the *Nation.* "Correspondents report that the Japanese are bitter about American bombings," observed the editors, "but when you mention Nanking or Manila they look pained, as if you had made an awkward slip of the tongue." The editors also quoted Admiral Halsey's remark at the time of the surrender ceremony that he wished he could kick every Japanese delegate in the face and commented: "Not elegant. Not polite. But very exact and satisfying — and somehow reassuring."

"Thank God, It's Our Atomic Bomb!" exclaimed Irving Brant in an essay by that title for *PM* on August 7. "Our atomic bomb! Do we realize, can we realize, what that little possessive pronoun means? Three little letters, o-u-r, to reflect the thankfulness of all Americans and of their allies that Germany or Japan did not produce this engine of inconceivable destruction." For the editors of *PM,* the atomic bomb "means the utter destruction of Japan — unless Japan capitulates" and they warned that "it will be followed by others to level all Japanese industry above ground unless Japan drops its weapons and surrenders." *PM* did not minimize the horror of the new weapon. It is "an engine so terrible," wrote Brant, "that it gives the world but two alternatives: *the end of war or the end of humanity.*"

Like the *Nation* and the *New Republic, PM* favored internationalizing atomic energy and making it the servant of peace. But it was also convinced that the bombing of Hiroshima and Nagasaki was absolutely necessary for speeding the war with Japan to an early end. When the Very Reverend William R. Inge, the former "Gloomy Dean" of St. Paul's in London, deplored the use of atomic bombs as a "revolting business," *PM* pointed out that Isamu Inouye, chief of the Overseas Bureau of Domei, the Japanese news agency, had announced that the atomic bomb was not as "good — or bad — as is claimed," and that B-29 raids over Tokyo on March 10 had done far more damage than the atomic raids. *PM's* editors also quoted Eleanor Roosevelt on how the bombs might shorten the war, agreed with the *New York Herald Tribune* in dismissing protests against use of the bombs as a "foolishly sentimental outburst," and reported that a third atomic strike might be necessary to force Japan to quit her "stalling" tactics.

*PM's* John P. Lewis thought that picking Nagasaki for the second atomic bomb was ironically appropriate. It is "pleasant to know," he wrote in one of his editorials, "that the city from which the Japanese announced the first of their modern aggressions, the conquest of Korea, was — Nagasaki." But it was left to *PM* columnist Max Lerner to give the most detailed defense of the atomic bombings. "The few people who thought up, made, and dropped the atomic bomb," he announced in the first of two lead editorials on the subject, "did more to bring Japan to its knees than the American fleet and (despite *Isvestiya's* recent denial) the massive Russian armies." And in a second piece, entitled "The Atomic Bomb and the Human Heart," Lerner summed up the views of many Americans on the non-Stalinist Left who were friendly to Russia: "There are many who feel that the bomb is Satan's missile, should never have been invented; and, when invented, should never have been used; and, now used, should be erased forever from the human eye and mind. There is no question that it is a terrible thing to wipe out whole cities at a time. But war is a terrible thing in itself, and the expansion of its technology is limitless. . . . Once you set your will on killing people, all the glories of science become the servants of the Devil. What differs then is not so much the mechanism as the spirit in which it is used. If it is used — as the Germans used the human furnace, or as some Americans wanted to use poison gas — out of hatred and sadism, it brutalizes the user. If it be used, as I think we used the atom bomb, to end the war quickly, and with a loathing for its needs, then the heart that uses it may be salvageable."

Support for the atomic bombings and insistence on unconditional surrender appeared to be two of a piece in August 1945. "We have the secret of the atomic bomb," *PM* quoted one faithful reader as saying, "so let us use our strength and hit this malignant foe into genuine unconditional surrender, with no strings attached." When Japan hinted it might capitulate if the emperor's prerogatives were retained, *PM* coldly quoted the statement of a Soviet commander: "Unconditional surrender is unconditional surrender. There can be no plainer words." Richard A. Yaffe called the emperor "the willing accomplice of the war-making ruling classes." John P. Lewis said he was "the most culpable criminal of all," and Alexander H. Uhl warned that "fooling around with the emperor may cost us the war politically."

I. F. Stone was in accord with Lewis and Uhl. In an article for *PM* on August 13, he deplored the fact that the United States "was prepared to wage total war, but is reluctant to make total peace. The atomic bomb was the logic of war carried to an extreme which, many people (the writer included) felt, was abhorrent. But no such remorseless logic is visible in the current surrender negotiations with Japan. . . . To leave the Emperor in power is to make considerably less than a total peace, to leave untouched the symbol and the rallying point of Japanese imperialism." Stone was willing to use the authority of the emperor in making peace, but once the war ended, he insisted, it was important to pin responsibility for the war on the emperor and to encourage revolutionary forces to overthrow him.

Lerner saw eye to eye with his colleagues on *PM* when it came to Hirohito. The "Emperor-cult and the Emperor institution" must both go, he announced; retaining the emperor "means keeping all the cement that holds the structure of Japanese power together." Like Stone, Lerner was critical of the State Department for encouraging the idea that the emperor bore no responsibility for the war. And when the war finally ended with the emperor still on the throne, he regretted "our long-distance wooing of his imperial majesty when we could so easily have stood flatly on the Potsdam Declaration."

The *Nation* and the *New Republic* were just as critical of Japan's emperor as *PM* was. The *Nation* conceded that there were advantages in using Hirohito to make peace, but, like *PM*, warned against a "soft peace," castigated State Department officials, especially Joseph Grew, for absolving the emperor of war guilt, and insisted that it be made clear that American occupying forces would have the full authority to do whatever was necessary to destroy Japanese militarism, even if it involved "the ultimate abolition of the monarchy" and the trial of the emperor as a war criminal.

The *New Republic* saw a real dilemma: if the United States guaranteed the emperor's prerogatives, it would preserve an autocratic regime that might in time plan new conquests; but if it flatly refused to retain the emperor, it would prolong the war. "One thing to note," said the editors, "is that Hirohito is certainly a war criminal, in every technical as well as moral sense. His apologists in this country, like the recent Under-Secretary of State, Mr. Grew, have a serious ambivalence in what they say about him. . . . Hirohito is in fact, and personally, of substantial importance in the Japanese government. This being the case, we do not see why he should not accept his fair share of the responsibility for the war crimes in which he participated."

Far East specialist T. A. Bisson felt the same way. Discussing the emperor for the *New Republic* on August 27, Bisson was scornful of "a policy which throughout the war studiously refrained from attacking the Emperor," but he, too, acknowledged there were advantages in using him, first, to bring about peace, and then trying him as a war criminal later on. But as things turned out, when the war ended with the emperor intact, Bisson was not happy. "The Imperial oligarchy knew what it was about," he lamented, "when it accepted the Potsdam terms." And in a September 10 essay for the *New Republic* on "Our Japanese Policy," Thomas F. Reynolds, like Bisson, regretted the "pragmatic utilization of the Emperor as a means of bringing a quick end to the bloody fighting in the Pacific."

Unlike the secular liberals writing for the *Nation,* the *New Republic,* and *PM,* American religious liberals for the most part felt sorrow, not elation, over the atomic bombings. *Commonweal,* a Catholic weekly with a liberal social outlook, published in New York, found nothing to say in defense of the bombing of Hiroshima and Nagasaki. In an editorial entitled "The Best Bad News of the War," the editors rejected the view of some liberals and radicals that the atomic bomb would make world peace a necessity. To underscore their skepticism, the editors presented a long passage from Eugene O'Neill's *Marco Millions* in which Kublai Khan expresses grave doubt about Marco Polo's assertion that gunpowder would be a means of preserving peace. And in an editorial entitled "Horror and Shame," they said flatly: "But we will not have to worry any more about keeping our victory clean. It is defiled. . . . The name Hiroshima, the name Nagasaki are names for American guilt and shame."

The editors of *Commonweal* thought the war could have been won without the use of atomic bombs. They were critical of the Soviet Union for having rejected Japanese peace bids at the time of the Berlin conference, presumably because Stalin wanted to get into the war before it ended. But they also criticized the United States for having dropped the bombs without warning. It was possible, they insisted, to have arranged a demonstration of the bomb's awesome power to the Japanese beforehand. "For our war, for our purposes," exclaimed the editors, "to save American lives we have reached the point where we say that anything goes. That is what the Germans said at the beginning of the war. Once we have won our war we say that there must be peace. Undoubtedly. When it is created, Germans, Japanese and Americans will remember with horror the days of their shame." *Commonweal* warmly praised conservative columnist David

Lawrence for his forthright condemnation of the atomic bombings in two long pieces for *U.S. News.* The editors also called an anti-bomb statement issued by "more or less the old familiar group of pacifist Protestant ministers and educators" an "eloquent" statement and said it "deserves praise."

Protestant pacifists — like all pacifists — naturally condemned the atomic bombings; but, then, they condemned the war itself as a horror and an abomination. Dovish — but not pacifist — Protestants, like the editors of the *Christian Century,* condemned the use of the atomic bomb while supporting the war itself. The editors of the *Christian Century,* leading spokesmen for liberal Protestantism in 1945, had been strongly anti-interventionist before Pearl Harbor. When the United States finally went to war in December 1941, the editors viewed it as an "unnecessary necessity," and gave it their critical support. The atomic bombings, however, they regarded as neither necessary nor justifiable. Like the editors of *Commonweal,* the editors of the *Christian Century* reacted to the news of Hiroshima with shock and revulsion. In its first editorial on the subject, the *Century* quoted German military theorist Carl von Clausewitz on war as an act of violence pushed to its utmost bounds and declared: "In the atomic bomb this doctrine comes to perfect flower. Short of blowing up the planet, this is the ultimate in violence. . . . Instead of congratulating ourselves on winning a race and achieving the impossible, we should now be standing in penitence before the Creator of the power which the atom has hitherto kept inviolate, using what may be our last opportunity to learn the lost secret of peace on earth."

The *Christian Century* acknowledged that the Hiroshima bomb brought Russia into the war and that the Nagasaki bomb brought Japan to her knees suing for peace; still, the editors regretted that "the bomb inventors did not destroy their creation" in the moment of birth. And in a lengthy essay, "America's Moral Atrocity," on August 26, the editors reported that the magazine had been flooded with letters denouncing the use of "this incredibly inhuman instrument" and went on to express the belief that the use the United

States had made of the bomb placed her in an indefensible moral position. The war was rapidly nearing an end, according to the editors; there were reports, they noted, that the Japanese had made peace overtures as early as January 1945 which the Roosevelt administration, hewing to its unconditional-surrender line, summarily rejected. And this meant unnecessarily prolonging the war.

But even in August 1945, the *Christian Century* insisted, the United States might have avoided the horror of Hiroshima. Like the editors of *Commonweal,* the editors of the *Christian Century* thought that the United States should have arranged a demonstration of the terrible effectiveness of the atomic bomb before using it on Japan. Only if Japan had refused to surrender at that point, said the editors, would the United States have been morally justified in using the bomb. But, they complained, "Our leaders seem not to have weighed the moral considerations involved. No sooner was the bomb ready than it was rushed to the front and dropped on two helpless cities, destroying more lives than the United States has lost in the entire war. . . . This course has placed the United States in a bad light throughout the world. What the use of poison gas did to the reputation of Germany in World War I, the use of the atomic bomb has done for the reputation of the United States in World War II." The editors printed scores of letters from their readers filled with expressions of horror, revulsion, shame, and guilt. They also heartily endorsed Providence clergyman Bernard Iddings Bell's vehement denunciation of the atomic bombings and described the use of the bomb as "impetuous, indeliberate, and wanton."

Not all Protestants with a liberal social outlook had been, like the editors of the *Christian Century,* anti-interventionist before Pearl Harbor. An influential group of Protestant leaders, headed by theologian Reinhold Niebuhr, had dissented from the dovish views permeating liberal Protestantism in the 1930s, insisted on all-out aid to the Allies after World War II broke out in September 1939, and established a biweekly journal of opinion called *Christianity and Crisis* to express their views.

Though Niebuhr and his colleagues tended to be New Dealish in orientation, they were critical of the sentimental view of human nature and uncritical faith in human progress which they thought dominated the thinking of both secular and religious liberals. They insisted on "Christian realism," that is, a forthright recognition of human limitations and an ever-present alertness to the way in which the "sin of pride" corrupts the behavior of even the best-intentioned human beings. It is perhaps not surprising, then, that *Christianity and Crisis* joined the secular liberals writing for the *Nation,* the *New Republic,* and *PM* in accepting the atomic bomb as a hard, though unpleasant, fact of life. "The secret weapon which has dwarfed old-time wars into relative insignificance has now been demonstrated," declared the editors. "We accept it, as we accept the mysteries of radio. The discoveries represented by the atomic bomb are here to stay. Whether these discoveries are to be used for the destruction or for the enlargement of civilized living rests ultimately on the attitudes of the people."

Still, Reinhold Niebuhr had grave reservations about the bomb. In an essay for *Christianity and Crisis* on "Our Relations with Japan" appearing shortly after the war ended, he confessed to "a strange disquiet and lack of satisfaction" over victory because it "was secured, or at least hastened, by the use of the atomic bomb." Niebuhr was bothered by the fact that the methods of warfare (including obliteration and incendiary bombing) used against Japan exceeded in ferocity anything used against Germany. The difference may not have been deliberate, he acknowledged; certain types of incendiary bombs were not perfected in time to use on Germany. "Yet," he added, "one is left uneasy by the difference; because we used more terrible instruments against the Japanese than they used against us." Though he did not say so, Niebuhr was undoubtedly thinking of the racial differences involved.

Niebuhr was also upset by the unconditional-surrender policy which Franklin Roosevelt (whom he otherwise supported) put forward early in the war, a policy militantly supported by such organs of opinion as the *Nation,* the *New*

*Republic,* and *PM.* Not only did he think that adherence to the unconditional-surrender policy prolonged the war, he also deplored the insistence by many Americans on the Left that unconditional-surrender meant reconstructing Japanese society and culture after the war according to American liberal conceptions of what was right, just, and necessary in the world.

"American liberalism," Niebuhr complained, "recently allowed itself an orgy of the most nauseous self-righteousness; for liberal journals were almost unanimous in warning against any possible peace which might emanate from Japanese capitalists. This type of liberalism would rather annihilate a foe completely than enlist the aid of any elements in an enemy country which are not absolutely 'pure.' The policy is usually accompanied by the foolish hope that if we can completely destroy we will also be able to build a more ideal social structure out of these complete ruins. There is no vainer hope in human history; and it is prompted by a peculiarly dangerous type of 'liberalism' in which the imperial power impulse has become strangely mixed with moral idealism. We will destroy nations in order to make 'democracies' out of them."

Niebuhr was pleased that, in the end, the United States backed down from Roosevelt's unconditional-surrender policy and allowed the Japanese to retain their imperial house. But he was aware of the fact that most liberal journalists and commentators violently opposed making this concession, even if it shortened the war, and that some of them even wanted to hale the emperor before a war-criminals court. Lamented Niebuhr: "We can hardly be proud of the sentiments expressed by Americans in general, and by 'liberals' in particular, in the fateful days during which the surrender was negotiated. The wine of success is a very heady wine. No nation has ever embarked upon the hazardous business of ruling the world, in company with two partners, with a more blithe ignorance of the meaning of customs and continuities, of sentiments and unique loyalties among the people to be 'ruled' than we. We have arrived at an ignorant idealism according to which the world is divided into two classes: American democrats and all the other 'lesser breeds without the law' who do not share our democratic creed and must therefore be fascists. If a man, such as Under-Secretary Grew, with his long experience in Japan, expresses the conviction that the emperor ought not to be disposed of, there are liberal journalists who request his removal by the president on the ground that he is an appeaser of fascists. Thus the passions of war have introduced poison into the sentiments of liberalism; and the pride of a powerful nation has blinded the eyes of large elements of our population, whose clear sight is necessary, if American power is to be used responsibly."

There were, however, a few secular liberals who shared Niebuhr's concerns; they were critical of the unconditional-surrender policy and expressed regret for the use of atomic bombs on Japan even more forcefully than he did. These were what might be called the "dovish" liberals, that is, liberals who had been anti-interventionist before Pearl Harbor and who, unlike the "hawkish" liberals (prewar interventionists), strongly doubted whether a Brave New World would emerge from the most terrible war in history, especially with Joseph Stalin throwing his weight around in the world.

Throughout the war, and after it ended, dovish liberals found an outlet for their views in the monthly *Common Sense,* published in New York, and the weekly *Progressive,* formerly *LaFollette's Weekly,* published in Madison, Wisconsin. When it came to the atomic bomb, *Common Sense* thought that it did not "augur well for the future" that man's first use of his newly acquired power was to destroy his fellow men. "It's a good thing, everyone agrees, that We and not They found it first," wrote one of the editors. "I think so too, but — ." *Common Sense* had many "buts" about the bomb. Stuart Chase, popular economist who wrote regularly for both *Common Sense* and the *Progressive,* conceded the possibility that atomic energy might produce an economy of abundance and the beginnings of a genuine world state, but he also pointed out that the surprise bombing of Hiroshima, "whatever the rationalization, will handicap the moral leadership of the United States for decades, if not for generations to come. We could have achieved our military objectives without this appalling slaughter of school children. We will not soon be forgiven by the world."

Milton Mayer, a pacifist who, like Chase, was a regular contributor to both *Common Sense* and the *Progressive,* was even stronger in his condemnation of the bomb than Chase. In the pages of *Common Sense,* he suggested that Justice Robert Jackson, American representative on the Allied War Crimes Commission, ponder the following question: "Was our destruction of Hiroshima and Nagasaki wanton, or was it needed, as a warning to Japan, to win a war?" Mayer himself clearly thought it was wanton. He heartily endorsed University of Chicago President Robert Maynard Hutchins' statement that when the United States dropped the bomb on Hiroshima it had lost its "moral prestige." But he also reminded Hutchins (another prewar anti-interventionist) that the University of Chicago was the "institutional daddy" of the atomic bomb and that it was "engaged, right up to its ears, in preparing the most stupendous atrocity of the war and the moral disgrace of the nation."

As a pacifist, Milton Mayer insisted that "war has no morals, no humanity, no victors, and no profit," and he quoted Randolph Bourne's famous statement at the time of World War I: "He who mounts the wild elephant goes where the wild elephant goes." But he also thought it might help some if the American people rose to a consciousness of their complicity in the collective guilt of mankind: *"Omnes peccavimus,* and not *omnes* Japs and *omnes* Germans, but *omnes* all of us, not just all of us who make and drop the bombs, but all of us who let them be made and dropped and stop up our ears and say anything from, 'My, what a big bang,' to 'Serves them right, the little yellow bastards.'"

For the *Progressive,* which saw eye to eye with *Common Sense* on many issues, one of the most thoughtful comments about the bomb was made by Richard L. Strout, Washington correspondent for the *Christian Science Monitor.* Editor Morris Rubin liked what Strout said so much, in fact, that he featured it in the *Progressive* for August 20. Strout, Rubin reported, thought that dropping the bombs on Japan was "a mistake" and "perhaps a calamity in its moral consequences." By its use, according to Strout, "the United States has incurred a terrible responsibility to history which now, unfortunately, can never be withdrawn." Rubin went on to quote Strout at length: "How can the United States in the future appeal to the conscience of mankind not to use this new weapon? It was the United States who first used it. Has not the moral ground for such an appeal been cut away from under our feet? It is true that Japan was warned either to surrender or to suffer fearful destruction. It is true that an object lesson may have been needed. But on the other hand, there was no fear that Japan would win the war. Japan was already defeated. In a moral decision as overwhelming as this, knowing already that the use of such a relatively minor weapon as poison gas has been avoided, it seems to this writer that Congress or the public might have been consulted."

Like the editors of *Common Sense* and the *Progressive,* American Socialists headed by Norman Thomas (a prewar anti-interventionist and a forthright critic of Stalinism) expressed serious misgivings about the bombing of Hiroshima and Nagasaki. In the pages of *The Call,* Socialist Party organ, for August 13, Thomas expressed irritation at the "statements of pious satisfaction" being made by many liberals about the bomb. Herman Singer criticized "America's ruthless use of the atomic bomb," and the editors deplored the fact that "science has been perverted to the extent that the bomb is used to blot out whole areas, cities, and helpless men, women, and children indiscriminately." And when the war ended, Thomas, in a long piece for *The Call* entitled, "History's Cruelest War," confessed that he could not "rejoice over this inestimable boon of the ending of a victorious war without a sense of shame for the horror which the atomic bomb released on earth. I shall be told that it was the bomb which ended the war. As things were that is probably true, but I shall always believe that the war might have been ended before the first atomic bomb was dropped on Hiroshima bringing death to at least a hundred thousand men, women and children." Like other critics of the bomb, Thomas thought there should have been a demonstration of the destructive capacity of the bomb at some designated point in order to persuade Japan to surrender.

Unlike the dovish liberals and the Norman Thomas socialists, the American Trotskyists, organized as the Socialist Workers Party, absolutely refused to support the war against Germany and Japan. They regarded World War II as an imperialist struggle like World War I, and they were as hostile to the government of Stalinist Russia as they were to the capitalist government of the United States. Any thesis appearing in the *Daily Worker* was likely to find its vehement antithesis in the pages of the Trotskyist *Militant,* published weekly in New York. Only in its gift for invective did the Trotskyist *Militant* have much in common with the Stalinist *Daily Worker*. The *Militant's* reaction to Hiroshima appeared plainly in huge headlines for August 11:

ATOMIC BOMBS IMPERIL EXISTENCE
OF HUMANITY
NEW IMPERIALIST WEAPON RAZES AN
ENTIRE CITY
WALL STREET MILITARISTS UNLEASH EXPLOSIVE
REACHING ULTIMATE DEPTH OF FRIGHTFULNESS

The *Militant* thought "barbarous capitalism" was responsible for the bomb. The atomic bomb was simply capitalism's "newest and most deadly instrument of destruction," harnessed by "the bloodstained rulers of capitalist society" to the "foul purposes of imperialist war," a "fiendish weapon which the rulers of our decaying capitalist society have devised for the more complete and efficient destruction of mankind." So strongly did the editors of the *Militant* feel about it that they praised such egregiously un-Marxist critics of the bombing as *The Pilot* (official organ of the Catholic archdiocese of Boston), Episcopalian minister Bernard Iddings Bell, and a group of Evangelical and Reformed Church leaders. For Bernard Baruch, who cited the bomb as another "evidence of the courage and foresight of Franklin Roosevelt," and for *PM*, which said, "Thank God, it's our bomb," they had nothing but contempt.

The *Militant,* like the *Daily Worker* and the *Call,* thought the atomic bomb made socialism — Trotsky's, not Stalin's or Thomas' — an absolute necessity. And when the war ended without the triumph of socialism, the *Militant* saw no cause for rejoicing. "There Is No Peace!" its front-page headline for August 18 reminded its readers. "Only World Socialism Can Save Mankind from Atomic Destruction in Another Imperialist War." The *Militant* could scarcely blame the Stalinists for the atomic bomb. Still, the editors regarded it as newsworthy that the Soviet Union's *Isvestia* reported the dropping of the atomic bomb on its foreign-news page without making any critical comment about it whatsoever.

The *Militant's* (and the *Call's*) condemnation of the atomic bombings of Japan was matched in fervor by Dwight Macdonald's radical little monthly, *Politics,* founded in 1944 and published in New York. Like the Socialist Workers, Macdonald (who had been a Trotskyist himself briefly) opposed the war, but he did so for pacifist, not Trotskyist, reasons. He was, in fact, a kind of pacifist-anarchist by the time World War II commenced; the ethics of personal responsibility which he was developing led him to deplore both the brutalities of Stalinism and the crimes of capitalism.

Hiroshima and Nagasaki horrified Macdonald. In a long essay on "The Bomb" for the September issue of *Politics,* Macdonald tried to make sense out of the way World War II had reached its climax in the horrors of the atomic bombings. He was struck by the fact that the men who produced and employed the bomb did not really know how deadly its radioactive after-effects would be, but went ahead with their work anyway. The bomb, in short, was a morally callous experiment; it was "undoubtedly the most magnificent scientific experiment in history, with cities as the laboratories and people as the guinea pigs." Macdonald was also appalled at the way vast numbers of citizens worked anonymously for the Manhattan Project which produced the bomb without knowing or caring about the fruits of their actions. It was a perfect illustration of the emphasis on collective responsibility and "individual irresponsibility" which Macdonald thought was at the root of the modern world's barbarousness.

Macdonald had nothing but scorn for the "official platitude" of American progressives that atomic fission "can be a Force for Good (production) or a Force for Evil (war), and that the problem is simply how to use its Good rather than its Bad potentialities." He thought that Marxian socialists, both revolutionary and reformist, accepted this platitude because it was based on a "fatuous faith in Science and Progress" that made it possible to overlook or minimize the evils growing out of the struggle to go forward. This way of looking at the bomb, he insisted, "blunts our reaction to the present horror by reducing it to an episode in an historical scheme which will 'come out all right' in the end, and this makes us morally callous (with resulting ineffectuality in our actions against the present horror) and too optimistic about the problem of evil." He also thought that people espousing the potentialities-for-good-or-evil platitude ignored the fact that atrocities committed in time of war "are right now brutalizing, warping, deadening the human beings who are expected to change the world for the better." And they refused to face the fact that modern technology had its own "anti-human dynamics" which had so far proved to be "much more powerful than the liberating effects the Marxist schema expects from it."

"What, then," Macdonald finally asked, "can a man do *now?*" How can he escape playing his part in a ghastly impersonal social process that produces Nazi death camps and atomic desolation? Macdonald had nothing but praise for the minority of scientists who refused to work on The Bomb and he found hope for humanity in their refusal. "All honor then to the as yet anonymous British and American scientists — Men I would rather say — who were so wisely foolish as to refuse their co-operation on The Bomb! This is 'resistance,' this is 'negativism,' and in it lies our best hope."

It is not surprising that pacifists like Macdonald condemned The Bomb; they regarded the war itself as an atrocity. Nor is it surprising that American Trotskyists, who dismissed the Allied cause as imperialistic in nature, denounced the use of The Bomb. It is not even surprising that dovish liberals like Robert Hutchins and Stuart Chase and dovish socialists like Norman Thomas were appalled by Hiroshima and Nagasaki. Though they supported the war effort, they were, as Bruce Bliven put it, "hang-back boys"; their pre-Pearl Harbor antiwar prejudices were still too deep-seated for them to muster the kind of moral fervor for the war that made it possible to justify (or overlook) cruel means on behalf of noble ends. But the American Stalinists and the non-Stalinist hawks on the Left most sympathetic to Stalinist Russia had no such qualms. Looking upon the war against Germany and Japan as an antifascist crusade with almost millenial possibilities for the future, they were among the nation's most fervent sponsors of the unconditional-surrender policy and The Bomb that went with it. If President Truman was engaging in "atomic diplomacy" against Russia in August 1945, as the New Left charges today, he had his strongest support for it from the militant Old Left that felt friendliest to the Soviet Union.

# 9

# Academic Anecdotes

**M**Y major interest as an academician was American intellectual history, or, the history of ideas in America, and most of the books I published during the first part of my career dealt with various aspects of American thought. But I was also interested in biography, and I never discussed the ideas of thinkers like Edwards, Emerson, James, Veblen, Holmes, and Dewey in my classes without first telling students something about their personal backgrounds.

I taught the survey of American history from time to time, too, and when talking about the social and political outlooks of presidents like Washington, Lincoln, Theodore Roosevelt, Wilson, FDR, and Kennedy, I always began with biographical sketches. I soon discovered that well-chosen anecdotes about the presidents not only enlivened my lectures but also summed up, in a nutshell, some of the general points I was trying to make about them.

In 1978, I completed a lengthy — and difficult — study of freedom and determinism in the history of American thought, and after that I was eager to do something of a biographical nature for a change and to direct my next book to the general reader rather than to the specialist. Struck by the number of stories — dramatic, funny, poignant — I had collected through the years about the presidents, it occurred to me that it might be fun to do a book making use of these stories and others that I might dig up. There were a number of books in print containing biographical sketches of the presidents, but they were largely factual summaries of the presidents' lives and work. What I proposed to do was something different; I wanted to concentrate on the presidents as human beings — on their characters, personalities, and temperaments — and I wanted to make use of anecdotes about them that illustrated, underlined, and even extended some of the points I planned to make about them in my biographical essays. The result was *Presidential Anecdotes* (1981), a book of essays and stories about each of the presidents from George Washington to Ronald Reagan, stressing personalities rather than policies. I did two more books organized in a similar fashion: *Presidential Campaigns* (1984) and *Presidential Wives* (1988). In 1991 I also did a book on Congress, *Congressional Anecdotes,* which contained essays and stories about members of the House and Senate from 1789 to 1989.

At this point it seems only fair for me, in a book entitled *Memoirs of an Obscure Professor,* to tell a few tales about my experiences in the groves of academe between 1935, when I entered Yale as a freshman, and 1983, when I retired from my position as Lyndon Baines Johnson Professor of United States History at Texas Christian University. "When a man falls into his anecdotage," wrote Disraeli in 1870, "it is a sign for him to retire."

★ ★ ★ ★

Misspelled

During my junior year in college I heard Robert Frost give a lecture and read some of his poetry, and I'll never forget the story he told about his experience as a teacher at the University of Michigan. Forced to give a final examination, he said, he simply asked the students to write down what they had gotten out of his course. Later he told a friend that one student wrote that he hadn't gotten a damned thing out of the course, and he gave him a "B." Asked why he didn't give him an "A" he said the student had misspelled "damned."

Substitute Teacher

One afternoon when I was an undergraduate, I heard the writer Stephen Vincent Benet speak in Yale's Wolsey Hall. I remember only the introduction to his lecture, in which he described his brief experience as an English teacher at Yale. A friend of his in the English department asked him to take over his fifty-minute class one day, when he had to be away, and the assignment was the first act of one of Shakespeare's comedies. Benet discussed the assignment, he said, but it didn't take long, so he went on to talk about the rest of the play. But he quickly ran out of things to say about it so he went on to discuss some of the other Shakespeare comedies, and before he knew it, he had gone through all of them. Glancing at the clock, he found he had plenty of time left, so he went on to talk about the tragedies, and then the histories. To his dismay, the period was still less than half over, so he branched out into a discussion of Chaucer, Milton, Pope, and Samuel Johnson, with occasional glances at the clock, and became increasingly worried about running out of material to talk about before the period was over. Finished with the eighteenth century, he went on to talk about nineteenth-century and twentieth-century English writers and at long last finally completed what turned out to be a grand survey of English literature from Beowulf to Aldous Huxley. At that point, eyeing the clock hopefully, he saw with immense relief that there was only a minute to go. Pausing to catch his breath, he exclaimed: "Are there any questions?" A hand went up in the back row. "Yes," he said. "Sir," said the boy, "is it too late for me to drop this course?"

Sects

One day my English history professor, William Dunham, gave a lecture on the radical religious sects that sprang up in mid-seventeenth-century England — the Ranters, Levellers, Seekers, Muggletonians — and in the outline he put on the blackboard he included a humorous title: "The Queer Sects." The lecture caught my fancy, and the following year, when I had to pick a topic for my senior thesis, I thought it would be fun to learn more about these unusual religious groups. My history adviser was Stanley Pargellis, a taciturn gentleman who invariably looked owlish and puffed his pipe a bit before responding to any remarks a student might make to him. I sought him out in his office one afternoon, and when he invited me to be seated and asked whether I had decided on a topic for my senior essay, I said eagerly, "I'd like to find out more about the Queer Sects." Professor Pargellis eyed me quizzically, puffed his pipe vigorously, and said nothing. At that instant the import of Professor Dunham's wry pun became apparent to me for the first time. "You know what I mean," I added hastily. "I want to study the Ranters, Levellers, and Muggletonians." Professor Pargellis relaxed.

Metaphysics

Yale is probably a better place now than it was when I was a student there. It's co-educational, for one thing; for another, you no longer have to wear coats and ties to class the way I did. But I was lucky to be an undergraduate at a time when there was a major emphasis on teaching. I'll never forget anthropologist A. G. Keller, a father figure with a genuine liking for students, whose lectures were entertaining as well as informative, and whose preaching of the conservative gospel (he adored Herbert Hoover) didn't bother me a bit, though I considered myself a liberal. From him I learned to admire Charles Darwin. From him I also learned that one could be a conservative and still be a firm supporter of freedom of speech and expression.

Professor John A. Timm, who taught a chemistry course designed for non-science majors, was another top-notch instructor. He discussed the big ideas as well as the nitty-gritties of chemistry and inspired me to start reading the science section of the *New York Times,* as well as books on science written for the educated lay person. He also handled student rudeness with good humor. One day he paused in a lecture and said: "Would those of you who are reading the *Yale Daily News* please put it on the floor and out of sight and read it from there? It makes it a little hard for me to lecture when I see you hold it up in front of your faces."

F. S. C. Northrop, in philosophy, was also a splendid teacher. His discussion of the philosophy of science opened up a new world for me and deepened my interest in twentieth-century science. In the logic course I took from him he was more interested in Boolean algebra than in Aristotelian logic, and one day he messed up a syllogism he was working out on the blackboard. "Frankly," he said, putting down the chalk and turning to the class, "this bores me." We laughed, but we understood.

Chauncey B. Tinker, who taught a course in English literature entitled "The Age of Johnson," conveyed his love of good writing to us but was something of a ham. When reading passages from Laurence Sterne's *A Sentimental Journey* he would pull out a handkerchief and pretend to cry. We thought it was corny but enjoyed seeing him enjoy himself. One day one of the students brought a young woman to class, and when Tinker spied her, he abruptly stopped his lecture and fixed his eye coldly on the couple. Finally they got up and fled. "I may be Victorian," he said sternly, before resuming his lecture, "but I do like privacy."

In my senior year, I took a course called "Philosophical Ideas in Contemporary Literature" from Wilbur Urban, a frail gentleman whose poor health forced him to drop out of the classroom during the last month of the course. Urban's class was important to me; it introduced me to Kant, Nietzsche, Ibsen, and Shaw, as well as to basic questions about the nature of things that still tantalize me. I'll never forget how the gentle Professor Urban turned suddenly vehement during one lecture and exploded: "I don't know how in hell you can have an ethics without a metaphysics!" I don't know how in hell you can either.

Pins and Needles

College students learn from their classmates (and from ex-
tracurricular activities) as well as from their classwork. They
also learn from show business — movies, radio, the theater,
and, since the 1950s, from television. I was a Shakespeare
buff as an undergraduate and still remember with pleasure
seeing Katherine Cornell in *Romeo and Juliet,* Maurice Evans
in *Richard II* and *Hamlet,* and a spirited performance of *Co-
riolanus* at a WPA theater in Manhattan. But I probably
learned more from *Pins and Needles,* a socially conscious musical revue, presented by the International Ladies' Garment
Workers' Union (ILGWU) in 1937, than from any other
show I saw when I was in college.

Until I saw *Pins and Needles,* first on Broadway and then
again at the Schubert Theater in New Haven, I was not much
interested in politics. Though I was vaguely liberal in my
social outlook and admired socialist leader Norman Thomas,
my main interests were music and literature; as far as my
major, English history, was concerned, none of the history
courses I took (until I had a class in modern British history
during my senior year) seemed to have any relevance to the
pressing issues of the day. I was, in short, a political naif.
Once, when I was a junior, someone asked me at lunch what
side I favored in the Spanish Civil War, and I ventured ten-
tatively, "I guess I'm for the Loyalists." At that, a senior
friend, staunchly anti-fascist, beamed with delight. "Boller
doesn't know much about these things," he seemed to be
thinking, "but at least his instincts are right." (Years later, I
learned that the Stalinists purged the non-Stalinist Left in
Spain and sullied the Loyalist cause, but even so, I can't imag-
ine ever being a pro-Franco fascist.)

*Pins and Needles* politicized me by sharpening my social
perceptions; it was crucial to my education as a young man.
Outspokenly anti-fascist and pro-labor, as well as extremely
friendly to FDR and the New Deal, the ILGWU production
presented its views with good-natured verve and exuberantly
high fun, and I watched it with glee and excitement the first
time I saw it on Broadway. Harold Rome's rollicking music

and lyrics were a joy and a delight: "Sing Me a Song with Social Significance," "Doing the Reactionary," "One Big Union for Two." So were the skits making fun of anti-labor society women, dishonest advertisers, and short-sighted conservatives like Neville Chamberlain who were, so to speak, "soft on fascism."

The *Yale Daily News* didn't like *Pins and Needles* a bit. Neither did my Republican friends whom I dragged off hopefully to a performance in New Haven. They were quite put off, in fact, by the play's left-wing bias, and some of them even thought it was offensively radical. But *New Republic* columnist Heywood Broun was right in noting that the temper of *Pins and Needles* was not revolutionary but one of enormous zest and high spirits. "The object is mockery," he observed. "The smug and conservative are held up to ridicule as persons blind to the nature of the world in which they live. Although the raillery is sharp and pointed, the wounds inflicted are not painful since the weapons are anaesthetized with humor."

After seeing *Pins and Needles*, I knew what I was: a New Deal Democrat. And the course in American history I took as a senior helped develop the social awareness that *Pins and Needles* had aroused in me. In the years to come, I was to learn to my surprise, that liberals could be as smug and humorless as conservatives were and as censorious of wayward ideas as well. But *Pins and Needles* taught me, once and for all, that one should bring high spirits and good fun, not ideological solemnity, to one's political preferences.

Our Line's Been Changed Again

In June 1941 Hitler double-crossed Stalin, contemptuously brushed aside the non-aggression pact and trade treaty he had concluded with Stalin in August 1939, and launched a surprise attack on the Soviet Union. At that point, the American Communist Party, which had been fiercely anti-interventionist during the Nazi-Soviet Pact period, when England faced Nazi Germany alone, flip-flopped overnight into a vociferous advocate of U.S. intervention in the war raging in Europe.

A few days after the abrupt switch in party line, my college friend, Bengt Carlson, and I, sightseeing in San Francisco, attended an anti-war rally in the Civic Center, and while walking through the crowd came across a zealous young Communist busily hawking copies of the *New Masses,* weekly organ of the American Communist Party on a street corner. "The *New Masses!* The *New Masses!*" he intoned, as he waved a copy of the magazine toward passersby. "Get the latest copy of the *New Masses!*" "Hey, man," I said, tongue in cheek, "I don't want the latest copy of the *New Masses.* I haven't finished reading last week's issue!" The party worker gave me a wry smile, knowing I was twitting him about the sudden change in party line. "I wouldn't bother with last week's issue if I were you," he said matter-of-factly. "Get this week's. *It's really up to date!*" Bengt and I walked on. Years later, after the party line somersaulted again, I enjoyed listening to Joe Glazer's satiric song about the zigzags in the Communist party line from the 1920s onward: "Our line's been changed again."

Switching Majors

I majored in English history as an undergraduate and got a job working part-time in my junior year for Wallace Notestein, one of the most distinguished U.S. historians in the field. The job involved making an index for a set of ancient volumes containing a record of debates in the House of Commons during the Restoration period. Notestein was particularly interested in parliamentary procedure; his article on the winning of the initiative in the House of Commons, published some years before, was something of a classic in the field. To try me out, Notestein sent me off to index a few pages of the first volume, and when I discovered some procedural point that intrigued him, he was so pleased that he hired me at once and took me under his wing as one of his favorite students. The job had side benefits. The eight-hour comprehensive examination in English history I was required to take as a senior had a question on the development of Parliament that was duck soup for me; the professor who graded my exam, not knowing about my work with Notestein, was astounded that I knew so much about the subject.

In my junior year I took a seminar on English history from 1603 to 1625, with Professor Notestein, and the class, about eight of us, met one evening a week at his house on Whitney Avenue, where he served us wine and beer on occasion. In my senior year I took another course from him in which I was the only one enrolled, and he put me to work with a graduate student from England reading microfilmed records of cases in the Court of Star Chamber during the early seventeenth century. He seems to have liked my paper for the course; he gave me a grade of ninety-nine at the end of the year. By that time I was wearing glasses; the hours I spent deciphering the seventeenth-century handwriting on microfilm had been a little rough on my vision.

In my senior year I applied for and received a fellowship to pursue graduate work at Yale in a special program called History, Arts, and Letters (English Studies). But in my last year as an undergraduate I took the first course I had ever taken in American history (at the prompting of my adviser, who thought I ought to know something about my own country), and I found the reading for the course so fascinating — Marquis James' *Andrew Jackson,* for example, and Matthew Josephson's *The Robber Barons,* Henry Pringle's *Theodore Roosevelt,* Frederick Lewis Allen's *Only Yesterday* — that I did a lot of reading in American history on my own during the summer following my graduation and began to contemplate changing fields.

By this time I had heard of Ralph Henry Gabriel's course in American Thought and Civilization, one of Yale's most popular undergraduate courses, and about a program in the graduate school called History, Arts, and Letters (American Studies), which seemed just up my recently discovered alley. At some point that summer I decided that American Studies rather than British was the field in which I wanted to do my work as a graduate student.

I still feel embarrassed when I recall how I made the change

from English to American Studies. It was a unilateral decision. With almost incredible naiveté I made the change without consulting anyone in either the English Studies or the
American Studies departments. It didn't even occur to me to
try to find out whether the fellowship I had received to pursue work in the English Studies program could be transferred
to the American Studies program without following some
kind of formal procedures. What I did, simply, when I returned to New Haven in the fall of 1939, was to drop by
Professor Notestein's office to tell him about the change I
was making. Notestein was extremely nice about it; he was
disappointed, he said, to lose me as a student, but, he added,
"We want our students to work in the fields that interest
them the most," and he wished me well. I then sought out
Stanley Williams, American literature specialist, then director of the American Studies program, to let him know that I
was enrolled for graduate work in his department. "I thought
I should introduce myself," I said amiably. "I'm Paul Boller.
I'm enrolled in your American Studies program." "Oh, you
are?" said Professor Williams, surprised and irked. "Who are
you, anyway? I don't know anything about you." I was shattered, and when he advised me to get a few letters of recom-
mendation to him before he made any decision about admit-
ting me to the American Studies program, I left his office,
crestfallen, and trotted down the hall back to Professor
Notestein's office. When I told Notestein about my chilly
reception by Professor Williams, he bristled. "Let me go
down and talk to him!" he exclaimed, jumping up and heading for the door. Then, as he stormed down the hall, he
muttered: "I never could get along with those American history people! Leonard Labaree is the only one I can stand!"

A little later, when I saw Professor Williams again, he had
a big smile on his face. "I apologize for being so unfriendly,"
he said. "I didn't know who you were." And so I was in the
American Studies program and I still had my fellowship too.
Working with Ralph Henry Gabriel (intellectual history),
Leonard Labaree (colonial history), Samuel Flagg Bemis

(diplomatic history), and Stanley Williams himself (American literature) was an extremely rewarding experience, and I never regretted shifting from English to American Studies, though I always valued the background I had in English history and literature.

Still, I am appalled as I look back on the shift I made in programs at how casual I was about it. All I can say in defense is that the academic world was, in fact, far more informal, permissive, and freewheeling in those days, at least at Yale, than it is today. Since World War II, and especially since the 1960s, universities, like American society as a whole, have gradually become bureaucratized to an extent that would have stupefied the professors with whom I studied a half century ago.

No Smoking

In the fall of 1948, when I arrived at SMU to begin my teaching career, I discovered that smoking by women was still frowned on there. The student newspaper was permitted to accept cigarette advertisements, but if a woman appeared in them, the cigarette she was holding had to be blocked out. I remember seeing a full-page cigarette advertisement in the school paper one day that showed film star Rita Hayworth holding her fingers up as if there was something in them. But there wasn't; her cigarette had been carefully erased.

Most Nearly Epic

In my early years at SMU I sometimes taught freshman English, and I was amused by the pro-Texas bias of the illustrative sentences appearing in the grammar book used in the course. To my delight, one day I came across the following sentence in the text: "Sam Houston was the most nearly epic figure in all American history." "You Texans!" I chortled, looking over at Catherine Perrine, English professor Larry Perrine's wife, then teaching freshman English and sharing an office with me. "Sam Houston, the most nearly epic figure in American history," I intoned with mock-solemnity. "Well," said Catherine calmly, "who do you think is the most epic figure? George Washington? Why," she reminded me, "he had false teeth!!"

William Faulkner and the Hoss

One of my best friends in my early teaching years was Hal Phillips, a native of Kossuth, Mississippi, who taught creative writing at SMU and published his first novel, *The Bitterweed Path* (1949), soon after he began teaching. Like so many young southern writers, Hal worshipped William Faulkner, and in the fall of 1948, when he attended a conference of college English teachers at the University of Mississippi in Oxford, he was eager to do some sightseeing in Faulkner's hometown and get a good look at Faulkner's home while he was at it. One of the senior members of SMU's English department accompanied Hal to the Faulkner home, and while they were looking it over, he suggested taking some pictures. "Perhaps we should ask permission," suggested Hal cautiously. So the two of them went up on the porch and rang the bell, expecting the maid to appear. Instead, when the door opened, there stood the great writer himself.

To Hal's delight Faulkner proved hospitable. Not only did he give permission for them to take pictures, he also invited them in for a chat. From Hal's point of view, however, the conversation didn't go very well. Hal's senior colleague launched at once into a name-recognition query, reeling off the names, one after another, of members of the English department at "Old Miss" and other Mississippi colleges, none of whom Faulkner seemed to know. Suddenly it dawned on Faulkner. "Oh, you mean the English professors?" he cried. "No. I don't know any of them." He added by way of explanation: "I ain't a literary man."

All along, Faulkner had been more eager to talk about his "new hoss" than about literary people, and he finally took his visitors to the backyard to show off his proud possession. After Hal and his colleague had admired the horse a bit, the latter suggested some snapshots and Faulkner stepped obligingly aside. But when Hal's colleague began motioning him back into the picture Faulkner expressed surprise. "You mean me?" he exclaimed. "Why, I thought you meant the hoss!" Hal's colleague then took shots of both Faulkner and the horse, and when the two of them took their leave soon after, Hal was in a glow. He could hardly wait to see the pictures his colleague took at Faulkner's place. But a day or so after he got back to Dallas he learned the bad news: his colleague had forgotten to put film in the camera.

Women in History

When Charles A. Beard died in the summer of 1948, I wrote his wife Mary to express my deep appreciation for his work as a historian and received a cordial letter from her inviting me for a visit. The following summer, when I was in the East, I drove up to New Milford, Connecticut, and spent an enchanting afternoon with Mrs. Beard talking about American history and politics and about her husband's work in the field.

When I saw Mrs. Beard in New Milford, I had read and reread *The Rise of American Civilization* and all the other books she had written with her husband, but, just before my visit, I had taken the trouble to read one of her own books — *Woman as a Force in History* (1946) — and found it enormously stimulating. Upon my return to SMU for the fall semester, 1949, I decided to prepare a special lecture for my History of Ideas in America class about Mary Beard and the role of women in history, based on my conversation with her as well as on her 1946 book.

In my Mary Beard lecture, I introduced a personal note, unusual for me in those days, when holding forth in the classroom. Not only did I say something about how important Charles Beard had been for me when I first took up the study of American history, I also told the class something about my trip to New Milford and about the lively conversation I had with Mrs. Beard about public issues, ancient and modern. The bulk of my remarks, though, centered on what Mrs. Beard had to say about the crucial part played by women in the development of civilization. After the lecture, I recall, three or four young women in the class came up to tell me how much they had enjoyed the lecture. I was a bit surprised, and of course pleased, but I didn't give it much thought at the time.

My Mary Beard lecture was a one-time event. I never gave it again. Why not? For one thing, I was a bit doubtful, back in those days, about injecting myself — the trip to Connecticut and my exchanges with Mrs. Beard — into a formal lecture. For another, when I jubilantly wrote Mrs. Beard afterward telling her about the lecture and the warm reception it received, her reply contained a mild rebuke for talking about her as a person in public and an admonition to stick to her published views. It reminded me of the displeasure John Adams' wife Abigail (an independent-minded woman like Mrs. Beard) expressed when a man quoted her during a New England town meeting one day: "What gentleman would quote a woman in public!"

Years later, a former SMU student, Patricia Wallace (history professor at Baylor University), gently chided me one day for not having done more with women in the History of Ideas course she took from me as an undergraduate in the late 1950s. "Pat, you're quite right," I told her. "I know I should have done more. But you must remember that I come from an entirely different generation than yours. There was no such thing as Women's Studies when I received my graduate training. In those days, in fact, mainline historians neglected women so much that when they wrote biographies of public figures like Washington, Clay, and Webster, they said next to nothing about any of the wives." But then, as I turned my thoughts back to my salad days in academia, I couldn't help remembering that I had, as a matter of fact, done something, if not nearly enough, with women in the course Mrs. Wallace took from me. "I lectured on Anne Hutchinson, the great Puritan rebel," I reminded her. "And on Ann Lee, the Shaker leader, and on Margaret Fuller and Dorothea Dix. Also," I went on to recall with glee, "I discussed the women's rights convention in Seneca Falls, New York, in 1848, and I even distributed to my classes copies of the Declaration of Feminine Independence adopted at that convention."

A day or so later, when Pat's kindly reprimand was still in my mind, I suddenly thought of the Mary Beard lecture I had given a few years before Pat came to SMU. Perhaps, I couldn't help thinking, if Mary Beard's letter had been less critical of the personal note I injected into that lecture, I would have continued to give the lecture, probably in a revised and expanded and more knowledgeable form. And as I look through the recently published collection of Mrs. Beard's letters — Nancy F. Cott, ed., *A Woman Making History: Mary Ritter Beard through Her Letters* (1991) — I regret very much that I did not do so.

500 Words

When I taught freshman English at SMU in the early 1950s, we used to ask for themes of 500 words every other week. Some students apparently counted as they wrote; their themes occasionally came to an abrupt halt in the middle of a sentence, with the number, 500, added in parenthesis after the last word, and underlined.

Party Line

Back in the early 1950s, when Stalin was still alive, there was a young woman in a class I taught at Dallas College (SMU's night school) who, it soon became clear to me, was a Stalinist fellow-traveller and faithfully followed the Communist Party line at the time. Chatting with her one evening during the class intermission, I couldn't resist taking a crack at people who followed the party line, and she at once flared up. American colleges impose "party lines" too, she exclaimed, and if students didn't hue to the line they wouldn't receive good grades. She was getting As in my course.

Learning Something

In the McCarthyite fifties I once asked students in one of my SMU classes what they thought about the idea of having a dyed-in-the-wool Communist come to our class to give a lecture on Communism. To make it hard, I added, let us suppose that he is intelligent, knowledgeable, and personally attractive. How many of you, I asked, think you would be won over to his line of argument? Since no one in the class raised a hand, I exclaimed: "In other words, you wouldn't have any objection to having a true-blue Communist come and address you in the classroom?" At that point I began to hear protests and objections. "We don't know enough about Communism," said one student, "to be able to argue with him." "Then," I said, "isn't it about time you started learning something serious about the subject?"

Eleven O'Clock Class

During the 1950s, members of the SMU faculty not only had heavy course loads (fifteen hours per semester), attended numerous departmental and general faculty meetings, and graded their own papers. They also gathered in Fondern Library for two or three days at the beginning of each semester to sign up students for the courses they were offering. One day a young woman needing an eleven o'clock Tuesday-Thursday class to complete her schedule, came over to the history table to ask me about an advanced course I taught at that hour. I gave her what I regarded as a splendid summary of what we covered in the course, and when I finished, she reflected for a moment and then announced: "Well, I guess I'll take it anyway."

Grade Points

Doris Johnson, who taught freshman English during the 1950s at SMU, told me one day about a young man who flunked the second semester of freshman English four times with her. The fifth time around — for some reason he kept reenrolling in her class — he did as poorly as ever, but since he needed to pass the course in order to graduate, Mrs. Johnson stretched things a bit and gave him a "D," which was a passing grade. A day or so after posting final grades she ran into the lad in the hall. "Mrs. Johnson," he cried, "that grade ain't gonna do me no good!" In somewhat better English he reminded her that a "D" carried no grade points and he needed them to graduate.

Kudos

Walking across the SMU campus one day I encountered a student majoring in psychology who had taken a course of mine the previous year and done "B" work in it. When she saw me, she gave a big smile and rushed over to tell me how much she had enjoyed the course. "I told my psychology prof the other day about how great I thought your course was," she exclaimed, "and he said that students usually like a course if they like the professor who teaches it. But," she added gravely, "I said no, no, it wasn't that! I really liked the course!"

Cliffhanger

One day I gave a "cliffhanger" lecture, quite unintentionally, in my Far Eastern history class. I was discussing the months just before the attack on Pearl Harbor, and after explaining that U.S. intelligence officers had cracked the secret Japanese diplomatic code just before World War II, I began shifting back and forth between the secret messages about Japanese intentions that U.S. officials were intercepting and deciphering, and the conversations that Secretary of State Cordell Hull was having with Japanese envoys in an effort to reach an agreement on the issues dividing the two countries. I was just getting to the breakdown in diplomatic relations and the surprise attack on Pearl Harbor on December 7, 1941, when suddenly the end-of-the-period bell rang loudly and I stopped talking. "Gee, whiz," cried a student in the front row, with a rapt expression on his face, as the class broke up, "I can hardly wait to find out next time how it turned out!"

Memorable

In a class of over 100 students at SMU one year, I couldn't help noticing a blonde fellow in the second row as I swept my eyes around the class during lectures. He was rosy-cheeked and baby-faced, and, somehow, every time my eyes passed him, the word, "dumb," came automatically into my mind. I got to know some of the students in that class, but he wasn't one of them. I couldn't help noticing, though, that he did not appear for the second semester of the course.

A year or two later the blonde boy turned up at registration to sign up for the second semester and I recognized him at once. "I took the first semester of your course a couple of years ago," he announced. "Don't you remember? I was the dumb-looking student who sat in the second row of your big lecture class." For a moment I was at a loss for words; then I cordially signed him up. He received what used to be called a "gentleman's C" that semester.

Shock

One SMU student whom I got to know fairly well for a time told me an unusual tale about himself. He entered the University of Texas in Austin a year or two before as a freshman, got converted at a revival meeting, and then spent all of his time visiting dorms and fraternity houses trying to convert his classmates. Because he neglected his studies, he flunked all of his courses and had to drop out of school. At this point, his father, a stockbroker, committed him to a mental hospital, where he received a series of shock treatments, at the end of which he was pronounced cured, enrolled at SMU, and did good work in all his courses, including mine.

Snide Review

In the spring of 1967, I received a call from *Time* magazine. The newsweekly planned to review my new book, *Quotemanship,* and wanted to get pictures of me to go with the review. I was a bit surprised; I hadn't been friendly to either *Time* or to its owner, Henry Luce, in the book, for they were hawkish about the Vietnam War, while I was opposed to American involvement. A few days later a couple of *Time* photographers appeared in my office at the University of

Massachusetts in Boston, took some pictures, and lingered for a pleasant chat afterwards.

Still puzzled by *Time's* friendliness to the book, I nevertheless looked forward to the review. The *New York Times,* the *Saturday Review of Literature,* and the *New Yorker* had given *Quotemanship* favorable notices, and I was naturally curious to see what *Time* would do with the book. But the weeks passed with no mention in the magazine. I finally concluded that the critical references in several places to Henry Luce had led *Time* to decide against running a review.

Then, a month or two later, the review appeared, but without any of the pictures taken in my office; instead, there were pictures of some of the people mentioned in the book, placed above the review. The review itself was unfriendly for the most part, and there was a clever little get-even ploy at the end. In the last paragraph, the reviewer presented a little test, based on material in the book, with the answers appearing, upside down, at the bottom of the page. One of the questions (the crucial one): "What is Henry Luce's middle initial?" Answer: "R, not C, as it appears mistakenly in *Quotemanship.*" I rushed to the bookshelf, pulled *Quotemanship* off the shelf, and hastily turned to the index. There it was — Henry C. Luce — wrong, it turned out, every time the name appeared in the text. How the error escaped me in galleys and page proofs I do not know to this day, but of course I bore the responsibility for it. I was humiliated; but I learned something: you'd better get the name straight when you're criticizing someone. I don't blame *Time* for being snide.

Black Studies

The University of Massachusetts at Boston was a new campus, only in its second year, when I joined the faculty in the fall of 1966, and enrollment was still small. This meant that classes were tiny, and, as it turned out, students were tongue-tied.

I had been used to large classes, formal lectures, and lively question periods at SMU, but I counted on a lot of class discussion in my little UMB classes. Unfortunately, the students, mostly lower-middle-class youngsters, felt ill at ease for a time in the college environment; they lacked the self-assurance of the middle- and upper-middle-class students at SMU, most of whose parents were college graduates. It was several weeks before I was able to develop the kind of animated class periods which were always my objective as a college teacher.

One of the students in my American history survey was a black. He was as reserved as the whites in the class. But one day I thought I had a way of getting him to talk and thus perhaps getting his classmates started too. The topic was slavery in the Old South, and my strategy was to talk about the subject for a while and then read the class a controversial passage about the slaves from *The Growth of the American Republic,* a widely used textbook written by Samuel Eliot Morison and Henry Steele Commager, and first published in the 1930s. The passage I read to the class (deleted in 1962 after NAACP complaints about it) went as follows: "As for Sambo, whose wrongs moved the abolitionists to wrath and tears, there is some reason to believe that he suffered less than any other class in the South from its 'peculiar institution.' The majority of slaves were adequately fed, well cared for, and apparently happy. . . . Although brought to America by force, the incurably optimistic Negro soon became attached to his country, and devoted to his 'white folks.'"

The minute I finished reading the Sambo paragraph, the hand of my black student shot up urgently into the air. "Yes," I said eagerly, nodding in his direction.

"Not true," he exclaimed. I waited for him to continue, but he lapsed into silence again. His classmates remained silent too. I couldn't help thinking of the laconic Calvin Coolidge, or, better still, of Unc Nunkie, one of L. Frank Baum's Oz characters, who always spoke (when he chose to do so at all) in monosyllables. In time, I did succeed in getting some of the whites to talk in my classes, but the black youngster, after his brief utterance that day, maintained his Coolidgean reserve to the end of the semester.

Well, the earth rotated a few hundred times more, and then the world was different. A year or two after I started teaching at UMB came the rise of black militancy, and, with it, demands for more blacks in the student body and on the faculty, as well as pressure on the administration to initiate independent Black Studies programs in the curriculum. By 1968 there were a fair number of blacks at UMB, though because UMB had increased its enrollment, they remained a small proportion of the study body. UMB blacks were all militants. They were especially eager to observe — "monitor" is too strong a word — what went on in American history classes. Even so, they rarely spoke up, at least not in the survey class on American History I taught in the fall of 1968. They sat together, five or six of them, in the back row, pointedly refrained from saying anything, and eyed me coldly and suspiciously when I was lecturing. From the beginning, the tension was acute; even white students who might have been inclined to speak up remained for the most part silent and looked uncomfortable during class periods. I couldn't help feeling that the black students were simply waiting for me to come up with some kind of faux pas — an unexpected tongue-slip — that would reveal me to be at heart an incurable racist, like all whites, despite my liberal credentials.

What was I to do? Class meetings, which should be joyous, were glum. There was no fun in meeting the class. I simply could not give my best as an instructor in an atmosphere permeated with doubt, suspicion, and distrust. To go out of my way to assure the blacks of my goodwill — take a loyalty oath, so to speak — would have been demeaning. To single the black students out for special attention, to curry their favor, would have earned me their contempt and confirmed their suspicions. I was in a bind. The weeks ahead promised to be bleak.

It was a book I came across quite by accident that saved the semester for me. While doing some research in the stacks of Harvard's Widener Library one evening, I suddenly spied a book on one of the shelves with an intriguing title: *The Life and Adventures of Nat Love, Better Known in the Cattle Country as 'Deadwood Dick' — By Himself.* I pulled the book off the shelf, started leafing through it, and to my astonishment found that Nat Love was a black cowboy, nicknamed "Deadwood Dick," who had plied his trade on the Great Plains during the heyday of the cattle kingdom from 1867 to 1890. The book was published in Los Angeles in 1907, contained a picture of Nat in his cowboy gear as a frontispiece, and, according to the stamped slip in the back of the book, was last checked out from Widener in 1924. I knew something about the rise of the cattle kingdom in the trans-Mississippi West from reading Walter P. Webb's *The Great Plains* (1930) when I was in graduate school. But the fact that blacks had worked as cowboys in those days was new to me, as it was to most students of American history at the time I stumbled onto the book.

When I finished reading about Nat Love, I knew what I must do. The textbook we used in the American history survey at UMB contained a chapter on the settlement of the "New West," as it was called, that came right after chapters on the Civil War and Reconstruction, and though I had never previously discussed the Great Plains in my classes, I most certainly intended to do so this time around. I went to work at once preparing a lecture; I reread Webb, consulted some books on cowboys, including one by my friend Joe B. Frantz, University of Texas historian, and took notes on Nat Love's book. A few days later, having finished with Reconstruction, I spent an entire period in my survey class on the settlement of the Great Plains after the Civil War.

In my lecture, I talked about the Chisholm Trail, about the long drive north from Texas to railheads like Abilene and Dodge City in Kansas, about roundups, and about stampedes, hailstorms, and Indian fights during the Long Drives. Above all, I described the hard life of the cowboy — with his high-horned Mexican saddle, broad-rimmed sombrero, spurs, high-heeled boots, leather chaps, and lariat — while he was on the cattle trail. Then, after pointing out that a few

*Nat Love, alias Deadwood Dick, in his fighting clothes (reproduced from* The Life and Adventures of Nat Love, *New York: Arno Press and the New York Times, 1968).*

cowboys wrote their memoirs upon retirement, I said I wanted to pick one cowboy in particular to talk about in some detail in order to give a more vivid picture of the day-to-day life of the cowpoke. I mentioned *The Log of a Cowboy* by Andy Adams and a couple of other cowboy memoirs, and then, with studied casualness, said I thought I would pick Nat Love, who retired in 1895 and published his memoirs in 1907, to talk about.

I enjoyed talking about Nat Love. Not only did I read passages from his book describing his experiences on the cattle trails; I also told them something about his encounters with Wyatt Earp and Bat Masterson, with Wild Bill Hickok and Billy the Kid, and with Jesse and Frank James, which, I told the class, were stock in trade for cowboy memoirs. "Nat Love seems to have enjoyed his life as a cowboy," I said when I finished sketching his life. "Here is how he ends his book." And I read a passage appearing near the end of his book: "I think you will agree with me that this grand country of ours is the peer of any in this world. . . . America, I love thee, sweet land of liberty, home of the brave and the free."

When I ended my lecture, the period was about over. I went on to announce the topic for the next meeting, the rise of industry after the Civil War, and urged the students to do the assigned reading on the subject. "Oh, by the way," I added, as if it were an afterthought, "I forgot to tell you. Nat Love was a black cowboy. He was one of many black cowboys who worked the trails during the flourishing of the Cattle Kingdom after the Civil War." At this, the blacks in the back row, implacably impassive until then, looked as though lightning had struck them. They exchanged startled glances and, as I left the room, went into a huddle. An hour or two later I encountered one of them in the hall while heading for another class. Her face lit up, she came running over, and shook her finger vigorously at me. 'You fox, you!" she cried gleefully. "You fox!!!"

The next time the class met the tension was gone. And though the blacks continued to sit together in the back row, they began speaking up during class meetings. The other students also began raising questions and venturing opinions. Before I knew it, the class had become my liveliest that year.

Mendacity

Faculty meetings at UMB became increasingly rancorous in the late 1960s and early 1970s, and when I joined the faculty of Texas Christian University in the fall of 1976, I looked forward to more peaceful departmental confabs. To my amazement, at one point during the second or third meeting of the history department, one of the senior members made a remark about some previous departmental action, and the chairman, Maury Boyd, ordinarily easy-going and good-natured, turned red and shouted: "That's a *goddamned lie!*" There was instant silence, a moment or two of awkward tension in the room, and then another member of the department turned the discussion to an entirely different matter. "Maury," I said amusedly a few days later, "I thought the UMB faculty was quarrelsome, but I never before heard a chairman, point-blank, tell a colleague, 'That's a goddamn lie'!" "Well, it was a goddamned lie!" Maury exploded, angry all over again. He insisted on explaining the accursed prevarication to me in some detail.

Visiting my friend Bob Smith, political scientist at Skidmore College in Saratoga Springs, New York, the following summer, I learned something about the tensions in his own department, and then told him that at least the Skidmore department had never had the kind of explosive confrontation that I witnessed during my first weeks at TCU. Bob enjoyed my tale. In fact, he enjoyed it too much. The following summer, when I visited the Smiths in Saratoga again, and Bob and I were hiking in the Adirondacks, he suddenly exclaimed: "Do you remember the story you told about how your chairman told off one of the members of your department at TCU?" "Sure do," I said. "Well, it almost got me in trouble," said Bob. He went on to tell me that one day he was making a point about Plato in his political theory class and one of the students raised his hand and said plaintively: "But Mr. Smith, what you're saying today contradicts what you said about Plato last week." "That's a goddamned lie,"shouted Bob. The students in his class were thunderstruck. He then hastened to explain that he was just teasing; and he went on to tell them the tale from TCU his friend Paul Boller had regaled him with some months before. The students found it all pretty amusing.

Bob's tale amused me too. "Maury," I told my chairman soon after I got back to Fort Worth for the fall term, "you're becoming famous. People are quoting you around the country." I went on to tell him about Bob's awkward moment in his Skidmore class when, almost to his own surprise, he suddenly quoted Maury: "That's a goddamned lie!" Maury immediately bristled. "Well, it *was* a goddamned lie!" he cried, turning red again. And he gave me more details about the mealy-mouthed mendacity.

Preliminaries

One day a Civil War expert turned up in Fort Worth, got in touch with TCU's history department chairman, Maury Boyd, and arranged to give a talk at the university early that evening. Maury made a series of frantic phone calls that morning and finally rounded up some graduate students for the event, as well as a few faculty members, and, to augment the audience, persuaded his mother, then in her seventies, to come too. The hastily assembled group numbered about twenty and Maury presided over the meeting.

Maury's field was European history, but he knew something about the Civil War, and while introducing the speaker he decided to put the talk in context. After he had expounded on the subject for two or three minutes, his mother, seated in the front row by herself, suddenly piped up: "Maury, get on with it!" Maury appeared not to notice the interruption; he went on amiably with his informal remarks. A minute or two later his mother spoke up again. "Maury," she cried, "why don't you get on with it!" "Well, I will, if you stop interrupting me," said Maury testily, while the Civil War expert looked bewildered and the rest of us exchanged smiles. There were a few more sharp exchanges between middle-aged son and "chronologically gifted" (as we say) mother, and then Maury finally yielded the podium. Afterward, we all agreed that we had enjoyed the punctuated preliminaries far more than the talk that followed.

Participatory Bureaucracy

In the old days, i.e., when I first began teaching, procedures were more informal in the academic world than they are today. Then came the drive for "participatory democracy" in the late 1960s and the development, in actuality, of what might be called "participatory bureaucracy": a proliferation of committees, faculty meetings, and paper work.

At TCU, though, Donald Worcester, history chairman from 1963 to 1972, stoutly resisted the trend toward bureaucratic busywork. To free members of his department, as well as himself, for research and writing, as well as teaching, he conferred individually with his colleagues about departmental matters, and for several years succeeded in avoiding departmental meetings completely. One day, however, he decided to have a brief meeting to dispose of some triviality. To his dismay, one member of the department got into a long discourse about something or other and ended by turning what Worcester expected to be a two-minute marathon into a two-hour talkathon. When the meeting finally ended, with nothing really accomplished, Worcester turned to one of his associates, as he headed for the door, and muttered: "Well, I'll be goddamned if I ever have another department meeting!"

En Route to BBC

One morning in the fall of 1981 I received a call from BBC. The program director wanted to set up an interview about my new book, *Presidential Anecdotes,* published by Oxford University Press a week or so before, and he said it would take half an hour. He didn't want a "phoner," that is, an interview by telephone to my home; he thought he could get a better recording if I went to one of the radio stations in the metroplex to do the taping. We finally agreed on 10 A.M. the following Tuesday, and, since I had an eleven o'clock class

*TCU's Don Worcester and Paul Boller (author's collection).*

that day, I asked my graduate assistant, David Monaghan, to start the class in case I wasn't able to get there on time after the interview.

When the day for the BBC interview arrived, I hopped into my Chevette at 8:55 A.M., over an hour early, and headed for the radio station that had agreed to tape the interview. But a minute or two after I started for the freeway, there was an explosion; one of those ferocious Texas cloudbursts broke forth in all its fury, with the winds roaring and sheets of rain hurtling down, and it became as dark as night. With my car lights on high and windshield wipers racing back and forth, I managed to get to the freeway and headed for Arlington. As lightning flashed and thunderclaps resounded, I crawled slowly through the torrent toward my destination. Scores of cars, I noticed, had given up and parked by the roadside, but it did not occur to me to stop. I had allowed plenty of time to reach the radio station and I was confident I could make my ten o'clock appointment despite my slow pace through the flooded highway.

At length I reached the exit I was seeking, got off the freeway, crossed the overhead bridge to the other side, and entered the access road on the left that would take me to the cluster of buildings where the radio station was located, which I saw dimly in the distance. Through the darkness I saw a fence running along the left side of the road, and I began looking for an entrance which would take me to the station. But I found no entrance. After driving along the access road for a couple of miles, I concluded I had missed the side road leading to the buildings, so I turned the car around and headed back. But I went too far; the next thing I knew I was back on the freeway headed for Fort Worth.

The error I had made irked but did not upset me. A quick glance at my watch told me I still had ten minutes or so left, and I was convinced that I could still reach my objective on time, even though the storm showed no signs of abating. When I reached the next exit, I left the freeway, crossed to the other side, started in the direction of Arlington again, and exited the freeway once more at the proper place. My car slid around some in the flood as I turned onto the bridge a second time, but I was proceeding slowly and carefully and managed to keep control of the vehicle. When I was on the access road again, I went along it even more slowly than I had the first time, peering intently into the darkness. But again I was frustrated; I simply could not find any way of getting over to the buildings where the radio station was housed, and after two or three miles I turned the car around and headed back, at a snail's pace, determined not to end up on the freeway bound for Fort Worth again.

"This is crazy!" I couldn't help thinking. "I know where those buildings are. There must be some way I can get there, even if my car can't!" It quickly dawned on me there was a way; I could walk. No sooner thought of than done. I drove onto the grass by the side of the road, parked the car in the grass, and stepped out into the storm. I was sopping wet in an instant, of course, but that didn't faze me, for I was sure, now, that I had a way of defeating the elements after all. I rushed over to the fence, tossed my briefcase over it, and started climbing. Unfortunately I had miscalculated. The fence was much higher than it had appeared to me through the rain and when I got part way up, I couldn't find any foothold above from which to boost myself over the top. At this point I was close, for the first time, to giving up the search and returning to Fort Worth. But at that exact moment (coincidences are always precise) a fire truck appeared, headed for the freeway, and when the firemen, clad in yellow raincoats, saw me clinging to the fence, they stopped the truck and yelled: "Hey, what's going on?" "I'm trying to get over to those buildings!" I cried. "I don't know how to drive over there." When one of the firemen began explaining how to find the road taking me there, it sounded so complicated that I interrupted him. "I haven't got the time!" I shouted back. "I have a ten o'clock appointment at a radio station. Why don't you just boost me over the fence? I'd really appreciate it. It would get me there on time." The firemen looked amused, but a couple of them got off the truck, came over, and gave me a good-natured boost to the top. I then jumped down to the other side, retrieved my briefcase, and ran as fast as I could toward the nearest building. It was now about three minutes to ten.

I soon found I was in the wrong building. When I asked a man in the lobby where the radio station was, he said: "I don't know. But it isn't here." Heart sinking, I rushed out into the storm again and headed for some buildings across the way. As I sloshed my way through grass, mud, and water, I passed a big truck, parked near the buildings, in which a man sat comfortably in the driver's seat, sheltered from the rain, eyeing me doubtfully. "Is KPLX over there?" I cried, pausing for a moment. "I don't know," said the driver, looking at me with some amusement. "But," he added, "KLIF is in that building," and he pointed. I was stunned. "It's *unbeleevable* (a TCU football slogan)!" I said to myself. "It looks as though I'm going to arrive on time — but at the wrong station!" Well, I had come too far to retrace my steps at that point, and it was high time to come in out of the rain in any case, so I continued my jog toward the building the truck driver had indicated. When I got close I could hardly believe my eyes: the station I was looking for was housed in a building next to KLIF's.

At exactly ten o'clock I walked into the entrance hall at KPLX. Some of the men there greeted me, came up with towels to dry me off, and then broke the news: because of technical difficulties, BBC had been forced to delay the interview.

BBC was only fifteen minutes late, and I had time to catch my breath and dry out. The interview went — dare I say it? — swimmingly. When it was over, KPLX's Mike Hoey gave me a ride back to my car. I was late for class, of course, but it was an hour and a half class and there was still time left in the period. I was in no mood to give the lecture on Jonathan Edwards I had scheduled, and, instead, spent the remaining class time describing my morning adventures. The students were amazed — and amused. So was I.

B-Minus

There were a number of reasons why I decided to retire from teaching in 1983, but grading papers was surely one of them. The "A" and "B" papers were a pleasure to read; but the "C" papers were usually boring, and the borderline papers ("To pass or not to pass") gave the most trouble of all. Grade inflation, which began in the late 1960s, made grading papers even more onerous, for "D" students now wanted "C", "C" students wanted "B", and "B" students demanded "A." A cop-out soon developed: to avoid friction (and maybe, even, lawsuits), instructors stopped giving "C" and began giving mediocre papers the grade of "B-minus."

One night I had a dream. I was grading a set of blue books and at one point angrily scrawled a big "B" on the cover of one of them and then started frantically adding scores of minuses after it. When I awoke that morning, I knew then it was time to retire.

Groves of Academe

There's as much foolishness in the academic profession as there is in other professions, but I never regretted spending my life in the groves of academe. "Where else," as my friend Bob Smith, a Skidmore College retiree, once put it, "where else do you get paid for reading?"

# 10

# Afterthoughts

- In the academic world it helps if you stuff your shirt a bit.
- Wisdom involves knowing when your opinion is worth something and when it isn't.
- The profundities of today are the simplicisms of tomorrow.
- There's just enough truth in some ideas to make them dangerously false.
- A closed system of thought imprisons the encloser.
- You are free to believe in determinism if you wish; I simply *have* to believe in free will.
- Historians tell us why things happened as they did, when it's too late to do anything about it.
- Ideologues have a tendency to transmute coincidence into conspiracy.
- He who can, does; he who cannot, signs petitions.
- If you read between the lines in some books, you don't find anything there.
- We are continually admonished to face reality, but never to face ideality.
- Honesty and ideology are immiscible.
- Do the means justify the ends?
- Science deals with processes; religion, with purposes.

- Never underestimate the cruelty of well-meaning people.

- I would hate to be operated on by a surgeon who was so filled with compassion for my plight that the tears streamed down his eyes as he performed the operation.

- Nothing becomes more quickly out of date than the immediately relevant.

- An optimist is a person who thinks things could have been better but might have been worse.

- Improbability: "We interrupt this commercial to bring you a news flash!"

- Sooner or later our present-day conservatives must come to realize that greed isn't the highest good, and our liberals learn that guilt isn't the only virtue.

- He labored like a mountain and brought forth a rat.

- He was so convinced they were wrong that he could afford to be fair about it.

- Some critics of our society assert that the people in our mental institutions are the really sane ones and it's those outside who are crazy, but they do not go on to show any compassion for the latter.

- Sometimes a piece of wit is the shortest distance between two points you're trying to make.

- Your view of the past depends largely on your vision of the future.

- Some music is more fun to play than listen to.

- A person who knows all the answers is asking the wrong questions.

- In some fields of inquiry so little is known that just about anything may be said.

- Hypocrisy pays lip service to virtue; cynicism denies its possibility.

- When we can't understand something, we give it a high-sounding name.

- A word always means a lot more than its dictionary definition.

- The question is not, Is it true? but rather, How much truth is there in it? The same with good.

- Sometimes being in the right isn't nearly enough.
- There are no easy ways to master a difficult subject, but some ways are more interesting than others.
- Some historians look down on the people they write about with the same kind of contempt they condemn those people for showing to some of their contemporaries.
- One person's aphorism is another's asininity.

# A Note on Sources

IN reconstructing incidents that took place during my years at SMU I utilized clippings I made at the time from the *SMU Campus,* the *Dallas Morning News,* the *Dallas Times-Herald,* the *Texas Observer,* and the *Park Cities-North Dallas News.* I also consulted Marshall Terry, "A Brief History of SMU" (typescript); Warren Leslie, *Dallas Public and Private* (New York, 1965); John Gates, *The Story of an American Communist* (New York, 1958); and Margaret Hartley, "The Subliterature of Hate," *Southwest Review,* Winter 1952. For the textbook controversy I reread the State Textbook Committee Hearing (September 14, 1961), as well as the lengthy reply which Jean Tilford and I prepared for Dr. J. W. Edgar, Texas Commissioner of Education, in response to attacks on *This Is Our Nation* (1961) by Texans for America. I also looked over letters from friends and foes during those years and the notes I took on the major events of the period. Some of these events remain vivid in my memory.

Like the chapter on SMU, "My Brush with History: Handling the Japanese Language during World War II," depends a great deal on memory, but also on information generously supplied me by friends and associates in the work of Japanese Language Officers (JLOs) during the war. There are general discussions of the Navy language school at Boulder in "U.S.

Navy Men Learn Japanese at School in Boulder," *Christian Science Monitor,* August 22, 1942, Section Two, p. 7, and Roscoe Fleming, "Our New Weapon — Japanese," *Collier's,* 117 (August 7, 1943), pp. 13, 41. For the work of JLOs in the Pacific Ocean Area I examined "History of JICPOA" (typescript), provided me by Harry Allen and Wendell J. Furnas; W. J. Holmes, *Double-Edged Sword: U.S. Naval Intelligence Operations in the Pacific during World War II* (Annapolis, 1979); Edwin T. Layton, with Roger Pineau and John Costello, *And I Was There: Pearl Harbor and Midway — Breaking the Secrets* (New York, 1985); and Quentin Reynolds, "You Too Can Capture a Jap," *Collier's,* 120 (February 17, 1945). p. 14. Robert Morris, with whom I worked while on Guam, described the project of dropping leaflets on Japan in *No Wonder We Are Losing* (New York, 1958), pp. 58 – 80, and there is also a brief discussion in Richard Hirsch, "Leaflet of Victory," *New York Times Magazine,* August 11, 1945. For life in occupied Japan I consulted letters I wrote home (with the end of wartime censorship I was able to give precise details), which my parents saved for many years and turned over to me upon retirement. For an amusing look at Japan right after the war, see two articles by JLO John Ashmead, Jr., "The Japs Look at the Yanks," *Atlantic Monthly,* 177 (April 1946). pp. 86 – 91, and "A Modern Language for Japan," *Atlantic Monthly,* 179 (January 1947), pp. 68 – 72.

There have been a number of studies of film music in general, and in writing chapter three, "Movie Music: the Sound of Silents" (which appeared in a somewhat different form in *American Heritage,* August/September 1985), I found the following the most useful: Irwin Bazelon, *Knowing the Score: Notes on Film Music* (New York, 1975); Mark Evans, *Soundtrack: The Music of Movies* (New York, 1975); Louis Levy, *Music for the Movies* (London, 1948); James Limbacher, *Film Music: From Violins to Video* (Metuchen, N.J., 1974); Kurt London, *Film Music* (London, 1936); Roger Manvell and John Huntley, *The Technique of Film Music* (London and New York, 1957); Roy M. Prendergast, *A Neglected Art: A Critical Study of Music in Films* (New York, 1977); and Tony

Thomas, *Music for the Movies* (South Brunswick and New York, 1973). For books dealing only with music for silent films, see Charles Hoffman, *Sounds for Silents* (New York, 1970) and Carl Van Vechten, *Music and Bad Manners* (New York, 1916). Even more informative were the columns on movie music appearing in the trade journals. The first such column, Charles E. Sinn's "Music for the Picture," appeared in *Moving Picture World* on November 26, 1910, and continued for several years thereafter. *Moving Picture News* initiated a column called "Picture Music," written by Ernest J. Luz, in 1912, and the *Dramatic Mirror* started one in 1917: "Preparing Programs for Photoplay Accompaniment," by M. M. Hanford. Seymour Stern discusses the score for *The Birth of a Nation* (1915) in *Film Culture* (Spring/Summer 1965), pp. 103 – 32.

For insight into the nature of silent movie music, however, the most enlightening (as well as entertaining) sources were the enormously solemn little manuals published for the edification of the young pianist and organist during the heyday of silent films: Eugene Ahern, *What and How to Play for Pictures* (New York, 1913); George Benyon, *Musical Preparation of Motion Pictures* (New York, 1921); Maurice M. Borodkin, *Borodkin's Guide to Motion Picture Music* (Maurice Borodkin, U.S.A., 1928); Edith Lang and George West, *Musical Accompaniment of Moving Pictures: A Practical Manual for Pianists and Organists* (Boston, 1920); Ernest J. Luz, *Motion Picture Synchrony for Motion Picture Exhibitors, Organists, and Pianists* (New York, 1925); May Meskimem Mills, *The Pipe Organist's Complete Instruction and Reference Work on the Art of Photo-Playing* (Philadelphia, 1922); and Lyle C. True, *How and What to Play for Moving Pictures* (New York, 1914). More fun, even, than the primly pedantic manuals were the musical compositions themselves: Lacey Baker, ed., *Picture Music: A Collection of Classic and Modern Compositions for the Organ Especially Adapted for Moving Pictures, with Practical Suggestions for the Organist* (New York, 1918); Erno Rapee's two collections, *Encyclopedia of Music for Pictures* (New York, 1925) and *Motion Picture Moods for Pianists and Organists: A Rapid Referenced*

*Collection of Selected Pieces Adapted to Fifty Moods and Situations* (New York, 1924), which E. B. White wrote amusingly about in "Onward and Upward with the Arts: Fifty-Two American Moods," *New Yorker,* 14 (March 26, 1938), pp. 21 – 24. And, above all, the prolific J. S. Zamecnik's indispensable contributions to silent film music through the years: *Sam Fox Moving Picture Music* (4 vols., Cleveland and New York, 1913 – 1923) and *Sam Fox Photoplay Edition: A Loose Leaf Collection of Motion Picture Music* (5 vols., Cleveland and New York, 1919 – 1929). For the comment on sound music pioneer Max Steiner, see George Anthiel, "On the Hollywood Front," *Modern Music,* 16 (November/December 1938), p. 62.

The prime source for stories about Calvin Coolidge, the subject of chapter four, is John Hiram McKee, *Coolidge Wit and Wisdom* (New York, 1933), which not only recounts stories but also discusses the twenty-ninth president's sense of humor. Edwin C. Lathem, *Meet Calvin Coolidge* (Brattleboro, Vermont, 1960) is also illuminating in this regard. For insights into Coolidge the man, *The Autobiography of Calvin Coolidge* (New York, 1929), which he actually wrote himself, is indispensable, as is Claude M. Feuss, *Calvin Coolidge: The Man from Vermont* (Boston, 1939), which attempts to distinguish between authentic stories and apocryphal ones. Donald McCoy, *Calvin Coolidge: The Quiet President* (New York, 1967) also adds to our understanding of the Vermonter, as does William Allen White, *A Puritan in Babylon: The Story of Calvin Coolidge* (New York, 1938). There are also several short popular accounts: Duff Gilford, *The Rise of Saint Calvin* (New York, 1932); M. E. Hennessay, *Calvin Coolidge* (New York, 1924); Cameron Rogers, *The Legend of Calvin Coolidge* (Garden City, N.Y., 1928); and E. E. Whiting, *President Coolidge: A Contemporary Estimate* (Boston, 1923). Three articles by Grace Coolidge, taken from her unpublished memoirs, throw light both on her husband's personality and his dry witticisms: "When I Became First Lady," *American Magazine,* 108 (September 1929), "How I Spent My Days at the White House," *American Magazine,* (October 1929); and

"The Real Calvin Coolidge," *Good Housekeeping,* 100 (March 1935). Ishbel Ross' biography, *Grace Coolidge and Her Era* (New York, 1962) is also useful. There are glimpses of Coolidge in the following memoirs: James M. Cox, *Journey through My Years* (New York, 1946); John Hays Hammond, *Autobiography* (New York, 1935); Irwin Hood (Ike) Hoover, *Forty-Two Years in the White House* (Boston, 1934); Lillian Rogers Park, *My Thirty Years Backstairs at the White House* (New York, 1961); Edmund W. Starling, *Starling of the White House* (New York, 1926); Henry L. Stoddard, *As I Knew Them: Presidents and Politics from Grant to Coolidge* (New York, 1927); and Charles W. Thompson, *Presidents I've Known* (Indianapolis, 1929). Kathleen Donald, "Coolidge Was Eloquent without Welliver," *New York Times,* February 18, 1987, p. 22, insists that Coolidge never had a ghostwriter.

"Purlings and Platitudes: Mencken's Americana" first appeared in the *Southwest Review,* Autumn 1965, and is based largely on Mencken's monthly column, "Americana," for the *American Mercury* from 1924 until 1933. In conception and organization it is also based on an examination of Mencken's major writings: the six books of *Prejudices,* published by Alfred A. Knopf between 1919 and 1927, *Notes on Democracy* (New York, 1926), *Minority Report: H. L. Mencken's Notebooks* (New York, 1956), and *The Letters of H. L. Mencken* (ed., Guy J. Forgue, New York, 1961). For Mencken's delightful autobiographical writings, see *Happy Days, 1880 – 1892* (New York, 1940) *Newspaper Days, 1889 – 1906* (New York, 1941), and *Heathen Days, 1890 – 1936* (New York, 1943). Mencken published one book of selections from his column, *Americana: 1925* (New York, 1925). There has been one detailed study of his work as editor of the *American Mercury* from 1919 until 1933: M. K. Singleton, *H. L. Mencken and the American Mercury Adventure* (Durham, N.C., 1962). Charles Angoff, who worked with Mencken on the *Mercury* presents a critical view of HLM in *H. L. Mencken: A Portrait from Memory* (New York, 1956).

In an essay on Mencken ("A Comedian Playing Hamlet") for the *New Republic* on May 21, 1956, Irving Howe dismissed the Sage of Baltimore, as he was called, as something of an anachronism. His "voice," wrote Howe, "no longer reaches us." Still, interest in Mencken, popular and scholarly, has continued undiminished. The publication of new Mencken material — *The New Mencken Letters* (ed., Carl Bode, New York, 1977) and *The Diary of H.L. Mencken* (ed., Charles A. Fecher, New York, 1989) — produced an outpouring of articles about him, especially the *Diary,* and revived the old controversy over whether HLM was a bigot or an emancipator. Special studies of Mencken's work as a writer continue to accumulate: Charles A. Fechner, *Mencken: A Study of His Thought* (1978); Fred C. Hobson, *Serpent in Eden: H. L. Mencken and the South* (Chapel Hill, 1974); Edward A. Martin, *H. L. Mencken and the Debunkers* (Athens, Ga., 1984); Charles Scruggs, *The Sage in Harlem: H. L. Mencken and the Black Writers of the* 1920s (Baltimore, 1984); John Dorsey, ed., *On Mencken* (New York, 1980); Douglas C. Stenerson, ed., *Critical Essays on H. L. Mencken* (Boston, 1987); and two shorter studies: W. A. Williams, *H. L. Mencken* (Boston, 1977) and Vincent Fitzpatrick, *H. L. Mencken* (New York, 1989). There have been no dearth of biographies: Carl Bode, *Mencken* (Carbondale, Ill., 1969); George H. Douglas, *H. L. Mencken: Critic of American Life* (Hamden, Connecticut, 1978); Edgar Kemler, *The Irreverent Mr. Mencken* (Boston, 1950); William Manchester, *Disturber of the Peace: The Life of H. L. Mencken* (New York, 1950); and Douglas C. Stenerson, *H. L. Mencken: Iconoclast from Baltimore* (Chicago, 1971). During one of the periodic brouhahas over Mencken's significance, historian Arthur M. Schlesinger, Jr., a liberal who disagreed with Mencken's conservative social views nevertheless praised him as "the Old Defender of freedom and intelligence" (*New Republic,* January 13, 1958, 3).

Lyndon B. Johnson hadn't been president very long before I noticed his habit of utilizing quotations from well-known people in his public statements and even carrying around with him well-chosen quotes on slips of paper which he could pull out of his pocket and read to reporters when it seemed appropriate. I began collecting LBJ's quotes, as reported in newspapers and magazines, and soon had enough of them to write an essay, "LBJ and the Art of Quotation," which the *Southwest Review* published in its Winter 1966 issue. In an expanded form the essay became chapter ten, "LBJ and Quotes," of *Quotemanship: The Use and Abuse of Quotations for Polemical and Other Purposes* (1967). For the present volume I have revised the essay once more to bring it to the end of Johnson's presidency in January 1969. All the citations appearing in the essay can be found in *The Johnson Press Conferences* (2 vols., New York, 1978) and in *Public Papers of the Presidents of the United States, Lyndon B. Johnson, Containing the Public Messages, Speeches, and Statements of the President,* 1963/64 – 1968/69 (10 vols., Washington, 1965 – 70).

"Beard and Batault: History and War," which first appeared in the *French-American Review,* 3 (Winter 1978/Spring 1979), is based on Georges Batault's *La Guerre Absolue: Essai de Philosophie de L'Histoire* (Paris, 1919) and on Charles A. Beard's references to Batault's military determinism and on his own ideas on war that appeared in several of his published works: *Cross Currents in Europe Today* (Boston, 1922); *Whither Mankind: A Panorama of Modern Civilization* (edited by Beard, New York, 1928); *The American Leviathan: The Republic in the Machine Age* (edited by Beard together with his son William, New York, 1931); *The Open Door at Home: A Trial Philosophy of National Interest* (New York, 1935); *The Rise of American Civilization* (written with his wife Mary, New York, 1937); *America in Midpassage* (written with Mary Beard, two vols., New York, 1939); *A Foreign Policy for America* (New York, 1940); *The American Spirit: A Study of the Idea of Civilization in the United States* (with Mary Beard, New York, 1942); *The Republic: Conversations on Fundamentals* (New York, 1944); *American Foreign Policy in the Making, 1932 – 1940* (New Haven, 1946); *President Roosevelt and the Coming of War* (New Haven, 1948); "Neglected Aspects of Political Science," *American Political Science Review,* 42 (April 1948). For critical studies of Beard's outlook as a historian, see Howard K. Beale, ed., *Charles A. Beard: An Appraisal* (Lexington, Kentucky, 1954); Bernard Boring, *The Political and Social Thought of Charles A. Beard* (Seattle, 1982); Richard Hofstadter, *The Progressive Historians: Turner, Beard, Parrington* (New York, 1968); Ellen Nore, *Charles A. Beard: An Intellectual Biography* (Carbondale, Illinois, 1983); and Peter Novak, *That Noble Dream* (Cambridge, 1988), pp. 95 – 278.

"Hiroshima and the American Left: August 1945," first appeared in *International Social Science Review* (Winter 1982). It begins with a quotation from Gar Alperovitz, *Atomic Diplomacy: Hiroshima and Potsdam* (New York, 1965), an influential book which presents the thesis (now conventional wisdom in certain leftist circles) that the United States dropped atomic bombs on Japan mainly to intimidate Joseph Stalin. In my research for the essay I examined the reaction of conservative publications to Hiroshima in the fall of 1945 (mostly approving), but devoted my major efforts to ascertaining what various journals of opinion on the left thought about that momentous event: Stalinists (*Daily Worker, New Masses*), liberals who were friendly to the Soviet Union (the *Nation,* the *New Republic,* and *PM*), anti-Stalinist liberals (the *Progressive, Common Sense*), religious liberals (the *Commonweal,* the *Christian Century*), socialists (the *Call*), Trotskyists (the *Militant*), and radical pacifists (Dwight Macdonald's *Politics*). From Macdonald's lively and provocative "worst seller" (as he himself admitted), *Henry Wallace: the Man and the Myth* (New York, 1945) came his wonderful description of liberal apologists for Stalinism as inhabitants of a region "of perpetual fogs, caused by the warm winds of the liberal Gulf Stream coming in contact with the Soviet glacier."

# INDEX